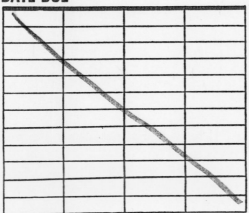

Political Development in Pakistan

PUBLISHED FOR THE

PRINCETON CENTER
OF INTERNATIONAL STUDIES

FOR A COMPLETE LIST OF THE BOOKS PUBLISHED FOR THE
PRINCETON CENTER OF INTERNATIONAL STUDIES
PLEASE SEE THE BACK OF THE BOOK

POLITICAL DEVELOPMENT IN PAKISTAN

Karl von Vorys

PRINCETON, NEW JERSEY

PRINCETON UNIVERSITY PRESS

1965

Dedicated
to my friend
VERNON VAN DYKE

Foreword

THE EMERGENCE of newly independent states in former colonial territories has generally been greeted with enthusiasm. Certainly most people in Asia and Africa were elated. Americans felt pleased and flattered that other people were following the example of 1776. Western Europeans quite probably sighed in relief. Enthusiasm engendered an atmosphere of optimism. Mankind, many believed fervently, was on the threshold of a brave new world. With the shackles of colonialism removed, progress was assured; democracy was sweeping the globe. Only recently have the full dimensions of the awesome task received attention. Since then, however, an uneasy feeling is growing that some of the newly independent countries—hopefully not most—may never develop into stable, modern nation-states, but submerge instead into anarchy, fratricide, and the barbarism of the darkest ages of human history.

The essential function of economic development in determining the prospects of the newly independent countries is widely recognized. Library shelves are packed with books on the subject. Economists supply a steady flow of theories. Governments proudly exhibit their planning commissions and devote much care and effort to detailed programs of resource mobilization and utilization. There is a similar appreciation—though perhaps less intense—for the requirements of an emerging national society. The literature is extensive. Social welfare agencies are diligently established, and public officials routinely discourse on social reform or the welfare state. Remarkably, there is little awareness of the crucial role of political development.

Until most recently it was generally held that independence and the constitution (often one bequeathed by the colonial power) completed the construction of the political system. Further changes would occur within this framework or could be handled through minor adjustments. Even those who recognized the inadequacy of this position were reluctant to take a public stand. One could detect a most pronounced aversion to any admission that these countries are not only economically underdeveloped and socially disorganized but also politically unstable. The struggle for and the achievement of independence evoked a pride which refuses to admit anything that would even remotely threaten the tenet of sovereign equality. Millions of tons of goods or thousands of technicians may be acceptable as foreign aid; sociologists and anthropologists may freely comb the countryside, but even a single political adviser is viewed with alarm as a return of colonialism. Most underdeveloped countries prefer to muddle along in the political arena, and scholars tend to respect their decision.

The position is clearly untenable. Recent history is littered with discarded constitutions. Unless one harbors the quaint notion that the maze of small-scale economic units with rudimentary specialization automatically and inevitably will expand into a large-scale industrial complex, or that a conglomeration of numerous disrupted traditional societies will necessarily reequilibrate in the form of a modern national entity, the crucial issue of initiative arises. This initiative, it is generally conceded, must come from the political system. Only an effective political system can possibly accelerate economic development by mobilizing and utilizing scarce resources efficiently. Similarly, only an effective political system can conceivably serve as the chief source of a new social control. The existing political systems in newly independent countries, however—and this is the crux of the matter—have nowhere near the capacities of coercion and persuasion necessary to direct the course and rate of economic and social change. These will first have to be developed. Until then their priority is clear.

Whether the political systems in these countries will ever develop these capacities is far from certain. The barriers to be surmounted are staggering. Interestingly —and this is a further commentary upon the close relationship of the various aspects of the task—progress toward economic development and a national orientation will facilitate the effectiveness of government initiative. Ultimately, however, political development will rest upon the emergence of political institutions (and leadership patterns) which are able to mobilize mass support. The academic communities throughout the world may doubtless aid the process by offering sound theories. These in turn require the correlation of empirical data and the performance of experiments. Hopefully, research in this direction will be intensified. My initial contribution is a study of the political development program in Pakistan.

In order to facilitate clarity this work is divided into two parts. The first includes a survey of the environment in which the political decision-maker must act and posits a series of propositions about the indigenous conditions that determine his range of alternatives. The second is devoted to a detailed discussion of the program of political development initiated and pursued by President Mohammad Ayub Khan.

The contention that political planning is in fact taking place in Pakistan deserves further comment. There is no intention whatever to suggest that President Ayub Khan had a detailed blueprint of specified ends *and means* which he rigorously followed. As a matter of fact, a major purpose of this study is to focus attention upon the very severe practical limitations faced by a capable, sincere, and hardworking leader, even though he does enjoy the confidence and support of a powerful army. He has had to make adjustments and compromises; he has had to witness the failure of some of his efforts. I do suggest, however, that his basic goal of a modern and effective political system remained paramount, and that his means were selected to serve this goal.

To establish the contention of political planning beyond a shadow of a doubt is clearly impossible. It is supported, however, by the following sets of facts. First, President Ayub Khan has claimed that political planning is taking place. From the very first days of martial law in the fall of 1958 he emphasized that he was not satisfied with short term, makeshift political improvisations. Instead, his primary efforts would be directed toward the long-range problem of gradually establishing a stable political system that could guide economic and social change. "I have definite ideas," he assured his countrymen. A personal note is of some relevance here. In the course of a conversation in December 1962, I asked President Ayub Khan why he pressed so resolutely for the restoration of constitutional government at the time when no effective opposition to his hegemony was in sight. I paraphrase his answer. To retain personal control over the country, the President explained, was not his primary purpose. The loyalty of the armed forces would assure so limited an objective. He held bolder ambitions. He sought to deliver his country from a chronic and devastating political instability by bestowing a constitution which would guide them for many generations. Along this line success would come only if his personal leadership and control could be converted gradually but surely into an institutional pattern sufficiently established to raise it above individual or partisan preference and which could effectively define the range of legitimate goals and means for the political arena. He would need time, concluded the President, to guide personally this transition from individual to institutional control.

Most revolutionary leaders pledge to establish a new and stable political order. Few have even a remote notion of how this could be accomplished; fewer still have thoughtfully formulated a definite program which they thereafter follow with any consistency. It is therefore of some significance that the contention of political planning in Pakistan is further supported by evidence indicating that long before martial law the President had considered in minute detail the political structure of Pakistan and had, in fact, arrived at some "definite ideas." The record further reveals a remarkable consistency in these "definite ideas" even though his own role in government has undergone substantial changes. Consider the following sequence. On October 4, 1954, Defense Minister Ayub Khan offered his views to the

Cabinet. His memorandum included not only an extended analysis of existing political difficulties, but also specific recommendations for remedies. He proposed a strong presidential system, separate provincial legislatures composed of 150 members each, a decentralized administrative system, and local development boards. Perhaps most interesting were his comments on the electoral process. He did not disguise his distrust of universal suffrage. At the same time he insisted that retreat from it in this stage of history would result in a disastrously unfavorable response from the citizens of Pakistan. To overcome the dilemma, Defense Minister Ayub recommended an electoral college system. Some four years later on March 5, 1959, President Ayub Khan expressed his views on political reconstruction to his Cabinet. The main ingredients of the 1954 position were retained: strong central executive, nominated provincial governors, elected national and provincial legislatures, administrative decentralization—all supported by universal suffrage channeled through an electoral college. One added feature of the 1959 memorandum was the President's concern about the legitimization of new institutions. He had little doubt about his duty to prepare a constitution but felt that somehow individual citizens and interest groups should also have an opportunity to contribute. Two alternatives suggested themselves: first, a referendum after the promulgation of the constitution and second, amendments by the new legislature which would reflect popular objections but would still be acceptable to the chief executive. In the spring of 1959 and again twenty-eight months later during the drafting sessions of the constitution President Ayub Khan preferred the latter choice. When it was finally completed, the new constitution (1962) was presidential in form. It provided for elected central and provincial legislatures and appointed governors. Suffrage was channeled through an electoral college. Finally the document was promulgated without prior popular ratification. Indeed one has to search with great diligence to discover differences between Pakistan's political institutions in 1964 and President Ayub Khan's blueprint of a decade earlier.

Given the validity of the contention of political planning in Pakistan, the second part of the study gains special significance. The environmental limitations upon the decision-maker may make Pakistan's case typical of the situations found in other newly independent countries. The record of a political development program makes Pakistan's case almost unique. Theoretical arguments perhaps suffice to demonstrate that drifting aimlessly never yields added political capacities. The effectiveness of a particular course, however, cannot be established by academic models. Only practical experience can do this. Thus the performance of specific experiments in the gigantic political laboratory called Pakistan—their success and their failures—may yield most useful lessons for those seeking to plot a secure course of political development in other parts of the world. It is of added significance that the political development program in Pakistan follows a non-totalitarian route. Its experiments may further demonstrate to what extent and in which form democratic institutions are adaptable to the conditions of the newly independent countries. Far, far more important—if indeed Pakistan's program will succeed—the pattern it would set may well save hundreds of millions of human beings from the agonies of revolution and the torments of terror.

++

Acknowledgments

++

THIS STUDY would not have been possible without the support of the Center of International
Studies, Princeton University. Although it was
commenced while I was a Fulbright Lecturer at
the University of Dacca (1961-1962), the Center
sustained it during the crucial year (1962-1963)
while its structure was taking shape.

I would also like to acknowledge major contributions to the conceptual foundations by Professors William W. Lockwood and Marion J. Levy,
Jr. of Princeton University, Charles Tilly of Harvard University, and Mr. Abdul Razzaque of the
University of Dacca. The manuscript was read
and commented upon at one stage or another
by Professor Mahmud Husain of the University
of Karachi, Professor Vernon Van Dyke of the
University of Iowa, Professor Charles Burton
Marshall of the School of Advanced International Studies, Johns Hopkins University, Professor
Manfred Halpern of Princeton University, and Professor Sidney Verba, formerly of the Center of
International Studies and now of Stanford University. Mrs. Ruth Madara, Librarian, South Asia Library, University of Pennsylvania, and her assistant Mrs. Panna Naik were most generous in their
bibliographic assistance. Mrs. Sally Aronstein and
Mr. Albert A. Thibault, Jr., graduate students at

the University of Pennsylvania, were instrumental in the compilation of election statistics. My wife, Barbara, contributed significantly to all phases.

I hope that none who helped in this effort will be disappointed.

Princeton, New Jersey   KARL VON VORYS
March 1965

Contents

List of Tables

xix

PART ONE

The Environment

Introduction

NOTHING but the pleasure of self-delusion can be gained from minimizing difficulties. These are the harsh realities of the environment from which Pakistan's decision-maker must fashion a modern nation-state. He has to guide a country bare in resources and scarce in human skills, a country moreover where national ties are extremely frail and where the small-scale social and economic units remain the foci of orientation. Perhaps more important, however, the decision-maker must act when he fully knows that the capacity for effective initiative is denied to the government. Communications, personnel, and ideological limitations exclude coercion as a useful tool. Persuasion is hardly more effective. There is little popular predisposition to conform to government decisions. Quite the contrary. An imperceptible rise in the standard of living and a rather apparent pressure against the traditional pattern have yielded resentment throughout the country and have even brought about a crisis of confidence in the East Wing. At the same time, the pattern of leadership offered by the government has been a combination of a façade of representative institutions and a hierarchy of socially isolated bureaucrats. It is not a particularly suitable pattern for the mobilization of mass support. That capacity continues to be reserved for the traditional hierarchies and has accrued by default to the three politicized interest groups, the *ulama* (religious leaders), the students, and the legal community, none of which

3

is favorably inclined to the government, and some are quite hostile. These indeed are terrible odds against the decision-maker. Yet if political development is to take place in this land of a hundred million Muslims, gradually perhaps but surely he must cope with them all.

Before spelling out in greater detail these propositions about the environment of Pakistan's decision-makers, a few words on supporting evidence may be helpful. Clearly Pakistan is among the few newly independent countries where a very considerable amount of data is available. The people are alert to their problems and spend a good part of their time discussing public issues. The Pakistani intellectual has an inquiring mind willing to probe into political and economic cause-and-effect relationships. In the universities a generation of young scholars is gradually emerging. They are schooled in the empirical methods and are willing to sacrifice their spare time for research. Substantial support by private foundations further stimulates interest in compiling accurate data about the country. Finally, in recent years the government has officially sponsored innumerable studies ranging from the report of the Education Commission to an analysis of rural credit. A related point should be noted here. A scholar sincerely interested in the country and engaged in productive research will find the political leadership most accessible. It is still amazing to me personally how much time and how often the President, members of his Cabinet, senior civil servants, and prominent party officials (or former party officials) made their time available to me for extended interviews. More important perhaps, these conversations were marked by a frankness and a sincere desire to help that have been almost unique in my experience. Even on sensitive political issues the person in question would bend over backward to supply as complete a documentation as propriety would permit.

In spite of these most robust efforts, however, there are some very significant areas of the Pakistani environment where data is scarce or not entirely reliable. This should not be surprising. Independence was gained only a decade and a half ago. Awareness that some questions are relevant is of relatively recent origin. There are, of course, additional difficulties such as the high rate of illiteracy, the rather rudimentary transportation and communications systems, and the sheer lack of personnel—all formidable barriers in the way of access to facts. Perhaps more significantly, even where empirical data seems to be available, it may well be of doubtful value. To cite only one example: The Central Statistical Office of Pakistan includes some of the most sophisticated and highly trained specialists in the world. They are familiar with the latest techniques. Yet all too often their skill is hampered and comes to naught. Consider the problem of calculating agricultural output. For their primary data the specialists of the Central Statistical Office are at the mercy of local officials. A substantial number of the latter do not send any reports at all affecting more than a third of the total land area. Even when reports are submitted, these are based on the impressions of village personnel who have neither the skill nor the facility for accurate calculations. They are moreover most vulnerable to the temptation of manipulating output figures for personal or political advantages. The CSO officials are quite aware of the fact that the method used is inadequate and that they will not approximate accurate output figures until the task of reporting is assumed by fully trained agricultural extension officers. This, however, will take time, a long time. There are some one hundred thousand villages in the country and less than three hundred young men per year who pass degree examinations in agriculture. In the meantime, the Central Statistical Office expert and the scholar must do the best they can.

Inadequate as some of the evidence may be, what are the alternatives? Firsthand impressions? It is undeniable that living in South Asia, traveling around widely and associating freely with all the population groups do provide the scholar with a "feel of the area." The experience of actually living in a Bengali village cannot be acquired through studying per capita income statistics or dietary patterns. Similarly, the different connotations of words in different culture patterns may escape one, unless he has extended personal contacts and some acquaintance with the indigenous languages. The difficulty with impressionistic evidence is its subjectivity. Personal preferences, ethnocentric prejudices, may creep perhaps unnoticed into the analysis. Moreover, the vastness and the complexity of Pakistan make it impossible to acquire adequate coverage in a reasonably limited time. The result all too often is an inclination to generalize from the impressions gained in one part of the country. Unfortunately this may lead to erroneous conclusions.

One possible alternative is reliance upon the personal impressions of other scholars and observers, both Pakistani and foreign. Yet even if such a composite were possible, the pitfall of the logic of the extreme case would still remain. There is no way to assure oneself or a reader that the impressions are based on a representative and relevant sample, not on the aberration of the extreme case. It is difficult enough to guard oneself against this danger regarding one's own impressions; it is infinitely more hazardous with someone else's impressions—particularly when these are received, as it were, in a distilled form.

Having drawn attention to the inadequacy of empirical data and the pitfalls of personal impressions, I now serve notice on the reader that I shall resort to both methods in the description and analysis of the decision-maker's environment in Pakistan. I propose to present all the empirical data available and augment these freely with personal impressions. To avoid misunderstanding I shall try to label each clearly. In the final analysis, however, the accuracy of the presentation will depend upon the merits of my professional judgment.

1

++

The Resource Base

++

PAKISTAN is a picturesque country. Snow-capped peaks tower majestically above the Khyber Pass and the bazaars of Peshawar. In Murree or Nathiagali one can breathe the clear mountain air and gaze down upon the gently coursing clouds. Descending into the soft green plains of the Punjab one is dazzled by the splendor of the Shalimar Gardens and the grandeur of the Badshahi Mosque at Lahore. Farther to the south stand the ancient towns of Hyderabad and Multan, and where the sparkling sands of Sind meet the azure of the Indian Ocean the modern port city of Karachi is located. A thousand miles across the Indian subcontinent is the lush tropical garden of East Bengal. Some of the world's mightiest rivers roll slowly across the lowlands past playfully bathing elephants, past prowling tigers. Primeval forests cover the Hill Tracts of Chittagong, while farther to the north neat rows of tea bushes garland the hills of Sylhet. Almost everywhere golden jute dries in the soft breezes.

Pakistan is also a very poor country. The land does not produce enough to feed the population. Mineral resources are scarce. Industry is in its infancy. The transportation network is rudimentary. The majority of the people, moreover, lack formal education or skills essential to the advance of specialization. The empirical data supporting these observations is clear and abundant. A condensed inventory, therefore, though tedious, may be appropriate.

Agriculture

As is true of most newly independent countries Pakistan's economy is primarily agricultural. Some 65 per cent of the labor force is engaged in this sector, contributing 56 per cent of the national income.[1] There is no shortage of land as such. The total territory covers some 365,529 square miles, four times the area of the United Kingdom. Arable land, however, is in short supply. In spite of extensive irrigation in regions like the Punjab only 20 per cent of West Pakistan and less than 27 per cent of the country is under cultivation.[2] Floods and other natural disasters periodically reduce the area sown in the East Wing. In West Pakistan waterlogging is a fairly constant and expanding threat. For example, in the Lyallpur District the waterlogged area increased from 137,000 acres in 1948-1949 to 274,000 acres in 1956-1957.[3] Most alarming, however, is the rapid advance of soil erosion and salination. The Photographic Survey Corporation of Canada, carrying out a soil survey of the Indus Valley, found that of a total of 15.6 million acres in the region only 1.8 million acres of irrigated land are comparatively free from erosion. Of the

[1] Government of Pakistan, *Economic Survey of Pakistan 1961-62* (Rawalpindi: Government of Pakistan Press, 1962), Statistical Section, pp. 7, 8, and Government of Pakistan, Planning Commission, *Statistics on Development Planning in Pakistan* (Karachi: Government of Pakistan Press, 1960), p. 3.

[2] Government of Pakistan, Central Statistical Office, *Pakistan Statistical Yearbook 1962* (Karachi: Government of Pakistan Press, 1962), pp. 70-72.

[3] *Ibid.*, p. 91.

9

balance, 13.8 million acres are affected "in varying degrees" and 4.3 million acres have been "rendered unproductive."[4] The Food and Agriculture Commission referring to this problem arrived at the following conclusion: "The gravity of the position may be gauged by the fact that unless a solution is found a very large proportion of the irrigated area may pass out of cultivation altogether in the comparatively near future."[5]

The substantial limitations on the availability of arable land are not offset by high fertility. Only in jute does Pakistan register comparatively high yields. As Table 1 indicates, even in her two most important staples, performance is far less impressive.[6]

Table 1

Yield of Wheat and Rice in Selected Countries
(kg per hectare)

Country	Wheat	Rice (paddy)
Denmark	39.0	—
France	25.3	31.6
Germany (West)	34.8	—
India	7.8	15.2
Japan	25.4	48.6
Pakistan	8.0	16.0
Poland	16.9	—
USSR	10.6	18.7
United States	17.6	38.4
Yugoslavia	17.3	36.5

There is evidence furthermore that over the years the

[4] Quoted in Government of Pakistan, *Report of the Food and Agriculture Commission* (Karachi: Government of Pakistan Press, 1960), p. 4.

[5] *Ibid.*, p. 43.

[6] Food and Agriculture Organization of the United Nations, *Production Yearbook 1961* (Rome: Food and Agriculture Organization, 1962), pp. 35-36, 50-51, 143.

fertility of agricultural land has not improved substantially. In jute, it is true, the average yield per acre of the 1956-1960 period was almost 10 per cent above the average yield of the previous five years. However, for rice the increase amounted to less than 3 per cent, for wheat and cotton less than 1 per cent.[7]

The combination of the scarcity of arable land and low yields is largely—though certainly not entirely—responsible for an inadequate food output. During the last three years of the First Five Year Plan (1957-1960) the cost of food imports reached Rs 15 crores, or almost exactly the amount of the country's trade deficit.[8] On October 15, 1961, Pakistan signed an agreement with the United States according to which she would receive American agricultural surplus goods with an estimated market value of Rs 25.5 crores over a three-year period.[9] Yet in spite of this supplement of domestic food resources the diet available to the average person remains far from satisfactory. According to a nutrition survey in East Pakistan, more than 25 per cent of the children up to the age of four years die of malnutrition.[10] Actually, the average daily calorie intake of 2,080 is not very much below the level in Japan (2,240) and somewhat above that in India (1,860).[11] The problem lies with the composition of the diet, which is almost exclusively starch. In fact, it contains less than half the

[7] *Pakistan Statistical Yearbook 1962*, p. 85.

[8] *Ibid.*, pp. 137, 147 [1 crore = 10,000,000].

[9] United States, Department of Agriculture, "Title I, Public Law 480.—Agreements signed from beginning of program (as modified by purchase authorization transactions) through September 30, 1962," SDS-12-62, p. 5.

[10] Dacca, *Pakistan Observer*, July 20, 1964, p. 1.

[11] Food and Agriculture Organization of the United Nations, *Production Yearbook 1961, op.cit.*, p. 245.

protein content of the rations given to inmates of German concentration camps during the period of April 1944 to February 1945 when food there was most scarce.[12]

Table 2

Annual Consumption of Some Non-Cereal Food Products in Selected Countries
(kg per year)

	Pakistan (1959-1960)	Japan (1959-1960)	U.S. (1959-1960)	German Concentration Camps (1944-1945)
Sugar	12	15	41	4.1
Meat	4	6	95	10.4
Fish	1	23	5	

To make matters worse, the cereal consumed is of an inferior variety. The main staple of the majority of the population is rice, and primary reliance upon it causes a condition known as *kwashiorkor*, among whose symptoms are lethargy and an extremely short attention span.

Food resources are not only inadequate but there is evidence that in per capita terms they may be declining. Naturally there are some short-term variations, but over a longer range the population is increasing at a rate almost twice that of the domestic output of food. Thus, for example, while the 1961 population census records a decennial increase of 23.7 per cent, the 1957-1961 average output of food grains exceeded average output of the 1947-1951 period by only 12.3 per cent.[13]

[12] *Ibid.*, pp. 247-249, and Eugen Kogon, *Der SS-Staat* (Frankfurt a/M: Verlag der Frankfurter Hefte, 1946), p. 115.
[13] *Economic Survey of Pakistan 1961-62*, Statistical Section, p. 16.

Mineral Resources

Under the mostly barren top soil of West Pakistan and the thin alluvial layer of the East Wing no great mineral wealth has so far been discovered. Since 1957 the geological survey of the country has been accelerated, but to date the results have been modest, to say the least. Preeminent in the exploration has been the search for gas and oil. Eighty-eight per cent of the fuels and minerals allocations of the First Plan was assigned for this purpose. The Second Plan has pledged to continue this pattern.[14] In the process substantial natural gas reserves were discovered—the richest fields at Sui and Mari in West Pakistan and near Sylhet in East Pakistan. Oil explorations, relying first on American, then on Soviet technical assistance, have yielded less encouraging results. The richest oil deposit discovered was near Balkassar, southwest of the capital, yet even there the reserves are small. Although domestic output of crude oil reached almost 101 crore gallons in 1961, it was still necessary to import Rs 31 crores worth of petroleum and petroleum products.[15]

There are scattered coal deposits in West Pakistan. Some have a high sulfur content which makes conversion into industrial coke unsuitable.[16] Others are located at inaccessible altitudes. Their extent and quality have not yet been ascertained. Somewhat more encouraging are recent reports indicating the discovery of "best quality coal" in the East Wing (Rajshahi and Bogra).[17]

[14] Government of Pakistan, *The Second Five Year Plan (1960-65)* (Karachi: Government of Pakistan Press, 1960), p. 269.

[15] *Pakistan Statistical Yearbook 1962*, pp. 131, 152.

[16] *Second Five Year Plan*, pp. 271-272.

[17] Karachi, *Dawn*, January 25, 1964, p. 1.

13

Total domestic output is now approaching one million tons and is augmented by imports costing Rs 5.2 crores a year.[18]

The story of iron deposits is very similar. Some reserves have been discovered in West Pakistan, but those which are high grade (Chagai and Dammar Nissar) are almost inaccessible, and the deposit closer at hand (Kalabagh) yields a much lower grade ore.[19] Total domestic output was only slightly in excess of four thousand tons in 1961.[20] Thus Pakistan, as yet, is almost exclusively dependent on imports of iron, scrap iron, and steel with an annual bill of Rs 36.5 crores.[21]

The country has other mineral resources as well. Table 3 indicates their current exploitation.

Table 3

Domestic Production of Selected Minerals, 1959-1961[22]

(in tons)

Mineral	1959	1960	1961
Asbestos	46	—	—
Barytes	508	635	437
Bauxite	2,139	574	1,411
Chromite	16,000	18,000	25,000
Copper	—	154	—
Lead	331	17	62
Magnesite	376	663	160
Manganese	29	180	344
Silica sand	22,000	26,000	15,000

Unhappily, these are not quantities capable of sustaining a substantial industrial complex. A final conclusion

[18] *Pakistan Statistical Yearbook 1962*, pp. 131, 152; and State Bank of Pakistan, *Bulletin*, March 1964, p. 82.

[19] *Second Five Year Plan*, p. 273.

[20] *Economic Survey of Pakistan 1961-62*, Statistical Section, p. 41.

[21] *Pakistan Statistical Yearbook 1962*, pp. 152, 154.

[22] *Economic Survey of Pakistan 1961-62*, Statistical Section, p. 41.

on this matter, however, must be delayed until the geological survey is completed.

Industry

Industry is not yet a substantial sector in Pakistan. It contributes only 13 per cent to the national income.[23] According to the Census of Manufacturing Industries, the value of fixed assets at the end of 1960 reached the very modest sum of Rs 196.4 crores, almost three-fourths of which were located in West Pakistan. Textiles, food processing, and the production of chemicals predominate, accounting for slightly more than 60 per cent of the assets. Industries engaged in the manufacture of machinery and transport equipment and metal goods still play only a minor role. Their combined assets, Rs 23.7 crores, represent only a 12 per cent share of the total fixed assets of the manufacturing industries.[24]

Industry, however, is a rapidly expanding sector. There are massive imports: in 1959-1960 some 70.3 crores of machinery and vehicles.[25] Accordingly, after partition industrial assets rose sharply from Rs 58 crores to Rs 502 crores in 1959.[26] More specifically, the fixed assets of the manufacturing industries increased by 28 per cent during the last three years of the First Five Year Plan. The assets of the metal industries and those of machinery and transport equipment manufacturers grew even more rapidly (34 per cent).[27] Whether this momentum can be sustained in the face of an apparent

[23] *Ibid.*, pp. 7-8.
[24] *Ibid.*, pp. 42-43.
[25] *Pakistan Statistical Yearbook 1962*, p. 148.
[26] Gustav Papanek, "The Development of Entrepreneurship," *The American Economic Review*, LII, No. 2 (May 1962), p. 51.
[27] *Pakistan Statistical Yearbook 1962*, pp. 108-109.

scarcity of mineral resources and some unfavorable economic and social conditions is, of course, a crucial question.

Transportation

"Rudimentary" is the kindest word to describe the transportation network and facilities of the country. Consider first the road network. According to official statistics the territory of Pakistan was serviced by 10,775 miles of "high type" highways in 1960.[28] This means that there are 34 square miles of territory for each mile of "high type" road in Pakistan. The comparable ratio is 9:1 for neighboring India and 1:1 for the United States of America.

These statistics, however, do not tell the whole story. To begin with, there are some very substantial regional differences. Less than 10 per cent of the "high type" road mileage is in East Pakistan.[29] The only long-distance roads in this province are the Dacca-Mymensingh (125 miles) and the Chittagong-Cox's Bazaar (100 miles) routes and the completed sections of the Dacca-Chittagong highway. Moreover, the designation of "high type" highways is perhaps somewhat extravagant. It refers to roads which are almost always single lane, that is, the entire pavement is scarcely wider than the width of a bus. Two motor vehicles can pass each other only if at least one of them partially leaves the pavement. The surface of these roads is uneven, with unrepaired cracks and holes. In places the hard surface is worn off altogether and has been replaced in a some-

[28] *Statistics on Development Planning,* p. 47.
[29] Government of East Pakistan, *Monthly Survey of Economic Conditions in East Pakistan,* xii, No. 1 (July 1961), p. 4.

what makeshift manner with crushed rock or brick. There are frequent detours, and in the East Wing constant ferry crossings are necessary.

Packed on these roads are motor vehicles of various sizes and varieties and ten times as many ox carts, camel carts, donkey carts, and rickshaws.[30] To this one must add the thousands of pedestrians who use the highways during market days and the early morning and late afternoon hours. Finally, there are herds of cattle, sheep, or goats driven over the roads, or individual animals wandering about. The result is that even where there are roads the traffic must move very slowly indeed.

Railroads were introduced on the subcontinent over a century ago, and until recently they were the chief means for relatively rapid and long-range transportation. Nevertheless, their conditions are similar to road transport. The ratio of square miles of territory to miles of railroad track is 52:1 in Pakistan, 32:1 in India and 17:1 in the United States. Here too there are striking differences between the two Wings. During the First Plan (1955-1960) the share of the Pakistan Eastern Railway in the total acquisition was 26 out of 135 locomotives, 294 out of 6,959 wagons and 146 out of 625 coaches and other rolling stock.[31]

As in the case of highways, railroad beds are predominantly single track. Operations are further hindered by differences in gauge. In East Pakistan, for ex-

[30] There are no detailed estimates available for West Pakistan. In the East Wing all motor vehicles (trucks, buses, jeeps, motorcycles, etc.) totaled 14,217 in 1960. At the same time there were 155,485 non-motorized vehicles in the municipal areas alone. (United States, Department of the Army, Corps of Engineers, *Transportation Survey of East Pakistan, 1961* [Washington, D.C.: Department of the Army, 1962], III, 201, 206.)

[31] *Statistics of Development Planning*, p. 47.

17

ample, the total route mileage of 1,712 is divided into 545.6 miles of broad gauge, 1,146.6 miles of meter gauge, and 19.8 miles of narrow gauge. The preponderance of meter gauge is a handicap in itself, but the prevalence of three different gauges in a relatively small network causes considerable delay and expense.[32]

Railroad equipment is scarce. Worse still, it is in poor condition and is inefficiently operated. The following data are illustrative. Almost two-thirds of the locomotives are more than 30 years old. The average speed for express trains in East Pakistan is 27 miles an hour; the average wagon mileage per day is 20 on the meter-gauge and 30 on the broad-gauge track. The average miles traveled by passengers *dropped* from 38 in 1951 to 26 in 1960. Finally on March 31, 1961, in Chittagong there were 1,131 unfilled requests for freight cars, 998 of which were outstanding for over a week.[33]

In the most recent past, air transportation has made its debut in Pakistan, but the high cost has so far prevented its extensive use. Capacity is small and remains only partially (61 per cent) utilized.[34] It performs, however, the essential function of serving as an important link between the two Wings. Within East Pakistan air bus and helicopter service extend rapid transportation to the less accessible areas.

Water transport requires a special mention in a survey of transportation in Pakistan. It is still the predominant means of carrying people and goods in the East Wing. Surrounded by rivers and most of the year by flooded

[32] *Transportation Survey of East Pakistan*, ii, 145, 160-161.

[33] *Second Five Year Plan*, p. 281 and *Transportation Survey of East Pakistan*, ii, 159, 160, 163; iii, 115-116.

[34] Pakistan International Airlines, "Annual Report, 1961-62" (pages unnumbered).

areas, 90 per cent of the villages must rely on boats to maintain contact with each other and with distant towns. During the recent decades motorized water transport has been introduced at a rapid rate. The increase in launches in East Pakistan from 58 at the time of independence to 450 in December 1960 is impressive, although somewhat modified by rapid depreciation due to poor maintenance and constant overloading. The preponderant share of water traffic, however, is carried by slow and short-range non-motorized craft. Some 203,072 such passenger vessels ply the waters, while 316,505 non-motorized cargo carriers annually transport over 6,360,000 tons of goods, or more than is carried by either the railroads or highway transport.[35]

Skills

Data regarding the resource of human skill reflect a similar pattern. Most fundamental is the skill to read and write; most dramatic is its scarcity. The 1961 Census of Pakistan defines literacy as the ability to "read with understanding a short statement of everyday life in any language," and reports that out of a total population of 93,720,614 only 15.9 per cent qualify.[36] A more rigorous test of functional literacy, requiring a minimum of five years formal schooling, eliminates all but 9.4 per cent of those ten years or older. The situation is further aggravated by the fact that a large percentage of functionally literate persons is concentrated in the younger age group. Thus while an estimated 15.6 per cent of the age group of fifteen to nineteen can be so classified, the

[35] *Transportation Survey of East Pakistan*, ii, 92, and iii, 60.
[36] Pakistan Census Commissioner, *Population Census of Pakistan 1961*, Census Bulletin No. 4 (Karachi: Government of Pakistan Press, 1962), p. vii.

figure drops sharply to 7.3 per cent in the category of twenty-five years and over.[37] There are also differences between rural and urban areas and between East and West Pakistan. Applying the official definition, literacy in urban areas (35.8 per cent) is substantially above that in the villages (16.6 per cent).[38] Similarly, the number of literates in the East Wing (17.6 per cent) is significantly above the figure for the West Wing (13.6 per cent). Combining these data, we find that in some rural areas of West Pakistan illiteracy must be appalling. In the Kalat Division less than 4 per cent of the population over five years of age can read a simple statement in any language.[39] Improvement, moreover, is expected to be slow. Currently only about 30 per cent of the relevant age group is attending primary schools,[40] and universal education is not considered feasible for another decade or two.[41]

There is an even greater paucity of more specialized skills. In the absence of an accurate manpower survey no direct data are available on the size of the skilled labor force. Its modest dimension, however, may be inferred from an estimate in the Second Five Year Plan that the annual output of all technical training centers in 1960 reached only 1,250. It was hoped that by 1965 the output of these centers plus that of polytechnics, monotechnics, technical institutes, artisan and trade

[37] Jamila Akhtar, "Literacy and Education: Fifth Release from the 1961 Census of Pakistan," *Pakistan Development Review*, III (Autumn 1963), pp. 430, 434.

[38] *Population Census of Pakistan 1961*, Census Bulletin No. 4, p. xiv.

[39] *Ibid.*, p. xix.

[40] *Pakistan Statistical Yearbook 1962*, p. 321.

[41] Pakistan, Ministry of Education, *Report of the Commission on National Education* (Karachi: Government of Pakistan Press, 1960), p. 183.

schools of varying grades and types, plus the number of those trained at industrial establishments, together would exceed 11,190.[42] In view of the fact that in 1951 the non-agricultural labor force was almost five and a half million,[43] this surely is a tiny fragment.

If we turn to advanced educational achievement, we find that college graduates amount to only a very small portion of the population. In 1961 they totaled 82,069, or only 4 per cent of citizens twenty-five years of age or older. It is significant, moreover, that this figure represents a decline from the 85,988 graduates recorded by the 1951 census.[44] The Second Five Year Plan also indicates inferentially that as a "rough estimate" there are some 2,000 "graduate engineers of various types."[45] The number of doctors reached 9,200 in 1959, or one for every 10,000 inhabitants.[46] In comparison, the same ratio in the United States is one qualified physician for every 750 inhabitants. Since most doctors are concentrated in the cities, this means no scientific medical attention in rural areas where the vast majority of the population lives. In all of Pakistan there were only 2,000 nurses in 1960, or a ratio of one nurse per 46,500 population.[47] Finally in 1959 there were 170,847 teachers in elementary, middle, and secondary schools.[48] A full use

[42] *Second Five Year Plan*, pp. 347-348.
[43] *Pakistan Statistical Yearbook 1962*, p. 11.
[44] *Population Census of Pakistan 1961*, Census Bulletin No. 4, p. xx.
[45] *Second Five Year Plan*, p. 370.
[46] *Ibid.*, p. 357.
[47] *Statistics on Development Planning in Pakistan*, p. 50.
[48] Government of East Pakistan, Education Directorate, *Report on the Ground Survey of Educational Institutions in East Pakistan* (Dacca: East Pakistan Government Press, 1960), Part I, p. 2; Government of East Pakistan, Education Directorate, *Report on the Ground Survey of Educational Institutions in East Pakistan* (Dacca: East Pakistan Government Press, 1961), Part II, p. 5; Government of

21

of training facilities during the 1960-1965 period would still leave, according to official estimates, a deficit of 70,000 teachers in the primary grades alone.[49]

Another skill, the skill of entrepreneurship, also requires special attention. That entrepreneurs are essential for economic development is generally accepted; identifying them is another matter. This we know: In June 1960 the number of proprietorships, partnerships, and joint stock companies in the manufacturing industries totaled 3,373.[50] There is also evidence that less than 250 industrialists control some 75 per cent of the capital in Pakistan.[51]

The quantitative data on personnel, however, do not fully reveal the extent of the scarcity of skill. A further critical aspect of the problem is that even those who claim qualification seldom meet requirements which, at least in the western part of the world, are normally regarded as essential. In the case of the entrepreneurs, for instance, we find the number of men occupying the position of manager of industrial plants increasing steadily. There is little evidence, however, that they stimulate rising productivity. Consider, for example, the performance of Pakistan's largest industry, cotton textiles. Its environment of high protective tariffs and massive imports of machinery could favor innovation. Yet the record of the 1953-1961 period reveals that while the

West Pakistan, Bureau of Education, *Educational Statistics for West Pakistan Province 1958-59* (Lahore: Government of West Pakistan Press, 1960), pp. 43, 49, 55.

[49] *Second Five Year Plan*, p. 344.

[50] State Bank of Pakistan, Central Directorate, "Memorandum #DR-MS/48/6849-62."

[51] Gustav F. Papanek, "The Development of Entrepreneurship," *American Economic Review*, LII, No. 2 (May 1962), pp. 48-49.

inputs of spindle hours, loom hours, and the consumption of raw materials (cotton) increased by 308 per cent, 257 per cent, and 298 per cent respectively, the output of yarn and cloth lagged behind, rising only by 241 per cent and 177 per cent.[52]

The qualification of teachers is similarly suspect. The total of 78,565 primary school teachers in East Pakistan includes 42,857 (54 per cent) who have not completed high school.[53] Similarly, 26,492 (70 per cent) of the 37,869 high school teachers in the country do not even hold a college degree,[54] although in Pakistan such degrees are awarded after 14 years of education rather than the 16 years customary in the United States. One may even wonder about the small segment of graduates in the profession, for a teacher has neither prestige nor a reasonable income in Pakistan. As an informal experiment I asked all the senior high school students in 19 randomly selected secondary schools what profession they hoped to enter. Not a single one answered "teaching." In rural areas of East Pakistan the top monthly salary for a teacher is Rs 65.50, and only the most senior of the trained teachers receive this amount. On the other hand, the personal servant (peon) of the Assistant Director of Public Instruction has a base salary of Rs 80 a

[52] There was also a change in the mix of fine, medium, and coarse cloth from a ratio of 10:76:14 to 12:47:41 (*Pakistan Statistical Yearbook 1962*, pp. 126-127).

[53] Government of East Pakistan, Education Directorate, *Report on the Ground Survey of Educational Institutions in East Pakistan*, Part I, p. 2. No comparable breakdown is published by the West Pakistan Directorate.

[54] Government of East Pakistan, Education Directorate, *Report on the Ground Survey of Educational Institutions in East Pakistan*, Part II, p. 5; The West Pakistan Bureau of Education, *Educational Statistics for West Pakistan 1958-59* (Lahore: n.p., 1960), p. 55.

month.[55] Perhaps it is not extravagant to assume that in most cases only the very worst of the graduates and matriculates who have no other prospects turn to teaching as a profession.

Doubts have also been expressed about the qualifications of graduate engineers. "Engineering education has not been of a high quality," observes the Second Plan.[56] "It is a common criticism that our present engineering graduates are often averse to working with their hands and do not even know how to repair a machine," reports the Education Commission.[57]

Finally the record is completed by Pakistan's medical graduates. In the March 1962 examinations administered by the (United States) Educational Council for Foreign Medical Graduates, only 49 out of a total of 158 Pakistani candidates scored 75 or over. This percentage of 31.0 is not only below the American performance of 95, but also less than the worldwide average of 43.9.[58]

Such indeed are the resources of Pakistan. Still the dimension of their deficiency represents only one feature of the environment that limits the political decision-maker's initiative. No less severe a restraint is the prevalence of disrupted small-scale social units which nevertheless continue to serve as foci of orientation.

[55] *Working Papers for the Seventh Meeting of the East Pakistan Development Advisory Council* (Dacca: East Pakistan Government Press, 1961), Part I, p. 13.

[56] *Second Five Year Plan*, p. 346.

[57] *Report of the Commission on National Education*, p. 64.

[58] Letter from G. Halsey Hunt, M.D., Executive Director of Educational Council for Foreign Medical Graduates, October 15, 1963.

2

++

The Focus of Orientation

++

U NDER INTERNATIONAL LAW Pakistan is a sovereign state. It sends and receives ambassadors; it is entitled to sue in foreign courts. In the halls of the United Nations or in foreign chancelleries its diplomats represent and protect its *national* interests. This external image of solidity, however, is the consequence of international definition rather than a reflection of internal cohesion. To the vast majority of its population national interest is a rather hazy and remote concept. Identification with fellow citizens in distant regions is most tenuous. Certainly a willingness to subordinate personal and parochial advantages to "national interest" is rare.

For centuries, perhaps millennia, a vast number of traditional societies—kinship groups and tribes—operated in a small-scale equilibrium in South Asia. Each was socially definitive. It made and enforced rules. It ascribed and rewarded roles. Each was also economically self-sufficient. It produced its own food and traded its modest surplus for other necessities with local artisans. Except for times of cataclysms it provided at least subsistence to all members. This is not to say that the small-scale traditional societies were free from stresses and strains. They were not. Their long term persistence was assured, however, by the absence of alternatives. There were few outside contacts and even in these, whether the subject was marriage or property, the critical criterion remained family identification. Ostracism was a most potent deterrent.

The traditional small-scale societies are no longer in equilibrium. They are no longer socially definitive. Increasingly, urbanization offers a new range of alternatives while traditional rules appear inappropriate and their implementation seems ineffective. Increasingly, the confidence in the hierarchy is sapped by men of inferior ascriptive standing, who through competitive accomplishments earn substantial increments in rewards. Increasingly, the authority of the hierarchy is undermined by a younger generation with more education than its elders and by women with a vote equal to that of their husbands. Nor are the traditional small-scale societies self-sufficient any more. With a massive increase in population in a relatively short time the size of the kinship group to be sustained by the small agricultural holding has multiplied many times over while the holdings themselves have been subdivided and fragmented. Simultaneously the introduction of industry has offered a formidable competition, gradually invading remote rural markets, reducing and in some instances eliminating altogether the income of artisans.

Disruption of the small-scale equilibrium, however, does not appear to be sufficient stimulus for reintegration on the national scale. The forces facilitating national cohesion, moreover, have not so far distinguished themselves by the potency of their appeal. In their absence—and this is a most significant paradox—the anomic pressures in fact reinforce the small scale as a focus of orientation. In rural areas, for example, this is expressed in a neo-orthodox reaction. Villagers increasingly aware of their own vulnerability respond with some anger to the disequilibrating pressures of "modernization" and seek refuge almost desperately in an intensified commitment to the values and organizational pattern of their fathers and their own childhood. Even urban residents, although physically removed from the confines of traditional societies, retain a considerable measure of commitment to them. Many, of course, have arrived only recently. Faced by the complexity and unfamiliarity of their new environment they naturally accentuate the habits acquired in the past. They seek security through social contacts with persons from the same kinship group or those from the same village. They seek security by applying as critical criteria in economic relations the traditional ascriptive identifications. Above all, these urban residents seek security through religious ritual. The mosque indeed remains one of the few familiar and reassuring sights which greet the urban immigrant. There are, of course, veteran city dwellers who for generations have had little contact with the rural communities. Still, for them as well, kinship ties are of primary importance. Beyond these, they turn to professional and class associations as a focus of their orientation. The net result is a Pakistan which is culturally and socially heterogeneous, economically proliferated, and held together internally only by frail national ties. Let us be more specific.

Cultural and Social Heterogeneity

Pakistan is indeed a rich mosaic of ethnic groups. Among them differences are not merely superficial; they involve fundamentals—language, customs, and mores. The groups have little sympathy for each other and less participation in common ideals. There is much suspicion and even hostility.

The Bengali are by far the largest ethnic group. They share the East Wing with a small group of Assamese around Sylhet and a few tribesmen in the Chittagong Hill Tracts. They are a thin, short, sentimental, and extraordinarily friendly people. The men routinely wear *lungis* (a sort of wraparound skirt) or loose white linen trousers. The women wear *sarees*. Their staple diet is rice. Vigorously, perhaps aggressively, they are committed to their language and cultural traditions. Across some one thousand miles of unfriendly Indian territory lies the West Wing. The people there are taller, calmer, and somewhat more reticent. The men wear *kamis* and *kurta* (long, high-collared coats with trousers) and the ladies *kamis* and *shalwar* (high-collared dresses with pajama-like slacks). Their main staple is wheat. In spite of some common elements which differentiate them from the Bengali those residing in West Pakistan do not form an ethnically homogeneous entity. They are Sindhis, Punjabis, Baluchis, Pathans, Kashmiris, and refugees from all over India and the Near East. Each group is committed to its own customs, its own language, and its own cultural traditions. To a Pathan the ways of the Bengali are different—perhaps even foreign; but no less different and no less foreign are the customs of Sind or the mores of the refugee metropolis of Karachi.

In turn, there are severe cleavages supported by tradition within ethnic groups. To begin with, there are caste distinctions. Among the Hindu minority identification with caste is rigid and insistent. Islam does not permit such differentations among its followers. Still, Muslims in South Asia divide themselves into castelike groups. There is a widely accepted separation between High Muslims and Low Muslims. A generation ago a study identified four castelike groups among Muslims in India based primarily upon descent from the Holy Prophet or from the ruling elites of foreign conquerors: the Sayyid, Shaykh, Mughal and Pathan.[1] More recent investigations in the Punjab revealed effective castelike distinctions between *zamindars* and *kammis*.[2] In East Pakistan, according to another study, High Muslim groups include the Khans, who are landlords by tradition, and the Khandkars, who monopolize religious activities in the villages. The lower Muslims in turn are divided into a maze of groups such as Shek, Shikdar, Kulu, Jolaha, Nikari, and Bediya, "which indicate the craft and profession which they have inherited from their ancestors and which will be practiced by their sons and daughters."[3] Between High Muslims and Low Muslims and among the Low Muslim groups there is little social interaction, less intermarriage, and virtually no social mobility. Deviation from inherited occupations is rare. An illustration of this last point is offered by yet another recent study. It found the Khandkars facing hard times. Their return from management of land is low; their fees from conducting religious rites are meagre. The study, however, also found that "not only do the Khandkars believe manual labour as being beneath their dignity, but also villagers feel that if a

[1] Murray T. Titus, *Indian Islam* (London: Oxford University Press, 1930), p. 139.

[2] Zekiye Eglar, *A Punjabi Village in Pakistan* (New York: Columbia University Press, 1960), p. 28.

[3] Fazlur Rashid Khan, "The Caste System of the Village Community of Dhulandi in the District of Dacca," in John E. Owen, *Sociology in East Pakistan* (Dacca: Asiatic Society of Pakistan, 1962), pp. 226-227.

Khandkar came to work in the field the crop is bound to fail."[4]

In addition to castelike groupings, village communities continue to play a prominent role in social control. Religious life is regulated by the village *mullah* (a religious functionary). Disputes are expected to be settled through village elders. Most potent, however, are family and kinship ties. Marriage arrangements are settled by the head of the family, and his decisions are rarely perceived as arbitrary. Individual incomes of members are contributed to joint family funds. Sacrifices for family security or family honor are routinely expected in frontier areas. Here families, perhaps more accurately "clans," live in their own fortresses armed with automatic weapons. Rifles, pistols, and knives are basic items of men's wearing apparel. A visitor to one family is by definition suspect to the occupants of the fortress only a few yards away. Feuds are continued as a matter of course.

Ethnic, caste, regional, and kinship alignments so predominant in rural areas are carried over to urban centers as well. In Karachi the refugee communities are organized along such lines. Rivalry between the great industrial families is perhaps not as sanguinary as are the feuds in the frontier areas, but it is no less predatory. In employment ascriptive criteria play a major role. That ethnic and regional origin is a crucial consideration becomes apparent from the fact that more than 90 per cent of the faculty of the University of Dacca are Bengali, and the ratio of the Punjabi at the University of the Punjab and the Sindhi at the University of

[4] S. A. Qadir, *Village Dhanishwar* (Comilla: Pakistan Academy for Village Development, 1960), p. 53.

Sind is similarly preponderant. The relevance of kin-ship affiliation is indicated by a survey of industrial workers in East Pakistan. No less than 43 per cent of the random sample were found to be related to each other.[5] In social contacts the same pattern prevails. In four randomly selected tea shops in Lahore I found most patrons clustered according to the villages from which they came. A survey at Khulna revealed that 84 per cent of the industrial labor force lives with relatives or with persons originating from the same village or region. Conversely, among the local population only 12 per cent of those interviewed admitted having friends among workers who were not born in Khulna.[6]

Economic Proliferation

Cultural and social heterogeneity is further reinforced by the extraordinarily small scale of the units of produc-tion. Consider first the condition of agriculture. In the East Wing the average holding is about one acre.[7] In West Pakistan large and medium estates are more com-mon, yet even in this Wing the small units predominate. The average is below seven acres of cultivated land.[8]

[5] A. F. A. Husain, *Human and Social Impact of Technological Change in Pakistan* (Dacca: Oxford University Press, 1956), i, 356.

[6] A. F. A. Husain and A. Farouk, *Problems of Social Integration of Industrial Workers in Khulna with Special Reference for Industrial Unrest* (Dacca: Dacca University Socio-Economic Research Board, 1961), Appendices B-38, B-39, B-42, and D-4(a).

[7] *Report of the Food and Agriculture Commission* (Karachi: Gov-ernment of Pakistan Press, 1960), p. 37 and Government of East Pakistan, *Report of the East Pakistan Land Reforms Committee* (Dacca: East Pakistan Government Press, 1960), p. 4.

[8] *Report of the Land Reforms Commission for West Pakistan* (Lahore: Government Printing West Pakistan, 1961), Appendix i; *Report of the Food and Agriculture Commission*, p. 17; and *Prelimi-nary Report—Agricultural Census, West Pakistan* (Karachi: Govern-ment of Pakistan Press, 1962), p. 13.

31

Small as these units are, they are rarely consolidated. More often the family holding is composed of bits and fragments strewn all over the countryside and mixed in with bits and fragments of the holdings of other families. In East Pakistan 53 per cent of the less-than-half-acre holdings and 88 per cent of the half-acre holdings are fragmented into two or more plots.[9] The regional average of plots per acre is estimated at two in Rangpur to four in Feni.[10]

The small scale is also characteristic of production in the industrial sector. This is the sector of artisans and small family concerns. Although no detailed survey is available, an official estimate concludes that "the percentage of self-employed industrial labour force works out to 80 per cent of the total labour force, including those engaged in Defense and Railway Workshops."[11] The countryside is dotted with a mass of cottage industries. These "employ" only a few persons, most often only members of the immediate family.[12] The census of 1951 lists 57,357 such units employing 180,189 in West Pakistan.[13] A more recent survey by the Small Industries Corporation discovered 312,504 cottage in-

[9] Government of Pakistan, *1960 Pakistan Census of Agriculture* (Karachi: Government of Pakistan Press, 1962), I, 86.

[10] Dacca University Socio-Economic Survey Board, *Rural Credit and Unemployment in East Pakistan* (Dacca: Pakistan Cooperative Book Society, 1956), p. 43.

[11] Government of East Pakistan, Planning Department, "Memorandum #573/C/Cord/11-12/62."

[12] In the sample of 1,290 cottage industries the total persons employed was 4,049, of which 2,780 were family members (Wiqar Husain Zaidi, *A Survey of Cottage Industries in Comilla Development Area*, Technical Publication No. 3 [Comilla: Pakistan Academy for Village Development, 1960], p. 55).

[13] *Pakistan Statistical Yearbook 1962* (Karachi: Government of Pakistan Press, 1962), p. 124.

dustries employing 937,572 workers in East Pakistan. This is about 75 per cent of the industrial labor force in the province.[14]

Even in urban areas a substantial segment of industrial production originates in small-scale units. In the East Wing such establishments employ 106,020 workers approximating the number (139,010) engaged in large-scale manufacturing industries.[15]

The same pattern persists in West Pakistan. The most highly industralized city, Karachi, with its 1,098 large plants still reported 752 registered small firms in 1960.[16] Actually the share of small industries is probably even higher than the statistics indicate. It is not unreasonable to assume that a considerable number have never registered with the government and hence are not reflected in official data. Moreover, the official definition of a large-scale industry is an establishment where "twenty or more workers are working, or were working any day of the preceding twelve months and in any part of which a manufacturing process is carried on with the aid of power."[17] As a consequence, a substantial number of units which may well be considered small by the standards of an industrial society are listed as large by the official census.

If the units of production are small in Pakistan, so are the markets. The overwhelming share of goods is produced and consumed within the same locality. Perishable agricultural products, the largest item in family

[14] Government of East Pakistan, Planning Department, "Memorandum #573/C/Cord/11-12/62."

[15] *Ibid.*

[16] *Pakistan Statistical Yearbook 1962*, p. 96.

[17] Quoted from Section 2 (j), Factories Act, 1934.

budgets, naturally originate from the immediate vicinity. Access to most villages is difficult; transportation is slow; refrigeration is not available. Meat, vegetables, and fruit are offered for sale in open markets, mostly by the producer himself. In the marketing of fish there is often an intermediary (usually a money lender), but since refrigeration is no more available to him than to the fisherman, his interposition does not significantly extend the market. The conditions are somewhat more elastic in regard to the four major crops of rice, wheat, jute, and cotton. Jute, of course, is the major export item and as such reaches the large scale of the international market.[18] The same to a somewhat lesser extent is true of cotton. Some wheat and rice are marketed regionally. Yet even in these products the primarily local character of the market is indicated by the wide variation of prices in the various centers. The indices of monthly retail prices for rice (medium) in August 1961 were the following: Dacca, 138; Chittagong, 169; Sylhet, 160; Saidpur, 145; Khulna, 150.[19] Clothing, furniture, kitchen equipment, even tools such as fishing nets and agricultural implements are supplied by the local artisans. Canned food, finer textiles, drugs, and appliances are distributed nationally, and demand for these items is

[18] There is a measure of controversy about jute marketing. The Report of the Food and Agricultural Commission states that the jute grower is forced by his financial position to sell his product immediately after harvest. In contrast, the Dacca University Socio-Economic Survey Board presents data indicating that the periods of maximum sales have been moving away from the harvesting season. (*Report of the Food and Agriculture Commission*, p. 37 and A. F. A. Husain, "Report of the Food and Agriculture Commission," *The Pakistan Development Review II* [Spring 1962], p. 98.)

[19] Government of East Pakistan, *Monthly Survey of Economic Conditions* (Dacca: East Pakistan Government Press, 1962), XII, No. 4, p. 21.

dispersed over a wide geographic area. However, since it is concentrated in the upper middle classes of the larger towns, it remains a narrow-based demand.

Pressures of Anomie

Although the small-scale units continue to predominate in Pakistan, there is evidence that they are no longer self-contained. To be sure, caste identification, village loyalty, and kinship ties retain a powerful appeal. Nevertheless, the trend is toward physical separation from the traditional societies. Adults in growing numbers are leaving their village homes and moving to the towns and cities. In recent decades the cities have accounted for a steadily increasing share of the population: 7.9 per cent in 1941, 13.1 per cent in 1961.[20] Moreover, the appeal of the cities is not restricted to their immediate vicinity. According to one survey, 65 per cent of the sample of industrial workers in East Pakistan originate in other parts of the province or in foreign countries. Another more recent study on Khulna sets this figure at an even more impressive 86 per cent.[21] Significantly, a large number of those who move into towns rarely, if ever, return to the villages. The above-mentioned surveys also indicate that 55 per cent of the first sample and 65 per cent of the second make two or less visits to their villages annually.[22] Meanwhile, among the masses remaining in the villages the control of the hierarchies is impaired. Though they still exercise con-

[20] Economic Survey of Pakistan 1961-62 (Rawalpindi: Government of Pakistan Press, 1962), Statistical Section, p. 3.

[21] A. F. A. Husain, Human and Social Impact . . . , I, 343 and Husain and Farouk, op.cit., Appendix B-9.

[22] A. F. A. Husain, Human and Social Impact . . . , I, 344 and Husain and Farouk, op.cit., Appendix B-16.

siderable influence, they no longer enjoy a monopoly.
An increasing number of children attend schools where
they are exposed to different ideas, to different methods
of role assignment and above all to a different—if not
competing—hierarchy. Enrollment in primary schools
rose by more than 50 per cent during the decade of the
fifties, the figure reaching 40 per cent of the age group
in East Pakistan in 1960.[23] Perhaps more important,
there is evidence that education now plays an essential
part in aspirations. A case study in 1960 asked the question: "What would you like your sons to do?" Of those
responding 82 per cent "spontaneously wanted education for their sons."[24] In the summer of 1964 in connection with another research project I asked a similar question from a random sample of 30 per cent of the male
adults in nine East Pakistan villages. The results showed
8 per cent either had no sons or chose not to answer,
19 per cent wished a "good marriage" or a "happy life,"
and 73 per cent hoped their boys would receive a good
education. In order to avoid possible misunderstandings
about the term "education," I asked the men in the last
category just where they expected the children to get
this good education. Less than 5 per cent suggested the
family, 28 per cent were satisfied with the local *mullah*
or the traditional *madrassah* schools, while 62 per cent
had secular institutions in mind even if *these were located in distant towns and cities.*[25] One final example of

[23] *Pakistan Statistical Yearbook 1962* (Karachi: Government of
Pakistan Press, 1962), p. 321 and *Report on the Ground Survey of
Educational Institutions in East Pakistan* (Dacca: East Pakistan Gov-
ernment Press, 1960), Part I, p. 1.

[24] S. A. Qadir, *op.cit.*, pp. 97-98.

[25] Slightly more than 5 per cent were unable or unwilling to
specify. For further details see my forthcoming study *The Political
Multiplier Effects of Foreign Aid.*

deviation from the traditional pattern reflecting the declining authority of the hierarchies of the small-scale social units should be noted here. Evidently the latter no longer enjoy monopoly in the settlement of disputes. In 1951 no less than 273,983 civil suits involving Rs 56,617,651 were instituted in the East Wing. A more recent figure (1961) sets the annual total of civil suits in the more traditional West Wing at 55,277.[26]

There is also evidence that the small-scale units can no longer assure even subsistence for the extended families. While industrial plants are still few in number,[27] their effect upon small and cottage industries is devastating. Most of the latter still manage to survive, but, as case studies in East Pakistan and the Punjab indicate, many suffer from chronic depression.[28] More specific are the data on agricultural landowners, by far the largest group in the country. In 1960 at least 77 per cent of the holdings in West Pakistan were below 12.5 acres,[29] the level defined as "subsistence holding" by the Land Reforms Commission. In the East Wing the situation was no better. There 78 per cent of the holdings were below five acres. The provincial Land Reforms Committee, moreover, conducted a survey which revealed that in its sample all two-acre, all three-acre, and 91 per cent of the five-acre holdings were deficit operations.[30] Meanwhile the population in rural areas is continually increasing. During the last decade alone the

[26] Letter No. 20327, Gaz/IX.A.5 from Qaiser Ali Khan, C.S.P., Registrar, High Court of West Pakistan, Lahore, October 22, 1963.

[27] *Pakistan Statistical Yearbook 1962*, p. 96.

[28] Zaidi, *op.cit.*, pp. 11ff.; Eglar, *op.cit.*, pp. 180ff.; A. F. A. Husain, *Human and Social Impact* . . . , I, 252-253.

[29] *Report of the Land Reforms Commission for West Pakistan*, pp. 66, x.

[30] *Report of the East Pakistan Land Reforms Committee*, p. 39.

villages had to accommodate an additional 13.5 million persons.[31] Since under Muslim inheritance law all children are entitled to share in their parents' estate and since the total cropped area[32] increased by less than 6 per cent,[33] we may assume that family holdings are getting even smaller. In any case, it is not surprising that recent studies by the University of Dacca conclude that 30 per cent of the adults in the sample are compelled to take employment seasonally in other parts of the province or in India to make ends meet.[34]

The Frailty of National Ties

Against a background of small-scale economic and social units which show signs of gradual and perhaps accelerated disruption, it is of vast importance to note that the appeals for national orientation and integration are far from compelling. Islam, the most prominent source of such appeals, may appear to be a most potent unifying force. For centuries religious bonds were reinforced by cultural and social ties as well. During the Muslim rule conversion to Islam became a means of escaping the rigid caste system of the Hindu and frequently the miseries and indignities of being untouchable. The penalty was ostracism by the majority community, but many a low-caste Hindu was quite prepared to pay this price. For all practical purposes he was ostracized under the caste system anyway, and Islam,

[31] *Population Census of Pakistan, Census Bulletin No. 2* (Karachi: Government of Pakistan Press, 1961), p. 14.

[32] "Cropped area" refers to the total area cultivated plus the area sown more than once.

[33] *Pakistan Statistical Yearbook 1962*, p. 70.

[34] *Rural Credit and Unemployment in East Pakistan*, pp. 66ff. and Dacca University, Bureau of Economic Research, *Pattern of Agricultural Unemployment* (Dacca: Paramount Press, 1962), pp. 9-12.

after all, was the religion of those who had conquered the high-caste Hindu ruling classes. In the face of ostracism by the Hindus, however, the compulsion upon Muslims to form their own communities with their own social rules and customs was understandably intense. They differentiated themselves from the majority in diet, in dress, even in their laws of inheritance. They ate apart, did not visit Hindu homes, and would not think of intermarrying. When they lost the prop of Moghul protection, their common faith remained the formula for cohesion. Later as British hegemony in turn waned, this common faith became the rallying call for the partition movement. Since independence, Islam has been hailed as the national ideology.

Islam had been a sufficiently potent force to extort from the majority community the recognition of a separate Muslim political entity. The common fate of ostracism and the common faith in a religious formula, however, are not necessarily convertible into the driving force of national integration in the sovereign state of Pakistan. There are several reasons for this. First, Pakistan, in fact, is not a religiously homogeneous country. Bengal and the Punjab were partitioned, and almost fifteen million persons were exchanged. Still, 12 per cent of the citizens of Pakistan and 20 per cent of the residents of East Pakistan are Hindu.[35] There are also deep religious cleavages among the various Muslim sects. Conflicts between the majority Sunni, on one hand, and the Shiites and the smaller Muslim communities, on the other, trigger some of the most bitter riots. In 1953 martial law had to be imposed to quell anti-

[35] *Population Census of Pakistan 1961, Census Bulletin No. 2* (Karachi: Government of Pakistan Press, 1962), p. 19.

Ahmadi riots in Lahore, and Ashura processions in Dacca, Karachi, and Lahore not infrequently end in bloodshed.[36]

There are other reasons as well for the limitations on the effectiveness of Islam as a national cohesive force. The call of Islam, as perhaps that of other religions, is basically universalist and somewhat exalted. To reach all mankind, or at least all the faithful, is its object. "Break down the idols of color and blood," wrote Allama Iqbal, "and be immersed in the *millat* [the brotherhood of Islam] so that there might not be left distinct people as Turani, Irani and Afghani."[37] When it comes to a political unit that is smaller in scope and founded on nationalist aspirations, Islam can offer little ideological help. The teachings of the Prophet do not easily adjust to a value pattern which has at its core the predominance of national interest. To many religious leaders nationalism is a pejorative. Maulana Maududi, head of the *Jamā'at-i-Islāmi*, at one point insisted that nationalism is the antithesis of Islam, for it sets up the nation as a god.[38] More modern Muslim leaders do not find nationalism contradictory to Islam, but they too have doubts about the latter's efficacy as a driving force for national cohesion. They share the concern of Mahmud Husain, who as the keynote speaker at the Seminar on Pakistani Nationhood wondered aloud: "After all there must be some explanation of the fact that in spite of the great cementing force of Islam, the world of Islam could not,

[36] A recent serious Ashura riot occurred in Lahore in 1963. (Dacca, *Pakistan Observer*, June 4, 1963, p. 1.)

[37] Quoted in *The Problem of National Character* (Lahore: Pakistan Philosophical Congress, 1961), p. 45.

[38] Leonard Binder, *Religion and Politics in Pakistan* (Berkeley and Los Angeles: University of California Press, 1961), p. 93.

except in the earliest times, be united into a single state during these so many centuries."[39]

Perhaps the most crucial weakness of Islam as a stimulus for national orientation is its inability to provide a national leadership. It has no priesthood, no strict hierarchy. In South Asia, even more than in the Middle East, the jurisdiction of religious functionaries and religious leaders is local and small scale in character. There is, to be sure, a political leadership of larger scale. This leadership, however, is secular, not Islamic. In spite of Akbar's claims of caliphate and Aurangzeb's vigorous military efforts, Islamic political leadership never developed fully, and by the twentieth century it was altogether atrophied. Even when the Moghuls were at the zenith of their power, they felt compelled to make very substantial concessions to the mass of their infidel subjects. One of these concessions was a civil government which, if not contradictory to Islam, was nevertheless not determined by the Holy Quran and Sunnah. The actual separation of church and state became even more pronounced when, with the arrival of the British, government passed over to the infidel colonialists. Although the latter preferred the method of indirect rule and were loath to disturb local customs and hierarchies, the more determined opposition of the Muslims, culminating in the Mutiny (1857), persuaded the government to shift much of the intermediate level of political and economic power from the Muslims to the Hindus. In the meantime, the establishment of a centralized administrative service reaching far down into the districts and also staffed mostly by infidels brought the

[39] Dacca, *Morning News*, November 6, 1961, p. 8.

existence of a separate civil government even more to the awareness of the average Muslim.

The civil leadership that emerged from the struggle for independence was Islamic in the sense that its members were Muslims. In general they accepted the prescribed religious tenets and observed religious rituals, but their intellectual and political heritage came from Western secular training. One Muslim leader described this condition in the following manner: "Talking of an Islamic system and thinking in terms of the Western system is an incongruity which is visible all around us. The spirit soars to the lofty heights reached in Omar's time, but eyes are fastened on the spires of Westminster."[40] With independence the unity of church and state was formally restored. The first five years saw much debate about the specific pattern of an Islamic state and considerable traffic between the political and religious leaders. A special board of *Ta'limat-i-Islāmia* was established and was asked to prepare recommendations. Apparently no practical arrangement could be evolved. The recommendations of the board were ignored, and the group was dissolved. Ritualistic gestures continued. In 1956 Pakistan was declared an Islamic Republic. The new constitution began with an appeal to Allah and included "Islamic provisions." The orientation of the secular leadership, however, remained Western.

Another possible pillar of national cohesion is the common experience of the struggle for independence. If so, it is surely a rather frail pillar. The efficacy of the anticolonial movement was clouded by the peculiar

[40] Quoted in Keith Callard, *Pakistan, A Political Study* (New York: Macmillan, 1957), p. 201.

character of the struggle. The Muslim League agitated for independence—but for independence of a special kind. First it demanded special privileges for the Muslim minority in a united India, arguing with the Congress at length about constitutional and administrative arrangements and quotas too confusing to an average citizen. Only in the 1930's did the idea of a separate Muslim state gain currency.[41] Among the latest and more reluctant converts was Mohammad Ali Jinnah, "Father of the Country." The Lahore Resolution demanding an independent Pakistan was passed in 1940, less than a decade before independence! There were frequent tactical maneuvers, some at least tacitly supporting the colonial rulers against the Hindus, others presenting a united front with the Hindus against the British. Until shortly before independence the territory of the proposed new state remained vague and contradictory. Rahmat Ali envisioned a country comprised primarily of the Muslims of Northwest India plus some neighboring states. The Lahore Resolution assumed a united Punjab and Bengal and spoke of Muslim states in plural.[42]

With independence the ambivalence of target was resolved. Britain retired across the seas, exuding good will and extending administrative, economic, and military support. The Hindu masses, however, were still present as a substantial minority within the borders and a formidable power across the borders. Periodic violence between the two communities and unfriendly ac-

[41] Iqbal in 1930; Rahmat Ali in 1933.

[42] Muin-ud-din Ahmad Khan, *Muslim Struggle for Freedom in Bengal* (Dacca: East Pakistan Government Press, 1960), p. 68. Compare also: Penderel Moon, *Divide and Quit* (Berkeley and Los Angeles: University of California Press, 1962), pp. 11-28.

tions between the two states reinforced the anti-Hindu hostility generated by the independence movement. The flags of Pakistan and India had hardly been raised on the masts of their respective government buildings when communal violence swept the subcontinent, to be followed by mass migrations almost unprecedented in human history. The most frequently accepted estimates of 500,000 dead in the riots and almost fifteen million refugees between 1947 and 1950 may well be on the conservative side.[43] In April 1950 the formal Minorities Pact (Liaquat-Nehru Agreement) eased the tension and reassured the population somewhat. Nevertheless, scars remain very deep and the prospect of communal riots hangs, like Damocles' sword, over the subcontinent.

In the meantime, other grievances strengthened the suspicion and fear that, having failed to prevent the creation of a separate Muslim state, India was ready to pounce upon and devour its neighbor. In 1948 for no apparent reason India diverted the flow of the river Ravi, a vital source of water supply for West Pakistan. The following year conflict was intensified when, after England devalued the pound, India followed suit but Pakistan refused. Ultimately the water problem was settled through World Bank mediation and the financing of the gigantic Indus River Project, and Pakistan devalued her rupee in 1955. However, another issue—

[43] Cf. W. Norman Brown, *The United States and India and Pakistan* (Cambridge: Harvard University Press, 1955), p. 143; Tibor Mende, *South East Asia Between Two Worlds* (London: Turnstile, 1955), p. 214; Pakistan, Ministry of Refugees and Rehabilitation, *The Evacuee Property Problem—Pakistan's Case* (Karachi: Government of Pakistan Press, 1950), p. 4; Moon, *op.cit.*, p. 293; J. B. Schectman, "Evacuee Property in India and Pakistan," *Pacific Affairs*, xxiv (December 1951), p. 406.

that of Kashmir—continues to fester. No purpose would be served in recounting the long and somewhat ambiguous record of this dispute. The point is that the continued military subjugation of Kashmiri Muslims by the Indian Republic is considered by most Pakistanis as an affront to justice and a demonstration of Indian hostility against the Muslim state on the subcontinent. All this generates resentment, resistance *and a common bond.*

It is not easy, however, to transfer this kind of "unity" into a national orientation. The Hindu threat of the present—like the Hindu threat of the 1940's—is perceived primarily in local terms. Now, as then, the response tends to be temporary outbursts of communal violence rather than an increased feeling of identification with fellow citizens in distant regions or a willingness to subordinate personal or group aspirations to national interest. A case in point: during the spring of 1962 resentment in the East Wing against the Central Government, the West Wing, and the existence of economic "disparity" was not allayed or distracted by communal violence at Malda, the assaulting of Dacca University students on Indian soil or the attention devoted to the Kashmir dispute.

3

++

The Range of Government Effectiveness

++

THERE APPEARS to be a consensus among scholars and observers that the Government of Pakistan must take the initiative to achieve integration of the small-scale social, cultural, and economic groups into a national entity and to assure maximum mobilization and efficient utilization of scarce resources. It is doubtful that either Islam or the threat of an external enemy can generate sufficient cohesion for a national orientation, and the government after all is the most comprehensive organizational structure on a countrywide scale. The success of government initiative in the West and the Soviet Union lends further support to such a contention. In any case, the Government of Pakistan seems prepared to assume the responsibility.

It is difficult to imagine an alternative to massive government initiative; it is easy to entertain extravagant expectations about its effectiveness. As a matter of fact, among the cold, hard realities of the Pakistani environment the problem of severe limitations upon governmental capacity to affect the social and economic pattern is no less critical than those of the scarcity of resources or the predominance and disruption of the small-scale social units. These limitations, moreover, cannot be explained away by the corruption of the leadership. Admittedly, during its short history Pakistan was led at times by men of little understanding and less commitment to a modern nation-state. Extreme individualism, even widespread corruption in high places, was rampant. These circumstances surely contributed to governmental ineffectiveness. It is of major significance, however, that the evidence supports the conclusion that governmental initiative is severely circumscribed even when (as seems to be the case in recent years) governmental authority is vested in men who are both patriotic and honest.

To be sure, there are some areas of substantial governmental effectiveness. With its modern, well-disciplined armed forces the government has assured the integrity of the country against foreign aggression. It has demonstrated its ability to restrain such centrifugal drives as Ghaffar Khan's Red Shirts, the Khan of Kalat, or a Baluchi tribal force estimated at thirty thousand men. In regulating economic relations with foreign countries it monopolizes foreign aid, enforces strict exchange control, and arbitrarily fixes the exchange rate of the rupee. By strictly regulating passports it controls the international movement of the population.

All these areas of government initiative, however, have two features in common. First, it is significant that the effectiveness of the Government of Pakistan in these matters rests to a large extent upon the capabilities and cooperation of other governments. Pakistan's control of foreign exchange or foreign travel, for example, is at least partially enforced by the Governments of Afghanistan, India, the United Kingdom, and the United States. In those instances where the foreign government also suffers from limited capabilities or is unwilling to cooperate, the effectiveness of the Government of

Pakistan is correspondingly reduced. Secondly, government control in these areas involves only a small fraction of the population. Recruitment into the armed forces, for example, affects only a few. There is no draft or universal military service, and the supply of volunteers always exceeds the demand. It is a moot point whether the same measure of effectiveness would be demonstrated by the government were it to involve directly larger masses of its population. The response might be quite different, for example, if the preservation of the territorial integrity of Pakistan would necessitate a general mobilization. The number of young men who would respond is anyone's guess. I think not very many. There are no data available on total foreign exchange applications, since the Government of Pakistan refuses to release this information.[1] A clue to its magnitude, however, may be found in the State Bank announcement that during the period of April 1960 to October 1963 the number of applications for foreign exchange in support of travel abroad reached 33,964.[2] In any case, the number of all requests is not likely to be large. The Foreign Ministry is somewhat more cooperative in the matter of information about passports. It can be established that in 1962 the total number of passports issued was 165,075, of which 117,304 (71 per cent) were special passports limited to India.[3]

Actually, even in these areas government effectiveness is a bit frazzled. Although no statistics are available on the subject, my impression is that a great deal of

[1] Embassy of Pakistan, Washington, D.C., Note F. 46, 63, September 9, 1963.

[2] Dacca, *Pakistan Observer*, December 15, 1963, p. 1.

[3] Embassy of Pakistan, Washington, D.C., Note CD 13/63, August 1, 1963.

back-and-forth movement of population is taking place in the tribal areas and in East Pakistan without official sanction. Administrators on both sides of the border admit informally that they can do little about it. Similarly, smuggling, a widespread practice, reached spectacular proportions shortly before the Revolution in 1958. Martial law did make a sizable reduction in such activity,[4] but more recently newspaper reports suggest resumption of the previous pace.[5] In any case, there are still villages in the frontier areas, such as Landikotal, where a person can buy at cut-rate prices a remarkable range of goods that never appeared on an import manifest. Currency regulations are similarly circumvented. Again it is difficult to estimate quantities, but it is not difficult to observe a brisk trade in Pakistani currency in Calcutta.

Given the support of the armed forces, the government may assure its own tenure. Yet whenever it is not content to bask in the security afforded by its pretorians but assumes the initiative in a program of political development, then it exposes an entirely different dimension of limitations upon its effectiveness. The maintenance of law and order as well as the implementation of economic development policy—cornerstones of a political development program—require a capacity to assure the compliance, if not the active support, of the vast masses of population. In this, however, as the following evidence indicates, government effectiveness is quite negligible.

[4] In 1961 Military Courts tried 1,312 cases of smuggling involving goods valued at Rs 6,357,000 (*Pakistan 1961-62* [Karachi: Pakistan Publications, 1963], p. 24).

[5] Dacca, *Morning News*, July 8, 1963, p. 1.

Maintenance of Law and Order

There is some range of government effectiveness in central law enforcement. In the frontier areas it approximates zero. The laws of Pakistan do not extend to the tribal belt. Instead, tribal laws administered by tribal hierarchies remain determinant. It is a case in point that the government does not interfere with the manufacture and carrying of arms in these areas and is rather helpless when rail lines are taken up by the tribesmen to serve as the chief supply of iron for the weapons. Nor does it try to interfere with the settlement of disputes. The kinship group adjudicates such matters, or in the case of interfamily discord the issue is resolved by the tribal council (*jirga*). Although time and again the tribes have agreed formally to refrain from harboring fugitives from justice, the fact is that very few such persons are turned over to the authorities. More often, when such a fugitive requests sanctuary according to *Nanawatai*, he is hospitably entertained and protected from arrest.[6] Occasionally in the North West Frontier region the pretense of central jurisdiction is abetted by both sides. In some instances of blood feud the government may assert its authority, and the "culprit" may agree to surrender. Then follows a formal trial during which a host of perjured witnesses are produced to confuse the evidence. In the end, the accused may be convicted, thus complying with the required ritual. At this point, however, it is not unusual for the sentence to consist of a Rs 1,000 fine, which the defendant dutifully pays after a government agent has informally passed him the money. The tribes are, in fact, quite

[6] Olaf Caroe, *The Pathans* (London: Macmillan, 1958), pp. 354-356.

tolerant toward the quaint ways of jurisprudence—as long as the end result does not interfere with their own assessment of right and wrong.

In non-tribal and non-frontier areas the government exercises a more direct role, but the results are not much more favorable. Statistics on law enforcement are very scarce indeed. For example, no data exist on the ratio between crimes committed and crimes reported. In all countries there is a gap between these two figures, but it is my impression that in Pakistan this gap is especially wide. Inferences from empirical data lend support to this conclusion. Thus, for example, the ratio of reported incidents in Pakistan to those in the United States is 1:2 for murder, but 1:30 for robbery and burglary.[7] Barring the alternatives that Pakistani are especially prone to murder or that Americans have a special disposition to crimes against property, the explanation of serious underreporting in Pakistan especially in categories less grave than murder seems plausible. This explanation is also supported by comparative data on theft. In the United States the average value per incidence of reported theft is $76, or roughly 3 per cent of the per capita income. In East Pakistan the same average is Rs 544.81, or almost twice the per capita income.[8]

[7] In 1961 the Government of Pakistan reported 4,073 murders, 3,011 robberies and dacoities, and 28,214 burglaries. In the same year 8,599 murders, 91,659 robberies, and 852,509 burglaries were registered officially in the continental United States. (*Pakistan Statistical Yearbook 1962* [Karachi: Government of Pakistan Press, 1962], pp. 367-368 and United States, Federal Bureau of Investigation, *Uniform Crime Reports—1961* [Washington, D.C.: Government Printing Office, 1962], pp. 34-35.)

[8] United States, Federal Bureau of Investigation, *Uniform Crime Reports—1959* (Washington, D.C.: Government Printing Office,

By itself the fact (if it is a fact) of substantial under-reporting of crimes demonstrates the severe limitations on the effectiveness of government law enforcement. Data on the disposition of reported crimes supply further substantiation. First, it is clear that the rate of recovery of stolen goods is negligible. Of almost Rs 3 crores property taken illegally in East Pakistan during 1959 only 2.2 per cent was recovered by the police.[9] Second, the rates of prosecution and conviction of those accused of crimes are rather modest. As Table 4 (based upon 1959 East Pakistan data) indicates, the odds against the conviction of an accused are better than 8:1.[10]

Table 4

Disposition of Criminal Cases in East Pakistan (1959)

Crime	Cases Reported 1959	Previous Cases Pending	Total Cases	Cases Brought to Trial	Cases Ending in Conviction
Murder	749	436	1,185	574	169
Grievous hurt	1,254	260	1,514	407	181
Hurt (Assault)	1,905	362	2,267	484	199
Dacoity*	923	606	1,529	556	230
Robbery	827	192	1,019	284	76
Burglary	22,566	1,785	24,351	3,296	1,393
Theft	15,580	2,303	17,883	4,652	2,663

* Robbery by a gang.

1960), p. 80 and Government of East Pakistan, *Report on the Police Administration of the Province of East Pakistan for the Year 1959* (Dacca: East Pakistan Government Press, 1961), p. 90.

[9] *Report on the Police Administration of . . . East Pakistan . . . 1959*, p. 90. In 512 American cities with a population of 25,000 or over, the rate of recovery was 52.8 per cent (*Uniform Crime Reports —1959*, p. 81).

[10] *Report on the Police Administration of . . . East Pakistan . . . 1959*, pp. 73-75.

The significance of the Pakistani statistics is not merely their suggestion that the performance of central law enforcement is decidedly below American levels. Far more important is the implication that at this crucial time, when social control is progressively weakening, it would be illusory to expect that government initiative can substantially reverse anomic disruption.

The performance of government when faced with more massive challenges to public order, short of attempts of secession or revolution, is no more impressive. Certainly central law enforcement does not appear to have much success in deterring mob violence. In 1961, according to official statistics, there were some 6,458 riots, or no less than 17 per day[11] triggered by land dispute, intrigue or jealousy, and political agitation. Even the imposition of martial law does not seem to have reduced the rate of major public disturbances. The annual average during the first decade of independence with all its democratic self-restraint and apparent inefficiency was 5,205. During the martial law years in spite of the presumed increment in efficiency and coercive capacity the annual average number of riots rose to 5,528.[12]

Efforts to control political agitation and demonstrations further expose the substantial ineffectiveness of the government. Consider the case of Suhrawardy. On January 30, 1962, H. S. Suhrawardy, a prominent political leader and former Prime Minister, was arrested. The official statement accused him of "openly associating with anti-Pakistan elements."[13] Two days later Pres-

[11] *Pakistan Statistical Yearbook 1962*, p. 368.
[12] *Ibid.*
[13] Dacca, *Pakistan Observer*, February 1, 1962, p. 1.

ident Ayub Khan "explained" that the government had "direct proof" that Suhrawardy was seeking to disrupt East Pakistan first and then the rest of the country. Mr. Suhrawardy, the President added, was "a very good man and very intelligent, but I don't think he has much love for Pakistan."[14] The exact nature of his activities remained vague, but it was officially suggested that the accused had access to foreign funds. Simultaneously, warnings were issued to "enemy agents" and elements "hostile to Pakistan" that forceful action would be taken against them.

If the warning intimidated anyone, this was not apparent in the response it engendered. The Dacca University campus, which had been reasonably tranquil for a few years, erupted. During the next few days the students went on strike, assembled under their traditional mango tree, passed resolutions condemning the arrest, beat up a police spy and assaulted Pakistan's Foreign Minister. The "forceful action" that followed was an order to the Vice Chancellor to declare a month's vacation at the University and subsidiary colleges. The morning this decision was announced the students in mass formation left the campus, manhandled policemen, overturned and set fire to a bus, stoned the firemen who arrived at the scene, and for the *first time* chanted derogatory slogans against the President. After much reinforcement the police lathi-charged[15] and resorted to tear gas. Some 27 persons were arrested, and the public was reminded of martial law regulations imposing a punishment of 14 years rigorous imprisonment

[14] *Ibid.*, February 2, 1962, pp. 1, 8.

[15] Lathis are long bamboo sticks that the police wield in order to disperse demonstrators.

54

for inciting political disturbances.[16] Nevertheless, demonstrations and violent clashes with the police continued in Dacca and rapidly spread over the province. Relying on the tips of informers, the government advertised in the newspapers the names of those to be arrested and requested them to call at the nearest police station.[17] This procedure had little effect upon the real agitators. They remained at liberty. Troops were also called out to cordon off the university area while the police moved in to make mass arrests. The catch of 89 non-students was slim, consisting primarily of a few bystanders and some unfortunate bearers (servants). The agitators, of course, had known of the raid well in advance and had long since cleared out.

The coincidence of the Muslim month of fast dampened the demonstrations somewhat. As the students started to reassemble after their vacation, the government issued further warnings. Major-General Khwaja Wasiuddin, the provincial Martial Law Administrator, publicly threatened that disturbance to peace and order would not be tolerated. "There would be no immunity from martial law for anyone," he thundered.[18] The Governor wrote letters to parents and guardians requesting their cooperation. Meanwhile Mr. Suhrawardy was spending his time in a Class A jail with his books, phonograph records, and tape recorder. On February 13 he caused some flurry when he filed a habeas corpus petition through a friend. Next day the President obliged by promulgating a martial law ordinance which debarred habeas corpus petitions in cases where persons

[16] Dacca, *Pakistan Observer*, February 8, 1962, p. 1.
[17] See, for example: Dacca, *Morning News*, March 30, 1962, p. 10.
[18] Dacca, *Pakistan Observer*, March 13, 1962, p. 6.

were arrested under the Security of Pakistan Act, 1952.[19]

Refreshed by celebrations of Eid, the students returned to the university community and resumed their demonstrations. Lathi charges, tear gas, and arrests were repeated.[20] The Vice Chancellor was again ordered to close the University. Arrested students meanwhile were approached several times by senior police officials who pleaded with them to sign pledges of good behavior so that they could be released. The students refused.[21] When eleven students were convicted by a martial law court, they were promptly pardoned by the Martial Law Administrator and officially assured that the record of conviction was removed from pardoned persons.[22] Meanwhile, the hue and cry for the release of the students who remained under arrest intensified. Ex-politicians, bar associations, even rural delegations pleaded, requested, and demanded. By May 3 some of the most influential people had taken their position behind the students arrested for rioting. Among them was the highly respected Moulvi Tamizuddin Khan, former President of the Constituent Assembly and soon to be elected Speaker of the new National Assembly. The following day the President granted clemency to all students arrested during the disturbances.[23] Sureties of good behavior were to be demanded as the price of release, but when the students again refused, this requirement was dropped. Thus those arrested for inciting

[19] *Ibid.*, February 15, 1962, p. 1.

[20] Dacca, *Morning News*, March 25, 1962, p. 1 and March 27, 1962, p. 1.

[21] Several of my students were among those arrested, and this was their testimony.

[22] Dacca, *Morning News*, March 13, 1962, p. 1.

[23] Dacca, *Pakistan Observer*, May 4, 1962, p. 1.

violence against the government, defaming and insulting the President, and destroying public property were released unconditionally in less than four months.

What about H. S. Suhrawardy? He was released on August 19, 1962, with a statement that the "government is now satisfied that Mr. Suhrawardy will not henceforth participate in any disruptive activities."[24] Just what the government achieved apart from laying bare its own ineffectiveness is difficult to see. The demonstrations continued unabated, and upon his release Mr. Suhrawardy promptly added his prestige and organizational experience to the antigovernmental agitation.

Other examples bear the same message. When Maulana Bhashani began a hunger strike, all restrictions imposed upon him were promptly removed. Quayyum Khan, summarily arrested on July 6, 1962, was released within three months.[25] Perhaps most eloquent of all is a relatively obscure case. On October 7, 1962, a train was attacked and damaged by political demonstrators in rural East Pakistan. By the time the authorities arrived, even the shouting was over, and the participants had melted into the community. When the provincial government imposed a "collective fine" of Rs 5,000 on an area within the town of Netrokona, it was a public admission of its helplessness.[26]

The Economic Development Program

Limitations upon government initiative to accelerate economic development and achieve self-sustained

[24] *Ibid.*, August 20, 1962, p. 1.
[25] Karachi, *Dawn*, October 7, 1962, p. 1.
[26] Dacca, *Pakistan Observer*, October 13, 1962, p. 1.

growth are strikingly apparent from the record of over-all performance. Consider first the heart of the program: the mobilization of domestic saving. When it comes to public borrowing, the response of the population is dismal. A case in point: in July 1962 the government floated two loans. The total subscriptions toward these loans amounted to Rs 38.73 crores. Of this sum only Rs 30,000 was subscribed by individuals. This is less than .01 per cent.[27] Nor is the performance of the tax program any more encouraging. Pakistanis are among the most lightly taxed people in the world. The total tax revenue amounts to slightly less than 7 per cent of the national income. This figure is low not only in comparison to Western Europe and North America, but, as Table 5 indicates, it is below the level of many Asian countries.

Table 5

Relative Weight of Taxes in Selected Countries[28]

Country	Year	Total Tax Revenue as Percentage of National Income
Burma	1959/60	23
Cambodia	1959	15
Ceylon	1959/60	21
Federation of Malaya	1959	18
India	1959/60	10
Indonesia	1959	6
Japan	1959/60	14
Republic of Korea	1959	16
Philippines	1959/60	11
Thailand	1959	13

[27] State Bank of Pakistan, Department of Research, Memorandum No. DR-MS/48/6849-62 (November 12, 1962).

[28] A. H. M. Nuruddin Chowdhury, "The Weight of Tax Revenue in the Pakistan Economy," *The Pakistan Development Review*, III, No. 1 (Spring 1963), p. 102.

Another relevant comparison between tax revenue and public expenditure reveals that tax yields simply cannot support substantial development programs. As a matter of fact, they do not even suffice to cover the current administrative outlays. During the First Plan period, for example, non-development expenditures of the central government exceeded total tax collection by an annual average of Rs 41 crores.[29] This condition, moreover, was not a temporary aberration; it continues. The 1963-1964 budget anticipated the same gap to reach Rs 44.41 crores.[30] In other words, the government must divert non-tax revenues to cover some 21 per cent of the administrative budget.

A somewhat more detailed look at the performance of the tax structure produces further evidence of severe limitations upon government initiative. The only broadly based tax in Pakistan is land tax. Although agriculture contributes about 56 per cent of the national income, land revenue collected is below 12 per cent of the total taxes.[31] One problem is assessment. Most landholders enjoy pre-World War II rates but pay in highly inflated currency. Theoretically, assessment occurs in thirty-year cycles. There are, however, large blocks of land without assessments in half a century. The task of bringing assessment up to date is a slow and cumbersome process. It is retarded by tax assessors who are low-level and poorly paid government agents. These men are not only unskilled, but are extremely vulner-

[29] *Economic Survey of Pakistan 1961-62* (Rawalpindi: Government of Pakistan Press, 1962), Statistical Section, p. 131.

[30] Dacca, *Pakistan Observer*, June 9, 1963, p. 1.

[31] Actually this figure also includes return on government irrigation in West Pakistan (*Economic Survey of Pakistan 1961-62*, Statistical Section, pp. 131, 134-135, 138-139).

able to bribery as well. In East Pakistan an additional complication prevails. The *zamindars* who collected taxes for the colonial power were mostly Hindu and left after independence. Their records have either disappeared or are in complete confusion. Collection is another problem. Even at the prevailing anachronistic rates the total amount of arrears is substantial, and the capacity of the government to reduce it appears to be negligible. In the divisions of Peshawar, D. I. Khan, Rawalpindi, Bahawalpur, and Kalat the total delinquency in land revenue (ordinary) amounted to some Rs 45 lakhs in March 1962.[32] In East Pakistan the situation is even more dramatic. In 1958 land tax arrears reached Rs 10.6 crores compared to only Rs 10.4 crores of current demand. Collection of current demand itself ran for years at about 34 per cent.[33]

Income tax, the other main source of direct taxation, is not broadly based in Pakistan. The number of assessees in 1955-1956 was actually less than 0.08 per cent of the population.[34] Agriculture is spared completely, and in urban areas exemption is extended to incomes up to Rs 6,000, i.e., twenty-five times the per capita income. Limited as the application of income tax is, here too delinquency is massive and evasion is widespread. In 1956-1957 arrears reached Rs 52 crores, or more than

[32] Government of West Pakistan, Revenue Department, "Statement Showing Figures of Arrears and Recovery made up to the end of November, 1958 (When the Directive for special drive was issued) and up to the end of March, 1962 (showing the latest available position)" (unpublished) [1 lakh = 100,000].

[33] Government of East Pakistan, *Report of the Land Revenue Commission of East Pakistan* (Dacca: East Pakistan Government Press, 1961), p. 76.

[34] Government of Pakistan, *Taxation Enquiry Committee Report* (Karachi: Government of Pakistan Press, 1963), I, 47.

twice the collection.[35] Understandably, exact statistical information on evasion is not available, but its extent can perhaps be deduced from the following fact. One of the initial acts of the Martial Law Government was to proclaim a short period of amnesty for income-tax evaders. In three months no less than Rs 134.03 crores of previously undeclared income was reported.[36]

In the face of this poor performance of direct taxation the brunt of tax collection is naturally shifted to indirect taxes—primarily those which can be applied to export/import items and which involve control at international frontiers. Thus customs duty, excise tax, and sales tax together account for over 72 per cent of central taxes.[37] Rates, although selective, are quite high. Some automobiles, for example, carry 250 per cent import duty. Excise tax on tea is 10 annas (Rs 0.625) per pound. Evasion appears to be relatively modest except in instances of sales or excise taxes imposed on domestically produced items. These taxes, however, reach only a very small segment of the population. Total imports on private account, for example, amounted to only 11.4 per cent of the total national income during the First Plan period. If the value of imported raw materials and capital goods is subtracted, this figure shrinks to 5.5 per cent.[38]

The severe limitations upon government initiative are indicated by the *performance* of the government in mobilizing domestic saving. The dimensions of these limitations, however, become even more fully apparent

[35] *Ibid.*, I, 349.
[36] Dacca, *Morning News,* January 18, 1958, p. 1.
[37] *Economic Survey of Pakistan 1961-62,* Statistical Section, p. 131.
[38] *Ibid.*, Statistical Section, pp. 8, 56.

through the observation of the *differential effect in performance* resulting from an increment of government stability and coercive power after the imposition of martial law. It is certainly of considerable consequence to note that this increment did not bring about a significant tax yield. Nor did it improve the results of government initiative in three major areas relevant to the economic development program: land reform, price control, and population control.

First, let us consider the differential effect upon tax yields. During the nine years preceding martial law the annual average tax revenue collected by the central government was 6.35 per cent of the national income. During the four years of martial law this average rose to 6.42 per cent, or marginally by 0.07 per cent.[39] More specifically, under martial law the reassessment of land-holdings was not accelerated, and the ratio of arrears to collection of land tax did not perceptibly decline.[40] The initial successes against income and corporation tax evasion were not pursued. On the contrary, it was the Martial Law Government that increased the income-tax exemption limit from Rs 5,000 to Rs 6,000. During the last three years of martial law the yield of income and corporation taxes dropped back to Rs 30.5 crores, or some Rs 3 crores below the 1958-1959 level.[41]

Somewhat more noticeable was the differential effect of martial law with regard to land reform. For a dozen years after independence much oratory played on the subject, but no action was taken. Then on January 24,

[39] A. H. M. Nuruddin Chowdhury, *op.cit.*, p. 104.

[40] In 1961, according to an unofficial communication from the Revenue Secretary, Government of East Pakistan, arrears remained at the Rs 11 crores level.

[41] *Economic Survey of Pakistan 1961-62*, Statistical Section, p. 131.

1959, President Ayub Khan announced a "minimum programme of land reform,"[42] a double-barreled effort affecting both the very large holdings and the uneconomically small holdings. One part of the ordinance limited land-holdings to 500 acres of irrigated and 1,000 acres of non-irrigated land. Under this provision some 2.3 million acres were taken over by the government by 1960.[43] This is certainly a lot of land. If placed in perspective, however, the magnitude of the achievement becomes far less imposing. Most of the area "resumed" by the government was uncultivated and uncultivatable. As late as 1962 only 384,009 acres had been transferred to tenants and small landowners. This is 1.3 per cent of the cultivatable land in West Pakistan and 5.1 per cent of the land owned by those landowners who had previously held 500 acres or more.

Regarding the other aspect of land reform, namely the uneconomic small holdings, the President in his land reform speech declared that "holdings below a certain economic or subsistence level will be forbidden . . . ," and the Land Reforms Commission promptly and valiantly defined "subsistence holdings" as 12.5 to 16 acres in West Pakistan and 3 to 5 acres in East Pakistan.[44] This part of the program never got off the ground. It is one thing to proclaim a new policy and an entirely different thing to enforce it when it entails the prohibition of the holdings of seven and a half million families.

[42] Mohammed Ayub Khan, *Speeches and Statements* (Karachi: Pakistan Publications, 1961), I, 47-51.

[43] This is a Planning Commission figure. Actually it was somewhat less—2,195,305 acres.

[44] *Report of the Land Reforms Commission for West Pakistan* (Lahore: Government Printing, West Pakistan, 1961), IV and Government of East Pakistan, *Report of the East Pakistan Land Reform Committee* (Dacca: East Pakistan Government Press, 1960), p. 6.

If the government could claim some, however modest, marginal achievement in land reform during martial law, its efforts at price control were not similarly rewarded. Admittedly, this is a very difficult matter even in highly industrialized countries. The record of Pakistan, nevertheless, is revealing. One of the first actions of the martial law administration was the imposition of price control on "essential products,"[45] and the maximum punishment for black-market activities was set at 14 years rigorous imprisonment.[46] This, however, did not prevent a booming black market in sugar throughout the country. Nor did it dramatically affect retail prices of such basic staples as wheat and rice. Although during the first two years of martial law net availability of wheat rose 37 per cent from 4.1 million tons to 5.6 million tons, and net availability of rice increased 24 per cent from 7.2 million tons to 8.9 million tons, wheat prices in West Pakistan declined only 10 per cent (Rs 14.75 to Rs 13.25 per maund) and the price of rice in the East Wing actually climbed 5 per cent (Rs 30.50 to Rs 32.02).[47] An upward trend is also discernible in the consumer price index constructed by the Institute of Development Economics in Karachi. The Institute noted a rise in their index for the first two years of martial law from 113.4 to 123.7 in East Pakistan and 109.4 to 119.9 in West Pakistan.[48] This rise in prices was not necessarily greater than during the preceding period. There were, in fact, wide fluctuations before the Revo-

[45] Dacca, *Morning News,* October 12, 1958, p. 1.

[46] Government of Pakistan, *Gazette of Pakistan Extraordinary,* October 15, 1958, p. 1963.

[47] Institute of Development Economics, *Monograph No. 4,* "A Measure of Inflation in Pakistan 1951-60" (Karachi: Institute of Development Economics, 1961), pp. 40, 76.

[48] *Ibid.,* p. 5.

lution of October 1958. The point, however, remains that during the first period of martial law when the threats of coercion were most seriously and earnestly heeded, their net effect on price fluctuations seems imperceptible.

The Family Planning Program is another case in point. The First Five Year Plan recommended "vigorous research and publicity programmes" and approved a Rs 5 lakhs lump sum appropriation for the year 1957-1958.[49] Under the martial law regime the program was ostensibly intensified. The President himself stressed family planning. The Minister of Health promised a vigorous effort. At one point the Finance Minister even claimed that the martial law regime would solve the population problem.[50] In January 1960 Drs. Balfour and Harper, at the request of the Ministry of Health and Social Welfare, presented specific recommendations requiring an outlay of Rs 330 lakhs over a five-year period. The Second Five Year Plan incorporated the recommendations but cut the amount slightly to Rs 305 lakhs. In January 1962 the first conference of the Indian Ocean Region of the International Planned Parenthood Federation was held in Dacca amid much fanfare.

There are, of course, very substantial barriers against the effectiveness of a family planning program. Ignorance about the biological process of reproduction, resistance to the use of contraceptives, the lack of facilities, the lack of personnel are all difficulties which cannot be overcome within a short period of time. Never-

[49] Government of Pakistan, *The First Five Year Plan, 1955-60* (Karachi: Government of Pakistan Press, 1957), p. 192.

[50] Karachi, *Dawn*, February 25, 1959, p. 1; February 28, 1959, p. 6; May 3, 1959, p. 10; July 24, 1959, p. 1; September 14, 1959, p. 1.

theless, against a background of such apparently intense government commitment, the results must surely be disappointing. Actual expenditure for family planning was less than Rs 8 lakhs annually, or not much above the pre-Revolutionary period and very, very much below the Second Five Year Plan projections or the Balfour-Harper formula.

We have some further revealing data on the program in East Pakistan. In 1961-1962 total public expenditure on contraceptives in the province amounted to Rs 86,-319. A quick calculation reveals that if every unit were used and used effectively this sum would provide contraceptives only for 10,047 regular consumers.[51] In comparison, it might be noted that there are 5.2 million married males and 7.6 million married females between the ages of ten to thirty-nine.[52] Hence under the most ideal conditions less than 0.2 per cent of the families could possibly be affected.

So much for the evidence available to support the proposition that there are very severe limitations upon the effectiveness of government initiative. Government effectiveness, of course, depends both on the measure of popular predisposition to conform and the ability of the government to compel compliance. There is a relationship between these ingredients, and in different countries at different times there is a substantial variation in the mix. The critical problem in Pakistan is that the government has serious limitations on its coercive

[51] During that year the Family Planning Agencies made available 1,185,600 rubber condoms and 10,000 tubes of jelly (Assistant Director of Health Services, Family Planning, Government of East Pakistan, Communication No. 000-C-16/63/156, February 5, 1963).

[52] *Pakistan Statistical Yearbook 1962*, pp. 6-7.

power at the time when its capacity to persuade is minimal. The government has yet to demonstrate its ability to serve as an efficacious vehicle for popular aspirations or as a suitable leadership structure for the mobilization of mass support.

4

The Governmental Capacity to Coerce

IN HER SHORT HISTORY Pakistan has had experience with a variety of political systems. None relied primarily upon force for the implementation of laws and policies. During the first decade of independence a whole series of safeguards restrained and regulated the application of coercion. Periodic elections were held. A measure of parliamentary responsibility and some federal division of power existed. The interim semi-Constitutional documents and the Constitution of 1956 guaranteed "fundamental rights." Islamic provisions were included to reinforce restrictions upon arbitrary government action by prohibiting laws which would conflict with the Holy Quran and Sunnah. Martial law and the Revolution in October 1958 summarily eliminated constitutional restraints. Absolute power was assumed by the Commander-in-Chief of the armed forces. Yet arbitrary as this rule may have been, it was certainly not repressive. Force was used rather sparingly; threats were rarely carried out. Most significantly, from the very beginning the martial law administration demonstrated a singular determination to reestablish constitutional government and thus to replace personal hegemony with institutional control.

The apparent disinclination to rely upon force as the primary support for law and public policy does not necessarily reflect an extravagant commitment to non-coercive means. It may well indicate a recognition by those who control the political system that the capacity of the government to coerce is severely limited. As a matter of fact, few governments can compel mass compliance if they, unlike viceroys in colonial dependencies or Communist bosses in Soviet satellites, cannot rely on external forces for support. The Government of Pakistan, in any case, is not one of them. Indeed a survey of available communications facilities and that of coercive personnel reveals such critical barriers to massive use of compulsion that even if all other restraints were discounted, an effort of massive coercion would still founder. At the same time, the peculiar ambivalence in the people's attitude toward force makes even its limited and sporadic application dysfunctional. It rarely advances the implementation of government policy but invariably activates counterpressures which undermine the already tenuous governmental capacity to control.

Limitation upon Communication and Coercive Personnel

One precondition for a successful effort of coercion is the existence of sturdy communications links between the government and the population capable of conducting information in both directions with speed and accuracy. The barriers to downward flow, that is, the facility to acquaint the population with the officially preferred and prohibited behavior, are immediately apparent. To be sure, there were 95 dailies in Pakistan with unspecified circulation in 1960.[1] In a country where

[1] *Pakistan Statistical Yearbook 1962* (Karachi: Government of Pakistan Press, 1962), p. 364.

functional literacy is below 10 per cent of the population, however, the utility of newspapers in familiarizing the masses with government policies is correspondingly limited. There were also 227,130 licensed radio sets. Although obviously the number of listeners exceeds this figure by far, they still form a small minority of the citizens. Moreover, sets are concentrated in the towns and cities. Few of the one hundred thousand villages have even one receiver. The scarcity of receiving sets is aggravated by the lack of electric power. In 1960 only 64 of the 186 small towns and 370 of all the villages were electrified.[2] Television is not available at all, though experimental stations are planned for 1965. The limitation upon governmental access to the population through mass communication is complemented by the remoteness of public officials. Even the lowest provincial administrator, the Circle Officer, rarely—if ever—sets foot in the villages over which he is supposed to exercise authority. An East Pakistan government study indicates that in 1960-1961 one-fourth of the rural areas were not visited by these officials at all, and an additional third was honored by only one or two fleeting inspections.[3] The result is that those living in villages, i.e., the overwhelming majority of the population, learn of government policies through hearsay and rumor which are rarely accurate—more often contradictory and confusing.

The barriers to the upward flow of information, especially on such matters as deviation from laws and

[2] *Ibid.*, p. 215 and *Second Five Year Plan* (Karachi: Government of Pakistan Press, 1960), p. 215.

[3] *Basic Democracy in East Pakistan* (Comilla: Pakistan Academy for Village Development, 1962), p. 51. See also A. T. R. Rahman, *Basic Democracies at the Grass Roots* (Comilla: Pakistan Academy for Village Development, 1962), p. 70.

government policies are no less formidable. As we noted earlier, most crimes are not reported, and criminals, political dissenters, and agitators are often hidden or protected. Yet even if information concerning these matters does become available, it travels very slowly indeed. There are less than 90,000 telephones in the country; only 13,000 of these are located in the East Wing.[4] None are available in the villages. It is even unusual for police stations to be so equipped. In West Pakistan, of the total of 1,184 police stations and police posts only 28.5 per cent have telephones.[5] In East Pakistan one classic, but not unusual, example is the border station at Tamabil. If the Pakistani guards find it necessary to communicate with their superiors by telephone, they have to cross over to the Indian side, call Shillong in Assam and place an international call through that exchange via Gauhati and Calcutta to either Sylhet or Dacca. If a crime or a disturbance occurs in the rural areas, the police officer will learn of it, if at all, either through his mail or more often through a messenger. Then if an investigator happens to be available, he may proceed with some constables to the scene. Given the existing transportation facilities, the trip through high mountains, arid deserts, or inundated plains takes another extended period. By the time the authorities arrive the culprits are long gone and so is any evidence.[6]

[4] *Second Five Year Plan,* p. 310 and *Pakistan 1961-62* (Karachi: Pakistan Publications, 1963), p. 78.

[5] Memorandum #1391/M, Office of the Inspector General of Police, West Pakistan, Lahore, January 22, 1963.

[6] Conditions are not much better in urban areas. According to a newspaper report, only one police station in Dacca has even a single automobile. If the police receive an urgent call for help—and they often do not answer phones at night—they must depend on public transportation, hired rickshaws, or just plain walking (Dacca, *Pakistan Observer,* July 5, 1964, p. 1).

71

The communications barrier to massive coercion is very solid indeed. Perhaps even more decisive, however, are personnel limitations. Pakistan has a remarkably small police force. In 1960, for example, the Government of East Pakistan had only 20,839 regular policemen at its disposal. In comparison, the City of New York, a much more compact area with a fraction of the population of East Pakistan, required 25,000 policemen with far superior equipment for its efforts to assure law and order. Another, perhaps more relevant, comparison reflects a decline of 2,443 (12 per cent) policemen on duty during the previous decade.[7] The police force is augmented by village watchmen (*chaukidars*) which in the East Wing number some 35,381.[8] These men, however, have very little authority in law enforcement, and in case of conflict between villagers and the police they almost always follow the lead of the former.

Restrictions in size are aggravated by limitations in reliability. It was one major advantage of the colonial ruler that he could import from England administrators, policemen, and even troops whose loyalty was assured. The Government of Pakistan, on the other hand, must depend upon its native sons, who are tied to their own communities by relatives, custom, and training. A British officer could with assurance order his British troops or British-dominated police to fire into a crowd of demonstrators. A Pakistani police officer always faces the threat that his men might turn on him. Thus it is really no surprise that in 1963 and 1964 the police displayed

[7] Memorandum, Assistant Inspector General of Police, Government of East Pakistan, May 24, 1962.

[8] Government of East Pakistan, Police Directorate, *Report on Police Administration of the Province of East Pakistan for the Year 1959* (Dacca: East Pakistan Government Press, 1961), p. 11.

72

a singular reluctance to intervene in political mass demonstrations, labor strikes, and communal riots.[9] Yet even in less extreme circumstances the reliability of the law-enforcement personnel is questionable. A small group of senior officers (PSP) are well trained and well paid. The vast majority—some 98 per cent in East Pakistan—are constables and rural policemen who have little training and less financial rewards. In 1959 the income of an average rural policeman in East Pakistan was less than Rs 17 ($3.57) and that of a regular foot constable in West Pakistan slightly over Rs 35 ($7.35) a month.[10] Moreover, salary payments are irregular. Some 6,664 *chaukidars* remained unpaid for various periods in East Pakistan. Needless to say, the state of morale leaves much to be desired, and corruption assumes fabulous proportions. Consider the following example, indicating both the corruption and the turnover. The total number of rural policemen in Natore Subdivision was 344 in 1959. In the same year official records reveal that 497 were punished departmentally for violation of police regulations. Although this is an extreme example, it is significant to note that each year 30 per cent of the rural police force are *caught* and convicted for dereliction of duty.[11] The record of the regular police is somewhat better, but during the special screening

[9] In August 1964, the day after the United States Information Service Library in Dacca was wrecked by demonstrators, I remarked to a senior Secretary to the Government of East Pakistan that although the incident could have been anticipated (it followed United States bombing of North Vietnamese torpedo-boat bases), the police were conspicuous by their absence. He conceded that the event was unfortunate and added that their only excuse was that, even in more serious incidents, the performance of their police was no better.

[10] *Ibid.* and Memorandum #1391/M, Office of the Inspector General of Police, West Pakistan, Lahore, January 22, 1963.

[11] *Report on the Police Administration of the Province of East*

conducted during martial law 665 policemen were punished *in addition to* those convicted by regular departmental procedures.[12]

At this point a few words should be said about the armed forces. Their position is rather different from the civilian law-enforcement personnel. By all indications they are well organized, well disciplined, well equipped, and well trained. They are amply rewarded both in prestige and material goods. This has not always been so, and much credit must go to the first Pakistani Commander-in-Chief. The armed forces are an effective instrument in their own domain. Some of this effectiveness may even be transferred to the civilian administrative machinery. It is another question, however, whether they could enforce a program requiring massive coercion. There is no indication whatever that either the government or the generals even consider such an eventuality. Thus conclusions must be conjectural. It should be noted, however, that the great superiority of the armed forces is in their firepower and hence their capability to overcome concentrated and organized opposition. They may be well suited to prevent anarchy, the seizure of government by a revolutionary group, or the secession of part of the national territory. In penetrating remote villages, ferreting out individual criminals, tax evaders or political dissidents, and coercing the performance of specific tasks by millions of people over an extended time, the armed forces face much the same limitations as the civilian police.

Pakistan for the Year 1959 (Dacca: East Pakistan Government Press, 1961), pp. 11-12.

[12] Dacca, *Morning News*, July 10, 1959, p. 1.

Limitations by Ideology

Restraints upon communications and coercive personnel render quite ineffective laws and policies resting primarily upon coercion for their effectiveness. This is not all. Even a moderate use of force by the government runs afoul on a double standard in the popular attitude toward force. Private violence as means to settle individual and group disputes or to support political demands against the government is routine and appears quite proper. In contrast, the legitimacy of public force is far from generally accepted. Invariably, it evokes intense resentment not only from those who are its targets, but also from the population at large. For a husband to kill his wife and her lover if found together or for a family to continue a blood feud is considered to be in the finest tradition. For the government to punish such murders is unacceptable. That a man should avoid paying taxes for years causes scarcely an eyebrow to be raised. The seizure and sale of this man's property evokes general condemnation. Students, labor unions, and political groups may strike, demonstrate, damage property, even assault policemen as a legitimate routine. When the authorities respond with arrests, lathi charges, or tear gas, they are roundly condemned.

There are many practical demonstrations of this double standard. President Ayub Khan himself referred to it in his presidential campaign in 1964, citing the example of a Karachi police official who, after having been injured by a brick, fired three pistol shots and killed a student. "On such occasions," the President observed, "neither the public nor newspapers helped or lent support to the Government."[12a] The attitude is perhaps most

[12a] Karachi, *Dawn*, December 13, 1964, p. 6.

dramatically epitomized by the experience of Nurul Amin, Chief Minister of East Bengal and senior leader of the Muslim League. Throughout the morning of February 21, 1952, Dacca University students were rioting against the prospects of Urdu becoming the single national language. The police were hard pressed in spite of their periodic lathi charges and tear gas shots. Students in a frenzy hurled challenges and barrages of rocks. There was rarely a more clear case of self-defense for the policemen. They fired several rounds; the demonstrators withdrew and dispersed. One student was killed, and two died later in the hospital.[13] The next day the Chief Minister introduced a resolution in the Provincial Assembly, which recommended to the Constituent Assembly that Bengali be accepted as one of the "state" languages of Pakistan. He also announced a judicial inquiry to discover whether police brutality had occurred. In spite of these efforts the Chief Minister and his party were held responsible for the violence. Two years later in the provincial elections the Muslim League was practically wiped out and Nurul Amin ignominiously defeated by an obscure student.

Under martial law some of Nurul Amin's political opponents who had defeated him in 1954 were jailed. He had learned his lesson well, however. When the new constitution (1962) was announced, Nurul Amin was the first to demand the release of all political prisoners. Commitment to democratic ideals may certainly have been one of his motivations. Another practical consideration, however, was the concern that his opponents, who in his judgment had already been discredited by 1958, were now gaining great prestige while in jail.

[13] Karachi, *Dawn*, February 23, 1952, pp. 1, 6, 8.

The only way to prevent them from becoming undefeatable public heroes was to get them out.

The sources of the prevailing attitude toward force are deeply rooted in tradition and reinforced by experience. Suppose we turn first to the negative public response to governmental coercion. We may start with the observation that throughout South Asia physical force was rarely, if ever, used as a social sanction. The traditional pattern was so well established and social control so effective that in case of intragroup conflict or violation of group rules punishment took the form of censures by public opinion ranging up to *de facto* ostracism. Such collective sanctions as imprisonment, flogging, or executions were quite unacceptable. Only when the transgression involved women, and then only in some areas, did the issue of violence arise. In such exceptional instances private violence may have been accepted and approved.

In any case, social sanction was the prerogative of the small-scale social units, a tradition which was preserved into the most recent past. The Moghul emperors, in general, favored indirect rule and exercised only limited control. They never sought to integrate the numerous small social units under their control. As long as their hegemony was not threatened, they permitted, even encouraged, local communities to settle their own disputes and allocate roles. With the advent of colonial rule the role of government changed little. Although the various India Acts provided for centralized authority and law enforcement, in practice Britain was content to continue the former pattern. The princely states preserved their traditional structure. In British India government was limited to three functions: maintenance of order, administration of justice, and collection of taxes. In fact, the first two activities were interpreted to apply primarily as restraints on those challenges to public order which were directed against overall colonial control; the third—tax collection—was administered through local intermediaries (*jagirdars, zamindars*). The traditional mechanisms of kinship patterns continued to allocate roles, settle disputes, and enforce rules, while the government remained remote from the activities of the population.

The acute resentment against the use of physical force by the government has another source as well. The image of the political system is not one of impersonal institutions, but rather a highly subjective ruler/subject relationship. Such was the tradition of the Moghul emperors and such was the practice of the colonial period. To be sure, the British did introduce a civil service, but from the point of view of the native population little change could be perceived. The bureaucrat on the subcontinent was far more than an administrator. His authority, like that of his feudal predecessor, was delimited more by geography than functional specialization. So wide were his discretionary powers that the District Officer was often described as "a monarch of all he surveys."[14] Laws and policies were made in the distant capital, but their application to a particular individual or group depended upon the personal estimate of the civil servant. It was he who as magistrate held court and settled disputes. The precedents of English common law were rarely applicable, so he used his own judgment in determining the extent to which revenue should be collected. As administrator he controlled government

[14] Ralph Braibanti, "The Civil Service of Pakistan, a Theoretical Analysis," *South Atlantic Quarterly*, LVIII (1959), No. 2, p. 271.

licenses. Since the number of those eligible by objective criteria often exceeded the number of licenses available, the approval of the application once more depended upon the District Officer's personal judgment. The point of this is not that the Indian Civil Service was corrupt; by most standards it was not. The fact remains that it perpetuated the image of government by men rather than by laws.

The relevance of an image of personal government is this: the ruler/subject relationship when translated into referents which are more familiar to the rural masses becomes analogous to a master/servant relationship. In the latter, however, rules of *noblesse oblige* are operative. Islamic injunctions are quite emphatic on the responsibilities of those who have been given wealth and power. British practice tended to reinforce this attitude. A husband may beat his wife; a bearer may strike a sweeper. It is the height of bad form, however, for a master to beat his servant. It is a curious consequence of this analogy that a policeman raised in a village, who has married a girl from the village and whose income is no higher than that of a villager, nevertheless has crossed the magic line of separation.

Turning now to the other aspect of this double standard in regard to force, we find a number of conditions supporting a predisposition to private and antigovernmental violence. There is, first of all, the frustration-aggression sequence, and certainly with a rapidly widening gap between aspirations and attainment the extent of frustration in Pakistan is rising dramatically. The experience that antigovernmental violence is so eminently effective gives it further impetus. For five years the East Pakistani had requested and implored the government not to force Urdu as a national language upon them. The response was invariably oratory about "one nation—one language," or dark accusations of Communists and separatists. Then came the violence of February 21, 1952, which settled the point. Bengali was accepted as a national language. Another example involves the report of the Commission on National Education (1960). Several provisions recommending greater governmental control over the universities and the extension of the bachelor's degree course from two years to three aroused the ire of the academic community. The summer months of 1962 were rather turbulent with considerable free-floating hostility. In September agitation focused on the implementation of this report. On September 17, East Pakistan observed a complete *hartal* (general strike) in support of the students' demands "for scrapping of the Education Commission's Report." Predictably violence broke out and spread. By noon the army had to be called out to restore what euphemistically was called order.[15] On the same day a committee of "officials and experts" met in Karachi and recommended a review of the report. By September 30 the government suspended the three-year course and encouraged the reversion to the two-year program.[16] Within days all universities announced that students who had completed two years of the three-year program would automatically and without examination be granted bachelor's degrees. In the same summer Dacca University students employed violence to support their demands for postponement of their examinations[17] and won. In the fall East Pakistan Government Class IV

[15] Dacca, *Pakistan Observer*, September 18, 1962, p. 1.

[16] *Ibid.*, October 1, 1962, p. 1.

[17] They explained that they had not had time to study because of their participation in the spring demonstrations.

employees and then the railroad workers used violence to support their demands for higher wages and also won. The examples could be carried on for pages.

Perhaps an equally important reason for a predisposition toward private and antigovernment violence is the general and intense conviction that it is right. By tradition social sanctions within the various groups are nonviolent. By the same tradition physical force is a preferred method in the treatment of *outsiders*, especially those perceived as hostile. Captured dacoits (bandits) are dealt with summarily and brutally by the villagers. Property disputes between kinship groups or villages often end in bloodshed. Blood feuds have been carried on for generations and are abating only gradually.

The use of violence against the government and its tax collectors or policemen was considered a legitimate expression of grievances for many centuries. This was reinforced by the struggle for independence. Mutiny, peaceful and not-so-peaceful demonstrations, as well as political assassination, became a mark of patriotism. It did not matter what the specific riot was about; it satisfied the requirements of virtue as long as it was directed against the government. Toward the end of the struggle, Direct Action Day (August 16, 1946) was organized to demonstrate the determination of the Muslims, and communal riots became the test of state lines between Pakistan and India. Then came independence with full-scale communal violence and a half-million people butchered in "righteous retaliation."

The habits and lessons of the past are difficult to unlearn in so short a time. Student demonstrators in Dacca, for example, are not easily persuaded that while violence against the colonial government was an act

81

of patriotism, similar violence against the Government of Pakistan is subversion—especially since to them the grievances of today are no less real and no less severe.

This then is the consequence of the ambivalent attitude toward force. Even a moderate use of force to preserve public order or implement development programs creates acute resentment and invites a response of violence by individuals and groups. Such response, in turn, places the government in a peculiar dilemma. It may acquiesce or it may intensify physical force. Significantly *both* alternatives escalate violence, thereby initiating a contest which the government in view of the limitation on communications and coercive personnel simply cannot win.

5

++

The Governmental Capacity to Persuade:
The Pressure of Aspirations

++

A FREE AND SOVEREIGN Pakistan less than ninety years after the last Moghul was indeed a massive accomplishment. In 1947 the majority of Muslims in India simultaneously freed themselves from foreign colonial rule and escaped domination, perhaps exploitation, by the Hindu "majority community." The stature and vigor of the leadership certainly played a major role in the achievement of this feat. Success, however, was not assured until mass support had been enlisted by presenting the objective of independence as a vehicle for the realization of two key aspirations: the urge for an improved standard of living and the desire to preserve tradition.

The state of Pakistan was born of, and for a while was carried along by, a rising tide of expectations. Yet gradually and inevitably the realization dawned that independence had brought no panaceas. The growth rate in the standard of living continued to lag behind the expansion of aspirations for material goods. Independent Pakistan had failed to safeguard, let alone reinforce, indigenous tradition. Perhaps this was inevitable. Nevertheless, as a consequence expectation has turned into frustration, and mass support has changed into a rising tide of resentment.

The Urge for an Improved Standard of Living

In retrospect it is difficult to identify and measure the progressive inroads of the international demonstration effect. The concept is a recent one, and so are the techniques of social sciences. It is evident, however, that by the end of the nineteenth century exposure to Western material achievements was spreading throughout the subcontinent. The introduction and rapid extension of the railroads exposed a growing share of the population to the fruits of Western technology. In turn, a steady stream of Indian students, who after the encouragement of Sir Syed Ahmed included a large number of Muslims, sought education in Britain and learned at firsthand the consumption patterns of an industrial society. It is not unreasonable to assume that they were attracted by it. In any case, ever since the beginning of this century, campaigns and agitations for independence have consistently played upon popular aspirations for material rewards.

As exposure to Western consumption patterns expanded, the Congress Party relied upon two major techniques to mobilize for its own purposes the dynamics of the international demonstration effect. First, it intensified awareness of the low level of material rewards on the subcontinent by identifying the causes of deprivation as removable. Previously in the small-scale societies of Hindus and Muslims human hardship was attributed to inevitable fate or perhaps divine punishment. The Congress Party insisted on more human causes. Mahatma Gandhi set the tone for this approach when shortly after World War I in a public letter "to every Englishman in India" he listed "the exploitation of India's resources for the benefit of Great Britain" as the foremost grievance.[1] Running parallel with the effort to blame foreign exploitation for the poverty and misery in India was a campaign to project vividly the universal benefits which would flow from independence. This technique may well have had its origin in Jawaharlal Nehru's early contact with the Kisan (Peasant) Movement. When he first "got entangled" with it in June 1920, he was greatly impressed. "They were in miserable rags, men and women, but their faces were full of excitement, and their eyes glistened and seemed to expect strange happenings which would as if by a miracle put an end to their long misery." Nehru ascribed the success of the movement to Ramachandra's habit of making "all manner of promises . . . , vague and nebulous but full of hope."[2] In any case, by the 1920's and throughout the thirties Congress Party agitation consistently inflated postindependence expectations for material rewards.

For a long time the Muslim League tended to tag along with Congress on strategy. The 1937 elections marked a radical turning point. As the ballots were counted the hegemony of the League over the Muslim electorate appeared tenuous, to say the least. Worse still, in the negotiations for provincial Cabinet seats the Muslim League discovered that the Congress high command had little inclination to share power with a separate Muslim party. It became quite clear that the survival of the League depended upon its ability to establish an image that would be clearly identifiable and have a special appeal to the Muslim masses. The

[1] Mahatma Gandhi, *Freedom's Battle* (Madras: Ganesh and Co., 1921), p. 288.

[2] Jawaharlal Nehru, *An Autobiography* (London: John Lane Bodley Head, 1937), p. 52.

new Muslim League approach did not reduce emphasis upon the material rewards to be expected after independence. "Personally I believe that a political organization which gives no promise of improving the lot of the average Muslim cannot attract our masses," wrote Allama Iqbal in a confidential letter to Mr. Jinnah.[3] Instead it substituted the threat of Hindu economic domination for colonial exploitation as the critical but removable barrier to the improvement in the standard of living for Muslims. From 1938 on, the Muslim League never tired of reminding its followers that without partition of the subcontinent after the withdrawal of Britain, Hindu economic development would be sustained by the exploitation of the Muslim minority.

The magic day of independence arrived, passed, and receded into history. The international demonstration effect continued to inflate aspirations. During the last decades educational opportunities at British and American universities for talented young men from the subcontinent expanded rapidly. In return, a swarm of foreign technicians, businessmen, scholars, and tourists descended upon Pakistani cities, towns, even villages. Newspapers and movies added further content to the image of Western consumption patterns. The expectations for an improved standard of living, however, have not been satisfied to any significant extent. A decade and a half after independence the estimate of per capita income is Rs 251, or, at the arbitrarily fixed official exchange rate, $52.73.[4] This income level is not only ex-

[3] *Letters of Iqbal to Jinnah* (Lahore: Shaikh Muhammad Ashraf, n.d.), p. 15.

[4] Government of Pakistan, *Economic Survey of Pakistan 1961-62* (Rawalpindi: Government of Pakistan Press, 1962), Statistical Section, p. 8.

tremely low, it reflects a singular lack of progress. Although there was considerable fluctuation in per capita income estimates during the 1950's, the increase from the 1950-1951 level does not seem to exceed a total of Rs 3.[5]

This gain of three rupees over eleven years is statistically a positive margin. Practically it is imperceptible. It is even probable that while some individuals and groups have accumulated considerable wealth, large segments of the population have found their income declining. There is, for example, some evidence that the lot of the people in the East Wing in general and that of the rural masses in particular has worsened during the last decades. An empirical study in 1956 revealed an average disinvestment of Rs 40-100 per rural family in East Pakistan.[6] A more recent study suggests further, though somewhat decelerated disinvestment.[7] Henry W. Fairchild, an American specialist who lived in Bengali villages for many years, concluded: "[The cultivator] is poorer than his father was. He is illiterate and it appears that his children must remain illiterate also. He owns only one bullock whereas his grandfather owned four. He has less than half the land his grandfather held. He is head over heels in debt on which he pays half his total farm production in interest. He is at the mercy of the wind, the flood and the drought. There

[5] Government of Pakistan, *Pakistan Statistical Yearbook 1962* (Karachi: Government of Pakistan Press, 1962), p. 266.

[6] Dacca University Socio-Economic Survey Board, *Rural Credit and Unemployment in East Pakistan* (Dacca: Pakistan Cooperative Book Society, 1956), p. 48.

[7] M. Habibullah, *Some Aspects of Rural Capital Formation in East Pakistan* (Dacca: Bureau of Economic Research, University of Dacca, 1963), p. 32.

is a black future ahead and little that can be done about it."[8]

The Desire to Maintain Tradition

Perhaps less often noted, but certainly no less significant than the impetus to expectations for material goods, is the traditionalist appeal of anticolonialist agitation. There appears to be a remarkably uncritical acceptance of the image that the struggle for independence was sustained by aspirations for a national political entity supported by a society on a national scale. Nothing could be further from the truth. The masses were mobilized for the struggle against the colonial rulers not so much because the latter were a barrier to an indigenous *nation*-state, but rather because they served as a vehicle to disrupt the traditional *small-scale* societies. The ideal that attracted the rural populations to independence was the expectation that with the departure of the British the strain on the traditional norms and organization would be relaxed. Anticolonial vocabulary abounded with traditional terminology: *Brahmacharya, Swaraj, Ahimsa.* The symbol of the Congress was the spinning wheel (*Charkha*). Mahatma Gandhi disapproved of industrial machinery not merely because it was owned by foreigners. He objected to it since, regardless of its owner, "it is easily turned to a bad purpose as we know."[9] He also appealed against centralization of government or the economy. "I suggest that if India is to evolve along non-violent lines, it will have to decentralize many things," and he added propheti-

[8] Quoted in A. Farouk, "Is East Pakistan Developing?", Dacca, *Pakistan Observer*, August 14, 1963, Independence Day Supplement.
[9] S. Abid Husain, *The Way of Gandhi and Nehru* (Bombay: Asia Publishing House, 1959), p. 47.

88

cally, "Centralization cannot be sustained and defended without adequate force."[10] Mahatma Gandhi's ideal was, in fact, a decentralized rural economy consisting of small, self-sufficient village communities.[11]

The appeal of the Muslim League to the tradition of decentralization is perhaps less clear-cut. While it consistently opposed centralization, the League tended to emphasize regional autonomy rather than the ideal of traditional small-scale village or kinship units.[12] When in 1940 the Pakistan Resolution was passed in Lahore, it called for " 'Independent States' in which the Constituent Units shall be autonomous and sovereign."[13] During the final negotiations with the British Mohammad Ali Jinnah publicly argued that the departure of the colonial power terminated paramountcy (a synonym for national jurisdiction) and that sovereignty should therefore revert to all constituent units.[14]

Government in Pakistan has sought to satisfy the popular expectation for an improved standard of living. To be sure, it has not succeeded so far, but at least it has tried and continues to do so. In contrast, the oratory about local autonomy and the support of the traditional small scale was quickly discarded. During the first decade of independence the government embarked upon an intensive effort of cultural assimilation and a determined policy of political and economic centralization. In view

[10] *Ibid.*, p. 45.

[11] *Ibid.*, p. 38.

[12] See Leonard Binder, *Religion and Politics in Pakistan* (Berkeley and Los Angeles: University of California Press, 1961), p. 67 and Wilfred Cantwell Smith, *Modern Islam in India* (London: V. Gollancz Ltd., 1946), p. 249.

[13] Binder, *op.cit.*, p. 62.

[14] Abdul Waheed Khan, *India Wins Freedom, The Other Side* (Karachi: Pakistan Educational Publishers, 1961), p. 335.

of the far-reaching consequences of these policies some elaboration may be appropriate.

Let us first consider cultural assimilation. The pressure indeed was great throughout the country, but nowhere was it more dramatic than in Bengal. According to the official census of 1951 only 7.2 per cent of the population of Pakistan spoke Urdu, while 54.6 per cent spoke Bengali.[15] Nevertheless from the very beginning of Pakistan's existence the national leadership was quite insistent about adopting Urdu as the single national language. In February 1948, for example, Prime Minister Liaquat Ali Khan retorted to a motion for permitting the use of Bengali in the Constituent Assembly: "[the mover] should realize that Pakistan has been created because of the demand of one hundred million Muslims in this subcontinent, and the language of a hundred million Muslims is Urdu."[16] Two years later the Interim Report of the Basic Principles Committee stated flatly, "Urdu should be the national language of the State."[17] The peak of the one-language campaign was reached in February 1952, when Prime Minister Nazimuddin, a Bengali himself, spoke on behalf of Urdu. The result was bloody violence in Dacca and thereafter a hasty retreat by the national government. Nevertheless, the efforts for cultural assimilation have continued. In the schools students are pressured into taking Urdu; in government offices Urdu appears to be preferred; and finally the national government's allocation for the propagation of Urdu language and culture far exceeds that

[15] Cited in Keith Callard, *Pakistan: A Political Study* (New York: Macmillan, 1957), p. 181.

[16] Constituent Assembly of Pakistan, *Debates*, Vol. 2 (February 25, 1948), p. 17.

[17] Callard, *op.cit.*, p. 183.

of the allocation for any other language, including Bengali. As if this were not enough, there is periodic sniping in the West Pakistani press about the inferiority of Bengali culture. A most recent example of this was an editorial in the Pakistan *Times* claiming that the popularity of poet Nazrul Islam in Bengal was due solely to the fact that Iqbal had never been translated into Bengali. It further suggested that the University of Dacca should take a lead in this effort and not be so much under the domination of Calcutta.[18]

At the same time, considering the heterogeneity of the country political centralization proceeded at an extraordinary pace. When first established, Pakistan was a veritable maze of political entities. The East Wing was composed of the eastern part of the former province of Bengal and a small segment of the former province of Assam. In West Pakistan, however, the situation was more complex. To begin with, there were the Governors' Provinces (the Punjab, Sind, and the North West Frontier Province). In addition there were Baluchistan, the Baluchistan States (Kalat, Las Bela, Makran, and Kharan), the North West Frontier States (Dir, Amb, Swat, and Chitral), the frontier tribal areas, the princely states of Khairpur and Bhawalpur, and finally the federal capital area of Karachi. Muslim League agitation, Mr. Jinnah's personal assurances, and the formal accession documents to Pakistan had promised a high measure of local autonomy. Legally the central government

[18] Lahore, *Pakistan Times*, May 25, 1962, p. 6. As a matter of fact, at the time the article was written, various translations of Iqbal's works into Bengali had been made by Maniruddin Yusuf, Ghulam Mustafa, Syed Ali Ahsan, Qazi Akram Husain, Syed Abdul Mannan, Farrukh Ahmad, A. F. M. Abdul Haq, Mizanur Rahman, Muhammad Shahidullah, Ashraf Ali Khan, Muhammad Sultan, and Aminuddin Ahmad.

could control only foreign affairs, communications, and defense.[19] Such expectations were soon to be dashed, while legal obligations were cavalierly discarded. In less than ten years, through central force and manipulation all the political entities in the western part of the country were consolidated into one unit.

As a matter of fact, from the very beginning the central government intervened directly and frequently in the administration of the provinces. Chief Ministers were deposed with startling regularity. No less than ten provincial ministries fell victim to national action in the first seven years of independence.[20] Invariably at such removals the central government justified its action in terms of national interest or by accusing the dismissed Chief Minister of irregularities and corruption. The hypocrisy of these charges, however, is laid bare by the record of Mr. Khuhro of Sind. Twice the central government dismissed him for corruption. Yet when in 1954 it sought a successor to Pirzada Abdus Sattar who was charged with maladministration and abuse of power, the choice fell upon none other than the twice-accused and widely condemned Mr. Khuhro.

Intervention in the administration of the provinces by the national government was not restricted to the dismissal of Chief Ministers and their cabinets. It extended to the seizure of direct control of the provinces. During the final days of colonial rule Mr. Jinnah, acting on his

[19] Wayne A. Wilcox, Pakistan, *The Consolidation of a Nation* (New York: Columbia University Press, 1963), p. 104.

[20] The sequence of dismissals is as follows: 1947—Khan Shahib and Rashid of the North West Frontier Province; 1948—Khuhro of Sind; 1949—Khuda Bakhsh of Sind and the Khan of Momdot of the Punjab; 1951—Khuhro of Sind; 1953—Mumtaz Khan Daultana of the Punjab; 1954—Pirzada Abus Sattar of Sind, Malik Firoz Khan of the Punjab, and Fazlul Huq of East Bengal.

own initiative, inserted Section 92A into the Independence Act authorizing the Governor-General in case of emergency "to direct the Governor of a Province to assume on behalf of the Governor-General all or any of the powers vested in or exercisable by any Provincial body or authority."[21] This clause, which was originally intended for emergency use only, became a normal part of the working of federal political relations in Pakistan. Under this article the central government administered the Province of the Punjab from January 1949 to April 1951, the Province of Sind from December 1951 to May 1953, and the Province of East Bengal from May 1954 to June 1955. In the following year when the first Constitution of Pakistan was approved, the same provision appeared under the new Article 193.[22] Two months after the proclamation of the new constitution the central government invoked this article in East Pakistan, and within a year it did the same in West Pakistan.

One final expression of political centralization to be noted is the concentration of political power in the federal executive. Ostensibly Pakistan had a parliamentary government until 1958. Yet during these crucial years of newly acquired sovereignty the national legislature was relegated to the role of a minor partner. For the first eleven years of independence it was in session for 338 days, or for an annual average of 30 days. The executive had a clear field for the remainder of the time. Another comparison is also revealing. During these years the National Assembly passed 160 laws; the Governor-General (President) issued 376 major ordi-

[21] See Callard, *op.cit.*, p. 160.
[22] *Ibid.*, p. 162.

nances.[23] Most important of all, when the Governor-General dismissed the ministry of Nazimuddin after the latter had successfully guided his budget through the Legislature and when shortly thereafter the same Governor-General also dismissed the Constituent Assembly, he blazed the trail for a complete executive takeover, which occurred in October 1958 under martial law.

The massive drive for centralization was not restricted to the political arena alone. It extended into the economic development program as well. The mobilization of resources, for example, was almost exclusively a central government affair. The latter monopolized foreign aid funds, controlled public borrowing and reserved for itself the lion's share of tax revenue. Local government, even provincial government, is financially at the mercy of the Centre. Thus in 1960-1961 when the total development budget for East Pakistan called for expenditures of Rs 55.1 crores, less than 10 per cent (Rs 4.86 crores) was raised through provincially controlled taxes, but nearly 30 per cent (Rs 15.18 crores) was contributed by the central government from its tax revenue *collected in East Pakistan.*[24]

Similarly, since the completion of the First Five Year Plan the Planning Commission, a central organ, has played an increasingly determining voice both in the preparation of the Plan and the approval of specific schemes (projects). An official "historical résumé" points to this evolution in planning procedure:

[23] Muneer Ahmad, *Legislatures of Pakistan* (Lahore: University of the Punjab, 1960), pp. 123, 127.

[24] Government of East Pakistan, Finance Department, *Economic Survey of East Pakistan, 1961-62* (Dacca: East Pakistan Government Press, 1962), pp. 43, 51.

While in the preparation of the First Plan a start was made by inviting from the Provincial Governments, Central Ministries, quasi-governmental agencies and others concerned details of proposals and schemes which they would like to be undertaken during the First Plan period and these proposals and schemes were later integrated and developed into a Plan, in the case of the Second Plan the Commission took upon itself as a starting point to determine broadly the tentative framework of the Plan, its probable size, the desirable physical targets and the sector-wise priorities. Subsequent work on the Plan was to be carried out within this framework.[25]

This change in procedure assumes even greater significance through the following observation. The preparation of the Second Plan extended over two and a half years. It spanned the final months of the Constitutional Government and the initial period of martial law. There were numerous meetings with provincial government officials. Private groups were asked for suggestions. Comments were invited from seventy-five "eminent persons." After all this time and activity, however, the final draft of the Second Five Year Plan did not include a single major deviation from the judgments presented by the Working Paper prepared by the Planning Commission and the Deputy Chairman's note on the "philosophic concepts" in August 1958.

The provincial governments play a somewhat more perceptible role in the preparation of specific projects. They enjoy some discretionary powers over those schemes where total expenditure does not exceed Rs 25

[25] Government of Pakistan, Planning Commission, "Preparation of the Second Five Year Plan (1960-65)—A Historical Résumé," a mimeographed circular, November 11, 1960.

lakhs. They also exercise the initiative in proposing new projects. Yet this measure of "autonomy" is largely illusory, for such "autonomy" is merely administrative, not political. The traditional hierarchies, provincial interest groups, or even local officials have nothing to do with development planning. Instead, the provinces are represented by members of the central bureaucracy, who frequently do not come from the same province and whose career objectives are the Central Secretariat. In addition, provincial initiative in the development schemes is further offset by the reservation of final determination to the National Economic Council. This is not a mere formality, and the Council permits no illusions about it. During the First Five Year Plan when substantial allocations were unutilized in East Pakistan because of the scarcity of proposed projects, the Planning Commission nevertheless rejected or delayed approval on a large number of proposals simply because they were not submitted in the proper form!

Probably the most far-reaching aspect of the centralized economic development program, however, is this: investment priorities are based upon the implicit assumption that to the masses of citizens the national entity is the focus of political and economic orientation. Otherwise it is difficult to explain the persistent insensitivity of the program to the political and economic exigencies of the subnational (regional) entities, and a consequent concentration of public investment in one part of the country. It was not by accident that the income index between 1953 and 1958 increased from 112 to 143 in West Pakistan, but only from 120 to 122 in the East Wing.[26] The Second Five Year Plan admits

[26] S. U. Khan, "The Measure of Economic Growth in East and

96

that "after Independence, for a variety of reasons, a larger flow of immigrant capital, enterprises and technical skills went into West Pakistan than into East Pakistan."[27] Yet instead of attempting to correct this imbalance government action has aggravated it. During the First Five Year Plan almost two-thirds of direct central government investment went to the West Wing.[28] At the same time, provincial government outlays in West Pakistan amounted to Rs 188.4 crores, or almost twice the Rs 98 crores level of the East Wing. Investment by semigovernmental institutions reflected the same pattern.[29]

Table 6

Regional Distribution of Investment
by Semi-public Institutions (1956-61)

Semipublic Institution	Share of Investment (Per Cent)	
	East Pakistan	West Pakistan
Industrial Development Bank	20	80
House Building Finance Corporation	12	88
Pakistan Industrial Credit and Investment Corporation	24	76
Pakistan Industrial Development Corporation	45	55

West Pakistan," *The Pakistan Development Review*, I, No. 2 (Autumn 1961), p. 50. Cf. Government of Pakistan, *Outline of the Third Five-Year Plan* (Karachi: Government of Pakistan Press, 1964), p. 11.

[27] *Second Five Year Plan* (Karachi: Government of Pakistan Press, 1960), p. 39.

[28] This was partially camouflaged by listing the "Federal Territory of Karachi" as a separate budget item (see *Second Five Year Plan*, p. 408). According to one estimate the ratio of allocations during the First Five Year Plan was 9 to 4 in favor of West Pakistan (H. S. Suhrawardy, quoted in Dacca, *Pakistan Observer*, November 7, 1962, p. 1).

[29] Dacca, *Pakistan Observer*, June 3, 1963, p. 4.

Some data on foreign aid complete the picture. A non-classified study by the United States Mission in Pakistan covering the 1949-1961 period reveals that allocation of foreign loans and credits on a regional basis was as follows:[30]

West Pakistan (including Karachi)	$519,886,426
East Pakistan	$127,876,526
"Common"	$132,125,928

In short, when the massive efforts of centralization are added to the insistent pressures of cultural assimilation, they all point to this conclusion: independence did not bring about the satisfaction of the popular desire to maintain tradition. Quite the contrary.

Rising Tide of Resentment

It is not entirely the fault of the Government of Pakistan that popular aspirations for an improved standard of living have not been fulfilled. To be sure, it must bear the consequences of the articulation and inflation of expectations for material rewards during the struggle for independence. On the other hand, it really has no control over the standard of living in America, and short of a total isolation of the country—a task beyond its coercive capacity—the government cannot prevent the expansion of the international demonstration effect. Nor can it be held responsible for the rapid increase of the population which eats away gross gains. To turn back Muslim refugees from India or to discourage improvement in health and hygiene is unthinkable. The government does have good intentions regarding the reduction of birthrates, but such efforts have been retard-

[30] These figures do not include military aid or grants. United States, Department of State, Airgram AID/W POAIB A-2426, from Karachi, February 13, 1963.

ed by the scarcity of resources, facilities, skills, and the habituated norms of the traditional small scale. Finally, the government cannot be blamed for concentrating first upon an overhead structure which absorbs much investment but, in the initial years at least, has little effect on family incomes.

Certainly it is not entirely the fault of the government that the popular desire to maintain tradition has not been satisfied. The argument that centralized planning and a concentration of investment are necessary steps for a maximization of economic development is most persuasive. Thus government efforts along these lines may well have been motivated by a desire to respond to the popular aspirations for a higher standard of living. The years following independence, moreover, were politically turbulent. Pakistan's mighty neighbor India has never accepted the legitimacy of a state based upon religion and has demonstrated time and again that she would not shrink from using force to achieve her ends. Internally, the rapid decline of the Muslim League accentuated the prevailing political instability and accelerated centrifugal forces. It was a major challenge to deter foreign aggression and to keep the country from disintegrating. Centralization and cultural assimilation may well have appeared the most effective methods. Having said all this and more, however, the fact remains that the expectations aroused during the struggle against the colonial power and the initial years of independence have been increasingly replaced by a rising tide of resentment.

Most critical is the situation in the East Wing. There the improvement of the standard of living has been especially tardy, and the pressure against the traditional small-scale units, and especially the Bengali ethnic component, is perceived as particularly acute. Possibly the concentration of investment in another province a thousand miles away might have been acceptable had the popular perception of threat against the traditional units been minimized. Conversely, resistance against centralization and assimilation might have been less pronounced had material rewards been more abundant. As it happened, the alienation flowing from both these unsatisfied expectations converged into a massive crisis of confidence. The onus of exploitation which had been fixed first on Britain and then transferred to the Hindu majority community has now shifted to a new target: the Government of Pakistan.

One clear indication that the government has become the target of resentment is the widespread determination to identify the central government as the culprit for the disparity of incomes between the Wings. Incessantly the newspapers and public speakers recite data supporting the contention that East Pakistan has consistently been denied its fair share.[31] This is not all. Whenever central government officials visit the East Wing, they are showered with questions on disparity, and their reputations rest primarily on their willingness to admit publicly the validity of this claim. In January 1962, when Foreign Minister Manzur Qadir visited the Dacca University campus, the students would not permit him to speak on any topic unless he satisfied them with his answers on economic disparity and also would guarantee that these answers could be reported in the

[31] From a random selection of such "reports" see, for example: Dacca, *Pakistan Observer*, February 24, 1963, p. 1; March 3, 1963, p. 1; March 12, 1963, p. 1; April 4, 1963, p. 1; June 1, 1963, p. 4; June 2, 1963, p. 4; June 3, 1963, p. 4.

newspapers.[32] It was a red-letter day when Finance Minister Abdul Qadir conceded that "there has been some disparity in the field of economic development between the two provinces."[33] Those less obliging invite an uproar. Decrying the issue of disparity Said Hassan, Deputy Chairman of the Planning Commission, declared in a radio broadcast: "The trend toward 'economic separatism' must stop, this madness must end."[34] The response was sure and swift. Mr. M. Ibrahim, former Law Minister, immediately retorted that "economic disparity . . . can no longer be missed or neglected."[35] The next day President Ayub publicly admitted that in the past East Pakistan had not received its due share.[36] The storm, however, continued unabated with editorials, public protests, and student demonstrations. Before leaving Dacca the President sought to assuage ruffled feelings by assuring the reporters that Mr. Hassan was a "well-meaning man having a sense of patriotism and love for the people of both wings."[37] Then came a statement by M. Nurul Huda, member of the Planning Commission. Disparity in per capita income between East and West Pakistan was not a "dead horse," he assured the Bengali. It was "very much alive, big and growing and would never die a natural death."[38] Finally, Hafizur Rahman, East Pakistan Finance Minister, issued what amounted to a formal apology. "The gentle-

[32] The Foreign Minister insisted that he could make public statements only on topics of his portfolio, and the meeting broke up in pandemonium.
[33] Dacca, *Pakistan Observer*, May 4, 1962, p. 8.
[34] *Ibid.*, December 21, 1962, p. 1.
[35] *Ibid.*
[36] *Ibid.*, December 22, 1962, p. 1.
[37] *Ibid.*, December 25, 1962, p. 1.
[38] *Ibid.*, December 28, 1962, p. 1.

man in question," he declared, "did not in any way reflect the views of the Government."[39]

Closely related is another expression of this crisis of confidence. The issue of parity between the Wings is no longer limited to public investment. It has become the acid test of legitimacy for *all* national endeavors. East Pakistani politicians, journalists, businessmen, teachers, workers, and students are alert to the slightest deviation. In the political arena an equal number of legislators represent the two Wings. If the President is from one Wing, the Speaker must be selected from the other. Cabinet appointments are to be divided equally. Civil Service appointments are made through equal quotas. The provincial government of East Pakistan was Bengalized. Still the government is indicted for permitting West Pakistani to outnumber East Pakistani in the army officers corps and in senior civil service positions.[40] Parity in foreign scholarships is an insistent demand and so is equal allocation for museums and the propagation of Urdu and Bengali.[41] One final example: In a recent meeting of the Pakistan Olympic Association the East Pakistani members threatened to walk out unless they were assured a quota of 50 per cent of all athletes sent to the Tokyo Olympic Games.[42]

Perhaps the most far-reaching expression of the extent of alienation is the apparent inability of the government to win a popular election. Already in the early fifties the

[39] *Ibid.*, January 1, 1963, p. 1.

[40] Only 5 per cent of the army officers were born in East Pakistan. Similarly there were only 52 Class I East Pakistani officers in the Central Government compared to 541 such officers from West Pakistan. (*Ibid.*, April 13, 1963, p. 1 and April 15, 1963, p. 2.)

[41] *Ibid.*, December 9, 1962, p. 1; December 12, 1962, p. 1; March 31, 1963, p. 8; July 7, 1963, p. 1.

[42] *Ibid.*, August 12, 1963, p. 8 and August 20, 1963, p. 6.

signs were sufficiently clear. For one excuse or another the government kept postponing provincial elections. It was unwilling to try its luck even with by-elections, and thus in the summer of 1953 no less than 34 seats out of 171 were vacant in the East Pakistan Assembly. When the elections were ultimately held, the ruling Muslim League, the only "national" party, was practically annihilated. Its leader suffered an ignominious defeat, and the League's share of the 309-member legislature dwindled to 10 seats. The victors ensconced in their ministerial seats, however, soon found their popular support evaporating. In two years by-election results indicated the upsurge of the Awami League.[43] In another eighteen months it too was discredited. Then came martial law, the Revolution, and the end of direct universal suffrage.

Resentment against the central government is considerably less drastic in West Pakistan. Perhaps understandably the issue of foreign danger remains the center of attraction. This province is, of course, more urbanized than East Pakistan[44] and hence may be expected to be more aware of international events. Moreover, some six million (15 per cent) of its population are refugees who were driven from their ancestral homes by alien power. Finally, Kashmir is close by and its occupation by India has direct military and economic effects upon the province. Agitation therefore often aims at foreign countries: India routinely, Italy when it was rumored that an Italian movie company was considering plans to

[43] Callard, *op.cit.*, p. 61.

[44] 22.5 per cent of the population of West Pakistan but only 5.2 per cent of the population of East Pakistan are urban (Government of Pakistan, *Population Census of Pakistan 1961, Census Bulletin No. 2* [Karachi: Government of Pakistan Press, 1962], p. 14).

film the life of the Prophet, or the United States for aiding India in the first instance and ever since the Sino-Indian conflict for sending military aid as well.[45]

Periodically a measure of hostility is also leveled at East Pakistan. At times the focus of attack is a prominent individual; at other times groups and even the whole population of the province is slandered. In 1952 the *Evening Times* of Karachi carried a series of editorials characterizing political parity between the Wings as a principle "conceived . . . by persons who cannot see beyond their noses, whose mental horizons spread no further than the thoughts of their jobs." The reason behind the demand for political parity, explained the editor, was "unmistakably the short stature and the small calibre of present Bengali leadership."[46] Two years later after the fateful defeat of the Muslim League a leading newspaper in Lahore described the situation in the following manner. "The Province [East Pakistan] swarms with Communist cells. University students in particular are affected with the germs. About 80 members of the newly elected Legislature of 309 are believed to be Communists or fellow travelers."[47] In 1955 during the debates in the Constituent Assembly, according to one observer, "some of the advocates of the superior merits of Urdu managed to convey the impression that the defense of Bengali was both un-Islamic and opposed

[45] While in the West Wing these demonstrations on foreign policy frequently entail a high degree of violence, parallel demonstrations in Dacca against United States military assistance to India were noted for their friendly atmosphere, and even those directed against India were relatively mild.

[46] Quoted in Z. A. Suleri, *Pakistan's Lost Years* (Lahore: Progressive Papers Ltd., 1962), pp. 48, 49.

[47] Lahore, *Civil and Military Gazette*, July 1, 1954.

to the interests of national unity."[48] The spring of 1962 brought the resignation of popular East Pakistan Governor Lieutenant General Azam Khan. The national news service (APP) saw fit to imply that Communists and Indian agents were behind the rousing and tearful farewells the General received. Taking its cue from this report the Pakistan *Times* felt compelled to editorialize on "the dark hand of subversive political intrigue" in East Pakistan.[49] In the most recent example of this chain, the *Morning News*, a paper published in Dacca but controlled from Karachi, charged widespread activity by Indian agents and Communists throughout the East Wing.[50]

East Pakistan and the foreign enemy, however, do not exhaust the targets of resentment. From Baluchistan to the refugee colony of Korangi in private conversations one may detect a measure of disappointment and bitterness toward the government. The first Prime Minister of Pakistan and the first Chief Minister of West Pakistan were assassinated in this province. Students and workers in Lahore and Karachi periodically demonstrate against government policies. Deputy Commissioners find it necessary to announce regularly the prohibition of the assembly of more than five persons under Section 144 of the Code of Criminal Procedure. In my estimate, roughly 90 per cent of the time since independence public meetings and processions have been prohibited in at least one part of the province. Bar associations level frequent criticism at the government and freely deride the system of Basic Democracies. Tens of

48 Callard, *op.cit.*, p. 181.
49 Lahore, *Pakistan Times*, May 11, 1962, p. 6.
50 Dacca, *Morning News*, July 17, 1963, p. 1.

thousands cheered opposition leaders H. S. Suhrawardy and Abdul Qayyum Khan when a few months after the new constitution (1962) they demanded its repeal. Admittedly in West Pakistan resentment against the government does not approach the intensity of that in the East Wing. Nevertheless, against a background of disappointed expectations the conclusion that the government is not recognized to be a vehicle for aspirations can safely be drawn.

6

++

The Governmental Capacity to Persuade:
The Pattern of Leadership

++

FATE was unkind to Pakistan. Its Great Leader (*Quaid-i-Azam*) Mohammad Ali Jinnah died a little more than a year after independence was achieved. Before another three years had passed, an assassin removed its first Prime Minister, Liaquat Ali Khan, from the new government. In consequence, the top leadership that had unified the masses of Muslims in India behind a common purpose and created the sovereign state of Pakistan was no longer present to guide the people in the task of converting this temporary unity into the massive solidarity of a nation-state. The continuity was broken, and a vast reservoir of confidence and good will was dissipated.

The void created by the untimely demise of Pakistan's great leaders was lasting. No man of similar stature and political sagacity was waiting in the wings. There were, of course, men with administrative talent and intellectual brilliance. There were also articulate men who could move and manipulate the masses. Few, however, combined these qualities; fewer still were prepared to subordinate their individual or group interests to national objectives. The Constitution Commission in 1960 observed with some distress: "Even in the first year of Pakistan, when the enthusiasm of the people

107

for building up a new country was at the highest, personal rivalry started amongst the members of the party in power."[1]

It is possible that the severe barriers to public confidence in the government would have proved insurmountable even if Mohammad Ali Jinnah and Liaquat Ali Khan had remained at the helm of the state longer. We shall never know. The barriers certainly proved insurmountable to their successors. A good deal of precious time was wasted. Worse still, during these misspent years a pattern of leadership was set which did not enhance the government's capacity to persuade. Political institutions were operated by a bureaucracy dedicated to the privileges of a small, exclusive elite and by politicians devoted to the unrestrained pursuit of personal interest. Neither group was particularly successful in generating popular support for national objectives. At least partially by default most people in Pakistan continued to look for guidance to the ascriptive leaders of the traditional societies and the articulate leaders of three key politicized pressure groups—the *ulama*, the students, and the bar. By the fall of 1958, more than ever, the government became a voice crying in the wilderness. When its message was clear, which was not often, it was heard by only a few, and even those who heard it remained unmoved. These points, however, need further elaboration.

The Bureaucrats

A major innovation in South Asia and the pillar of colonial rule was the bureaucracy. From the beginning

[1] Government of Pakistan, *Report of the Constitution Commission* (Karachi: Government of Pakistan Press, 1961), p. 9.

of the nineteenth century Britain meticulously shifted control from its military commanders and band of adventurers to trained civilian functionaries. Gradually she constructed an administrative system extending over all of British India. Gradually Indians were recruited and given official assignments. Very gradually Indians were introduced into the senior services and admitted to the highest posts. After five generations of evolution, by the time of independence a central administrative structure in which indigenous personnel had had extended experience was an accomplished fact.

As it emerged under colonial rule, the bureaucracy had several noteworthy features. First, it was remarkably small in size. As late as 1939 the strength of the senior service was some 1,299 officers including the 130 assigned to Burma.[2] Second, there were clear and decisive demarcations among the various categories of civil servants. Lower cadres supplied the clerical requirement of government offices. Specialized cadres provided for the police, the railways, or the post and telegraph. An elite corps, the Indian Civil Service (ICS), filled top decision-making positions as well as key posts on all levels. There were differential material rewards, differential privileges, and differential rates of promotion. The cadre pattern was further reinforced by a formidable *esprit de corps* of each service (and especially of the ICS), which was carefully fostered by the government.

Another feature of the colonial bureaucracy was its independence. The tenure of a bureaucrat, once he was appointed, was assured. His promotions were regular.

[2] Philip Woodruff, *The Men Who Ruled India* (London: J. Cape, 1954), II, 365.

Neither the traditional hierarchies nor the representative institutions clouded his clear responsibility to his administrative superiors and ultimately to the Secretary of State for India. In rural areas—and almost all of India was rural—he enjoyed wide discretionary powers.

Finally, a most important characteristic of the bureaucracy was its orientation to Western values. Throughout the colonial period many, and for a long time most, administrators were English.[3] The others, the Indian personnel, however, also shared in this commitment. They were recruited at an early age when they were still malleable enough to acquire new values and loyalties. The selection process and the entire training program were organized to separate the young men from their native roots. The English language was their basic skill; Shakespeare, Locke, and Blackstone were their basic referents. Their task was to rise above the small-scale orientation of their native society and dedicate their lives to the administration of the central, albeit colonial, government.

The crisis came with independence. Partition brought relocations and dislocations. The already sparse bureaucracy—recruitment had been suspended during World War II—became a thin gray line when the new country inherited only a small fraction of senior administrators. Only a total of 82 officers of the Indian Civil Service and the Indian Police Service opted for Pakistan; only one had the rank of Secretary to the Central Government.[4] Worse still, the loyalty of the bureauc-

[3] In 1909 there were only 60 Indian officers in the ICS cadre of 1,142. In ninety years their number rose to 540 out of 1,299 (*ibid.*, II, 363).

[4] Cited in Keith Callard, *Pakistan: A Political Study* (New York: Macmillan, 1957), p. 289.

racy to the new state was suspect. These officials, after all, were those who had implemented colonial policy and only a few years before had jailed the patriots.

Independence, however, also provided an unequaled opportunity for the bureaucracy to prove its mettle. Communal riots rent the countryside; millions of refugees were standing at the city gates. Even the semblance of law and order had vanished. Faced with utter chaos, *Quaid-i-Azam* Jinnah turned to the bureaucracy as the only organized structure that could reverse disintegration. "You will no doubt agree with me," he explained to the Constituent Assembly, "that the first duty of a government is to maintain law and order, so that life, property and religious beliefs of its subjects are fully protected by the State."[5] The small group of bureaucrats who had chosen Pakistan met this challenge. They established a framework of administration and with the help of the army restored a measure of public order. In the process they effectively shifted their loyalty from the colonial power to the Government of Pakistan and reinforced their traditions.

The bureaucracy remains small in size. In January 1961 there were only 357 officers in the Civil Service of Pakistan (CSP), the successor cadre to the ICS.[6] They were supported by a total of 2,741 administrators

[5] Constituent Assembly of Pakistan, *Debates*, I (August 11, 1947), p. 18.

[6] This figure includes 28 newly appointed officers still in training at the Civil Service Academy in Lahore and some 50 officers who were on deputations as judges, board members of public and semipublic corporations, diplomats, or as students for advanced degrees (Government of Pakistan, *Civil List of Class I Officers Serving under Government of Pakistan* [Karachi: Government of Pakistan Press, 1961], pp. 345-369).

in the other Class I central and provincial services.[7] This adds up to an administrative structure of less than 3,100 persons in a country of one hundred million inhabitants.

The bureaucracy in Pakistan retained its strict hierarchy of cadres. During the immediate postindependence period some accountants were given senior administrative assignments. A Secretary to the Central Government (G. Ahmed) and a recent Chief Secretary of East Pakistan (Kazi Anwarul Huq) had been members of the police service. These were exceptions. As a rule there are few exchanges among the central services. Provincial Class I officers are rarely promoted above the level of deputy commissioner. Seventy-five per cent of the highest posts are specifically reserved to the CSP. Any change in the pattern is vigorously opposed. In August 1959 President Ayub Khan appointed a Pay and Services Commission under the chairmanship of Chief Justice Cornelius to "review the structure and organization of and powers and methods relating to civilian services. . . ." When its report was completed and presented to the President in July 1962, it apparently included a recommendation to integrate the various cadres into a single service. After considerable delay for "further study" the report still languishes in an administrative limbo.[8]

The separation of administrators into cadres occurs at the very outset of their careers. It starts with the

[7] These are the individual totals. Pakistan Audit and Accounts Service—69; Pakistan Taxation Service—173; Pakistan Customs and Excise Service—70; East Pakistan Civil Service—708; and the Class I officers of the West Pakistan provincial services—1,521.

[8] See, for example, Dacca, *Pakistan Observer*, July 26, 1962, p. 8 and November 15, 1962, p. 1.

process of recruitment. All Pakistani citizens between the ages of twenty-one and twenty-five who have graduated from a recognized university are eligible to appear for the entrance examinations of the central and provincial services. Most candidates for an administrative career, in fact, tend to compete in both tests in order to increase their chances for success.[9] The examinations include written and oral segments with the latter accounting for about 25 to 30 per cent of the marks. Candidates are then ranked according to their scores. In the Centre as well as in the provinces the more senior services have first choice from the lists.[10] As a rule, merit is the determining factor for appoint-

[9] The differences in the academic records of those successful in the central services examination and those who passed only the provincial services examination are not very pronounced. Both sets of candidates include the entire range from third class B.A.'s to first class M.A.'s. Insofar as there are distinctions, these are in the distribution between the extremes. In the 1960 examinations of the successful central candidates 18 per cent held first-class master's degrees, 50 per cent held second-class master's degrees and only 4 per cent achieved merely a third-division bachelor's degree. The comparable figures for (West Pakistan) Provincial Civil Service (PCS) are: 4 per cent first-division masters, 50 per cent second-division masters and 4 per cent third-division bachelors. The East Pakistan Civil Service (EPCS) recruits included 4 per cent first-division master's degree holders and 47 per cent second-division master's degree holders, but also 22 per cent who hold only third-division master's degrees and another 20 per cent with only third-division bachelor's degrees. (Unpublished data collected from official personnel files.)

[10] The superior central services include Civil Service of Pakistan, Pakistan Foreign Service, Police Service of Pakistan, Pakistan Audit and Accounts Service, Pakistan Railway Accounts Service, Pakistan Military Accounts Service, Pakistan Taxation Service, Pakistan Customs and Excise Service, Telegraph Engineering Service Class I, Post and Telephone Traffic Service Class I, Telegraph Traffic Service Class I, Pakistan Postal Service Class I, Pakistan Railway Service of Engineers, Pakistan Railway Transportation (Traffic and Commercial) Service, Central Engineering Service Class I, Pakistan Military Lands and Cantonments Service.

ment, but there may be some special quota arrangements within the services which would modify priorities somewhat. In the CSP, for example, there are two major deviations. First, there are provisions for regional representation. After 20 per cent of the annual quota of appointments have been made from the top of the list, the remaining 80 per cent are divided evenly between the two Wings. It is therefore possible for one candidate to be rejected and another with a lesser score to get the appointment in order to fill the quota of his Wing. Another modification of the merit system is the special provision which calls for 10 per cent of the CSP appointments to be nominated from the armed forces. In the early and middle 1950's this requirement was rarely fulfilled. More recently military nominations have exceeded 10 per cent.[11]

The results of the examinations as modified by the quota system will largely determine the young administrator's cadre. If he fails to pass the central examination but passes the provincial examination, he is offered an appointment in the provincial services. Given this opportunity, after some soul-searching he usually accepts. The successful candidates of the central and provincial services then spend a year at their respective academies, at the end of which time their final list of seniority is fixed. From then on their progress is based upon the progress of their class and their seniority within the class. Those who have been rejected at the time of the entrance examination may repeat until they pass the age limit; after that time their prospects in the bureaucracy are at an end. There is no entry into the

---

[11] In 1960 and 1961 five out of 28 and 27 appointments respectively were military nominations.

public services except through the examinations between the ages of twenty-one and twenty-five.

The bureaucracy of Pakistan also retains its independence. The first constitution (1956) included a separate section on the public services guaranteeing protection from "arbitrary treatment" and defined in some detail the role of the Public Services Commission and such procedures as examinations, disciplinary action, and claims. The new constitution (1962) contains very similar provisions. Job security is almost complete. Only one CSP officer was dismissed from 1959 to 1961,[12] and even this was a formality as he, in fact, had deserted. Efforts were also made to protect the bureaucracy from the "interference" of politicians. In October 1954 Iskander Mirza, Minister of the Interior, later President of Pakistan, declared: "You cannot have the old British system of administration and at the same time allow politicians to meddle with the civil service. In the British system the District Magistrate was the king-pin of administration. His authority was unquestioned. We have to restore that."[13] Later when the martial law authorities tried the politicians of the previous regimes, prominent among the charges was the "crime" of interfering with the administrator's right to make appointments and to enforce policy. Mr. Dhirendra Nath Dutta, former Health Minister, for example, was disqualified from political activity on charges including (a) the forced retirement of the Surgeon-General of East Pakistan, (b) the transfer of a midwife, (c) upgrading the post of pediatrician, and (d) the removal of a Public

[12] Government of Pakistan, President's Secretariat, Establishment Division, D.O. No. 6/1/60. S.O. (A. VI) June 15, 1962.
[13] Karachi, *Dawn*, October 31, 1954, p. 1.

Service Commission appointee.[14] Finally, outside of the big cities in his district or subdivision the bureaucrat continues to remain the ruler of all he surveys. He exercises wide discretionary powers and is largely independent even from his administrative superiors.[15]

Perhaps most significantly, the bureaucracy of Pakistan remains separated from the masses of citizens. This is especially true of the CSP. In the critical entrance examination English and English composition, rather than Punjabi, Pashtu or Bengali, are compulsory subjects and account for about a third of the written tests. During their training at the Lahore academy the newly selected public servants are constantly reminded of their special position in society and their role as "guardians."[16] Until recently Lahore was followed by a year's study at Oxford or Cambridge. Now in their first assignment they move into the rural areas as assistant commissioners. After a short apprenticeship CSP officers in West Pakistan take charge of some aspect of district administration, while in the East Wing they assume control of one of the fifty-four subdivisions. At the age of twenty-three or twenty-four they are still too young to command the respect of a community which places high premium on seniority. They are also too inexperienced to cope smoothly with adjustment problems in a society which has its own ascriptive pattern of authority and where they are viewed as strangers with some fear and much suspicion. Many of these young officers fail to understand that while their appointments properly

[14] Dacca, *Morning News*, August 5, 1960, p. 1.

[15] A. H. Aslam, *The Deputy Commissioner* (Lahore: University of the Panjab, 1957), pp. 21-27.

[16] Ralph Braibanti, "The Civil Service of Pakistan," *South Atlantic Quarterly*, LVIII (1959), No. 2, 280-282.

gazetted may grant them authority to rule, these do not endow them with leadership. The Bengali describe this phenomenon in their own picturesque way. "When the officials come to our villages, they bring along a chair and sit down in it and expect that this will entitle them to our respect."[17] The isolation of these young men is aggravated by two additional factors. First, compared to local standards they live in luxury. Their bungalows are sturdy structures; their furniture is extensive; their food is plentiful. Second, they have to maintain a certain aloofness in their personal relationships, or they become targets of frequent and intense efforts at covert and not-so-covert bribery attempts.

As the bureaucrats proceed up the administrative ladder and reach the post of deputy-commissioner, their authority expands and their contact with the population shrinks. Even if they would be so inclined, they have little chance to get acquainted with their districts. There is a shortage of CSP's, and lateral entry into the cadre is anathema. Consequently there is a brisk turnover. In January 1962, in West Pakistan, of 51 deputy-commissioners and political agents only five had held their assignments for more than two years, 19 for more than one year but less than two years, 13 for more than six months but less than a year, and 14 for less than six months. At the same time in East Pakistan of the 17 deputy-commissioners no less than 11 had been on their assignments less than six months, and only three had held them for over a year.[18] Finally, there are secretariat appointments in the major cities, and contact with

---

[17] The ceremony of asking someone to sit is an important one, and it signifies respect. The point is that it is the host who offers the chair.
[18] Unpublished data collected from official files.

the villages is reduced to official dossiers and perhaps at times to nostalgic memories.

In short, a decade and a half after independence the bureaucracy has consolidated its position. It has emerged as a nationwide organization without peer or competition. Highly competitive selection and advanced training assure that the administrators are usually capable and skilled. They are loyal to the central government, or more specifically to the central executive, and in general they are free from the taint of corruption. Yet in one area their qualifications are less impressive. As a small, socially isolated group their prospects of mobilizing mass support behind national objectives are not good.

The Politicians

The colonial period also saw the emergence of the professional politicians. They came from various social and economic groups and from the four corners of the subcontinent. They were articulate and excelled in the mobilization of the masses. Significantly they had little tradition of participation in the political system.

It is a myth, although a persistent one, that Britain bequeathed representative political institutions to the subcontinent. If the contention is not entirely unwarranted, it is certainly exaggerated. Such institutions were established hesitantly, belatedly, and in an emasculated form. This was certainly the case with local government. Admittedly, rural and urban boards were introduced at the end of the nineteenth and especially the beginning of the twentieth century. It would be extravagant, however, to call them representative institutions. In 1918 only 0.6 per cent of the rural populations enjoyed the vote; 92 per cent of the district boards

118

had appointed chairmen, and with the exception of Bengal and Bombay they could in any case be overruled by the District Magistrate. The following year brought the Montague-Chelmsford reforms (1919) with their ambitious steps toward the establishment of village councils (*panchayats*) throughout the subcontinent. To assure a representative base, franchise in the election for council members was to be expanded radically. Chairmen were to be elected, and the bureaucrats were to withdraw from local government activity. It did not work out quite that way. Bengal did achieve a complete system of village councils, but in the Punjab only one in twenty-five villages had a *panchayat*. In the other areas which now comprise West Pakistan the ratio was even less favorable. Again in the Punjab the members of the councils and their chairmen were appointed by the government. Finally, even in Bengal the decisions of local bodies remained under the supervision of the bureaucracy.[19]

On the central and provincial levels the evolution of representative institutions did not gain momentum until the final phase of colonial rule. The executive and the judiciary were always appointed. For ninety years after Clive's decisive victory there was no legislature. Then in 1853 the Charter Act established a "Legislative Council" which could be called representative only by the most extravagant stretch of the imagination. The entire membership was appointed and was composed of the Governor General, his executive council, a number of bureaucrats, and two judges. If this were not enough, the executive retained fundamental legislative powers

[19] Hugh Tinker, *The Foundations of Local Self Government in India, Pakistan and Burma* (London: Athlone Press, 1954), pp. 109, 198-202.

by its authority to issue and enforce ordinances. When toward the end of the century similar councils were widely introduced on the provincial level, they followed the same pattern.

The conclusion of the first World War brought a new Government of India Act and the system of dyarchy. Theoretically the colonial executive was to share its power of law- and policy-making with a bicameral legislature. The majority of seats in both houses moreover were to be filled by popularly elected members. In fact, however, the new act did not substantially impair the hegemony of the executive branch and its colonial administrators. Suffrage was restricted to a handful of voters who were easily accessible to the persuasion of officials. Then when the legislature still attempted to assert itself, the executive simply decreed its dissolution. In 1935 the next Government of India Act was promulgated. It continued the trend of apparent liberalization. Specifically, it proposed to transfer some political power from the colonial executive to provincial legislatures and to reinforce the power of the central legislature by exempting the upper house (Council of State) from dissolution. Accordingly, a decade before independence provincial elections were held, and Indians formed provincial ministries. On the central level, however, the Act was never implemented. In short, during the entire colonial record South Asia never experienced a legislature which was sovereign as in Britain or independent as in the United States.

If the politicians had little opportunity to participate in the political system, they had less loyalty to it. Most were products of an environment where the focus of orientation was the small-scale unit. Those who sought to represent necessarily had to reflect the parochial commitment of their constituents. Those who sought to enlist popular support necessarily had to curry favor with the traditional hierarchies which dominated the electoral base. The struggle for independence, moreover, further reinforced this unfavorable predisposition to the political system and elevated it to a tradition of opposition.

By the time Britain was prepared to introduce colonial institutions based upon popular support, popular aspirations could no longer be satisfied with colonial status. Responsibility to constituents became incompatible with loyalty to the political system. A few politicians chose to support the colonial power consistently; some held office in the provinces sporadically after 1937. On balance, however, their record was that of non-cooperation and resistance. In representative assemblies politicians used legislative processes to subvert the government. In the streets by "direct action" they mobilized the masses to overthrow the institutions.

Though not loyal to the political system, the politicians directing the campaign for the independence of India were committed to the Congress Party. The charismatic appeal of Mahatma Gandhi offered a common focus. Party organization led by Pandit Nehru provided cohesion. Patronage assured discipline. No similar commitment restrained the proponents of Pakistan. Patronage was scarce. The ambivalent position on independence fostered ambiguity. Loose organization vitiated effective direction. Their chief source of cohesion and coordination was the personal prestige of *Quaid-i-Azam* Mohammad Ali Jinnah, supported among other things by his control of the newspaper *Dawn*.

121

The politicians did recognize, however, some responsibility to their constituents. They may have used various methods to enlist support, but they did seek votes. They may have had their own objectives but, especially after the electoral disaster of 1937, they did formulate these in terms of popular aspirations. Unhappily, during the first decade of independence this frail link between politician and the population was first impaired, then severed. To begin with, partition itself had an adverse effect. Many Muslim politicians (some of the most prominent) had their homes and constituencies in the United Provinces, Bihar, Gujarat or Bombay—areas which became part of the Republic of India. They left these for Pakistan to "represent" districts where they had no roots and where they were considered strangers, if not foreigners. Perhaps more significantly, independence brought a radical transformation in their role. They were no longer in opposition. Almost overnight they took control of the political machinery. It was no longer enough to project promises; the time had come to deliver. Yet economic development remained as elusive as ever, and tradition seemed no more secure than in the past. Their lack of roots in their constituencies inspired suspicion. Their inability to satisfy popular aspirations which they themselves had helped to kindle spurred resentment and set them up as scapegoats.

Evidently the politicians had no illusions about these developments. They promptly proceeded to insulate themselves from the vicissitudes of popular favor. Accordingly, the First Constituent Assembly, which doubled as national legislature from independence until September 21, 1954, was not elected by universal suffrage. The rulers of princely states nominated their representatives. Some seats, as the seven additional seats of Sind, were filled through election by the national legislature itself. Most others were elected by the provincial assemblies whose members in turn were selected by an electorate of 15 per cent of the total population.[20] The Second (Interim) National Assembly which sat from March 25, 1956, to September 9, 1958, did have one member who was elected by direct universal suffrage: the representative of Karachi. Most others were selected by the provincial assemblies. In the provinces, where universal suffrage was conceded, polls were postponed for various contrived excuses. When they were ultimately held, according to the report of the Electoral Reforms Commission, "it was widely and persistently complained that these elections were a farce, a mockery and a fraud upon the electorate."[21]

The authority of the politicians continued to rest theoretically upon their capacity to mobilize masses; they continued to claim popular support. In fact, however, their sole qualification was their capacity to enlist support among fellow politicians. Mohammad Ali Jinnah must have been aware of the pitfalls of such an arrangement. He did not propose to rest his government upon so uncertain a foundation. When given a choice, unlike Jawaharlal Nehru he preferred being Governor General to Prime Minister. In this way he proposed to rise above parliamentary responsibility and direct from his own heights the evolution of Pakistan's political institutions.[22] When all too soon Liaquat Ali

[20] Muneer Ahmad, *Legislatures in Pakistan* (Lahore: University of the Panjab, 1960), p. 14 and Callard, *op.cit.*, p. 77.

[21] Government of Pakistan, *Gazette of Pakistan Extraordinary*, April 24, 1956, p. 922.

[22] From a strict "constitutional" point of view the Governor Gen-

Khan assumed command, he set out in a radically different direction—one which was pursued by him and his successors for nearly ten years. He accepted the parliamentary pattern and in consequence forced upon his successors and their cabinets the daily task of rounding up at various prices sufficient supporters in the legislature to remain in office. The stakes were indeed high. Restraints of institutional loyalty, party organization, popular responsibility were inoperative. The only guide to action which remained, and remained by default, was individual self-interest. Holding office became the highest goal. Those in power, insecure in their position, would make almost any deal to improve their position. Meanwhile they were prepared, just in case, to make hay while the sun shone. Those out of power in turn were inclined to accept almost any deal to acquire office. Meanwhile, they were prepared, just in case, to revert to the more accustomed role of the politician to use legislative processes to subvert the government and to mobilize the masses to overthrow the political institutions.

The short history of Pakistan is replete with examples of politicians, even very prominent politicians, who sacrificed previous commitments, the interest of their party, and the stability of the political system in order to obtain personal advantages. There was, for example, the remarkable instance of the fate of the man who

---

eral lost his powers to act independently of the Cabinet by Section 3(2) of the Pakistan Provisional Constitution Order, 1947. Yet even before this order was promulgated, *Dawn* editorialized: "Whatever the constitutional powers of the Governor-General of a Dominion may nominally be, in *Quaid-i-Azam's* case no legal or formal limitations can apply" (quoted in Callard, *op.cit.*, p. 132).

inherited the mantle of Muslim League leadership from Liaquat Ali Khan. In April 1953 Khwaja Nazimuddin, Prime Minister of Pakistan, was holding a comfortable majority in the National Assembly. Having successfully passed the budget and restored order (by martial law) in Lahore, he suddenly found himself dismissed by the Governor General. For a successor the latter turned to Mohammad Ali of Bogra, a man who had been out of the country for five years. Yet in spite of this, the Muslim League accepted the humiliation of its leader with little concern, and six members of the outgoing ministry promptly joined the new cabinet. The following year in Sind the Chief Minister Pirzada Abdus Sattar faced similar difficulties. In a signed statement 74 of the 110 members of the provincial legislature pledged him their support in his campaign against the unification of West Pakistan. For his efforts he was dismissed by the central government. Two months later in a remarkable conversion his successor, M. A. Khuhro, was supported by 100 votes to 4 on the One Unit resolution.

The destruction of Muslim League control of West Pakistan is another classic case in point. Dr. Khan Shahib, the first Chief Minister of the recently unified province promptly proceeded to undermine the Muslim League's majority in the provincial legislature by organizing his own Republican Party from those members of the Muslim League who, according to the Constitution Commission, "left it not on any principle but on personal grounds."[23] The showdown came on the election of the Speaker of the West Pakistan Assembly. A tie vote of 148:148 was resolved by the acting chairman in favor of the Republicans, and Khan Shahib's ministry was

[23] *Report of the Constitution Commission*, p. 9.

saved. Curiously, Pirzada Abdus Sattar who before the vote had fought hard for the League reappeared next day as a minister in the Republican cabinet. While all this was going on, Chaudhri Mohammad Ali, Prime Minister of Pakistan and nominal head of the Muslim League, watched the destruction of his party with singular lack of concern and in the end found nothing improper in endorsing Dr. Khan Shahib.

One final example: In February 1956 H. S. Suhrawardy walked out of the Second Constitutional Assembly. He refused to sign the new constitution and initiated a vigorous campaign inciting popular resentment against it. A year later, however, he showed no hesitation in becoming Prime Minister under the same document, which he now swore to preserve and defend. There are numerous other illustrations, and the Constitution Commission took the trouble to recount several others.[24] The significance of this record is that these instances go beyond isolated aberrations. It spells out a routine pattern of political intrigue. When the Revolution of 1958 arbitrarily excluded politicians from decision-making, it did not abolish representative institutions or a leadership structure with a significant capacity to mobilize popular support behind the political system. What it did, and this was surely not its purpose, was to unify the politicians and force them into their more accustomed position of agitation against the political system and the government.

Three Politicized Pressure Groups

The continued absence of national political institutions with popular foundations tended to reinforce, by

---

[24] *Ibid.*, pp. 7-13.

default as it were, the attraction of the small-scale social units and to enhance the appeal of the ascriptive pattern of leadership. At the same time, this vacuum raised to special prominence three groups of men with a demonstrated capacity to mobilize mass support. For some time the *ulama*, the students, and the legal community had played a significant role in Pakistan's political evolution. In the midst of an illiterate and inarticulate population the members of these groups were literate and articulate. During the struggle for independence they were instrumental in mobilizing mass support. Their organizational scale was countrywide, and so was their appeal. They were inclined to assume the role of a vanguard of the population and at times even advanced their own group structure as an alternative to the leadership pattern of the government. The disappointing record of representative institutions and political parties lent support to their claims and solidified their clusters of mass support. Since these three groups apparently have no intention of letting anyone (including the government) forget their strategic position, they merit a somewhat closer examination in this analysis.

Perhaps the oldest and certainly the most traditional of these groups is that of the *ulama*. Islam has neither priests nor sacraments. It does have religious functionaries who administer ritual. The most prominent among them are called *ulama*. These "men of knowledge," well versed in the Quran, informally coordinate the religious life of the faithful. More important, they are recognized as authorities on Islamic law (*Shariat*), and in this capacity they assume a political role. To be sure, they have little appreciation of politics in a modern, dynamic sense. In their view society is an essentially static ar-

127

rangement. This static society, however, is subject to a strict and specific application of natural law. "God," they believe, "has not left His servants without guidance even in the most minor every day acts."[25] They are not usually concerned with the personnel of the secular government. They do insist, however, that secular law not be repugnant to Islamic law, and they propose to determine just when such cases might arise.

Among Muslims in India the *ulama* were natural leaders. They had more education than their coreligionists. Their firm monastic stand set an example. When the Moghul Empire was destroyed by infidel arms and the secular prop of Muslim solidarity was removed, the religious leadership stepped into the breach and sustained cohesion. The formation of a Muslim community on the subcontinent was largely their accomplishment.[26] The record of the *ulama* in the struggle for a Muslim state, however, was more ambiguous. Almost certainly they played an important role in the organization of the mutiny and rebellion of 1857-1858. They were less enthusiastic about Sir Syed Ahmad and the Aligarh Movement. Some extremely vocal religious leaders in fact continued their skepticism concerning a drive for independence led by westernized secularists up until the final days of the struggle. "Expediting the so-called Muslim national state" was characterized as "a foolish waste of time" by Maulana Maududi, the head of the *Jamā'at-i-Islāmi*.[27] Another strong contingent of *ulama*, organized as *Jami'at-al-Ulamā* since 1919 and led by

[25] Leonard Binder, *Religion and Politics in Pakistan* (Berkeley and Los Angeles: University of California Press, 1961), p. 12.

[26] W. W. Hunter, *The Indian Musalmans* (London: Trübner and Co., 1872), pp. 152, 181.

[27] Callard, *op.cit.*, p. 200.

Maulana Abul Kalan Azad, supported the Indian National Congress and pressed for the independence of a united Indian state. Finally, some prominent *ulama* such as Maulvi Nazir Ahmad and, for a time, Maulvi Shibli Numani did cooperate with Sir Syed Ahmad's efforts to increase the political consciousness of the Muslim masses. This section, including Maulana Shabbir Ahmad Usmani, later supported the Muslim League and in 1940 endorsed the Lahore Resolution. They helped accomplish partition by organizing massive civil resistance and even by inciting communal violence.[28]

The establishment of Pakistan opened for the *ulama* prospects of direct participation in the building of an Islamic state. The Muslim League contingent in the First Constituent Assembly included several prominent religious leaders.[29] The government promptly (April 1949) established a Board of *Ta'līmaat-i-Islāmīa* (Teachers of Islam) to advise its various committees on the religious requirements. In addition, several special Islamic parties were organized and directed by *ulama*. Perhaps a peak of their direct participation in secular politics was reached around 1953. By then the argument over "repugnancy" was in full swing. Most religious leaders accepted the contention of the President of the *Jamī'at-al-Ulamā-i-Pākistān*, Maulana Abul Hasanat: "Our law is complete and merely requires interpretation by those who are experts in it."[30] They saw

[28] Callard asserts that Pakistan was won largely in spite of the men of religion. W. C. Smith, on the other hand, credits the religious leadership with major contributions to the mobilization of Muslim masses behind independence. (*Ibid.*, and W. C. Smith, *Modern Islam in India* [London: V. Gollancz Ltd., 1946], pp. 262 and 270.)

[29] For example, Maulana Shabbir Ahmad Usmani, Maulana Abdullah-el-Baqui, and Maulana Mohammed Akram Khan.

[30] Quoted in: Government of the Punjab, *Report of the Court of*

little purpose in a secular legislation. In any case, they insisted, a special board of the *ulama* must retain veto power to assure that no law which is repugnant to Islam be enacted. In the same year the religious leadership spearheaded an attack upon the Ahmadi sect demanding their exclusion from high government offices. When the Prime Minister refused to dismiss Zafrullah Khan, his Ahmadi foreign minister, the All-Pakistan Muslim Parties Convention—controlled by the *ulama*—demanded the resignation of Khwaja Nazimuddin himself. Worse still, they threatened *rast iqdam* (direct action) if their demands were not met.

The offensive of 1953 was not a notable success. The Prime Minister did not resign. The ensuing disturbances at Lahore were crushed in six hours by the military commander in the area, Major General Mohammad Azam Khan, without the latter's popularity being visibly affected. The investigation into the unrest produced a most comprehensive indictment of the *ulama*'s political activity.[31] The issue of "repugnancy" was settled in the first constitution by a general declaration which left the implementation and enforcement vague. The Board of *Ta'līmaat* was dissolved. Several of the *ulama* in the Muslim League withdrew from the political arena. Finally, Islamic parties met with disappointment at the polls. The *Jamā'at-i-Islāmi* had a single vote in the 197-seat Punjab Legislative Assembly. In the 1954 elections of East Pakistan the *Nizam-i-Islam* captured 20 seats and the *Khilafat-i-Rabani* an additional one seat from a total of 309.[32]

Inquiry to Inquire into the Punjab Disturbances of 1953 (Lahore: Government of the Punjab Press, 1954), p. 211.

[31] *Ibid.*, especially pp. 237-254.

[32] Muneer Ahmad, *op.cit.*, pp. 130-131.

If their excursion into practical politics was abortive, the prestige of the religious leaders has not suffered. They seem to have retained the respect of the community, especially in the rural areas. This general personal observation is confirmed by the single available empirical study. The residents of the East Pakistani village of Kailine (population—1,637) were asked to rate thirty-nine occupational groups according to a five-grade scale. Eighty-eight per cent listed the *mullah* (local religious functionary) in the highest category. If one considers that the *mullah's* income of Rs 43 ($9.03) a month is below the income of the rural clerk, deed writer, grocer, or betel-nut trader and that nearly 16 per cent of the population is Hindu, the above figure becomes even more impressive.[33]

The *ulama* may not have succeeded in forcing into the Constitution the recognition of their veto power over governmental decision-making; in point of fact, however, they exercise veto power over the implementation. Whenever they decide to define a law or a government policy as involving moral issues, their influence is decisive. Consider the fate of government officials who with Quran in hand try to prove that birth control is not un-Islamic. After a detailed, scholarly presentation the official may assume that he is making progress. While he prepares his glowing report to the Department of Health, his audience casually saunters over to the local *mullah* and asks his judgment. "Birth control is against Islam," is the routine reply. The *mullah* rarely bothers even to argue his case or to offer citations from

[33] K. M. Ashraful Aziz, "Social Status and Relation to Income," in John E. Owen, *Sociology in East Pakistan* (Dacca: Asiatic Society of Pakistan, 1962), p. 187.

the Holy Book. With a simple sentence he buries effectively all the erudite labors of the government official. Another case in point is the Muslim Family Laws Ordinance. In 1961 when the martial law government sought to tighten controls over polygamy and divorce, the opposition generated by the *ulama* was so widespread that its implementation had to be postponed. When the legislature met, total repeal was prevented only by the determined resistance of the President. Meanwhile, the effectiveness of the ordinance in the countryside is at best spotty.

The ability of the religious leadership to mobilize masses is not restricted to preventing the implementation of laws and policies they consider repugnant. They are quite prepared to demonstrate their power to mobilize masses by periodically instigating massive demonstrations in urban areas. Mostly the issues appear to be religious, and their targets may be religious minorities. Such was the case during the Ahmadi riots in 1953 and continues to be during the annual *Ashura* violence. The situation was a bit more confusing on May 18, 1962, in Peshawar. Inflamed by reports that an Italian movie company was preparing to produce a biography of the Prophet, the religious leadership led a demonstration against the movie houses of the city and the only modern hotel. In the process the Dutch ambassador was assaulted and the American Consulate was besieged.

More progressive and certainly politically more active are the students. Like the *ulama* they are literate and articulate; unlike the *ulama* the students are not individuals of high prestige or possessing extramundane authority. Although some graduates from West Pakistan's exclusive schools may decide to attend Pakistani universities, most students come from humbler, rural circumstances. Their political effectiveness is based largely upon their access to the rural population. During vacation these young men fan out all over the provinces turning into living communications links. They return to the villages not as outsiders bringing along their government commissions as their authority; nor do they come as candidates seeking popular support. They come home to their parents and relatives recounting their experiences in the big city. Their version may not coincide with that of the government; it may not even coincide with the facts. Still they are likely to be believed.

The political effectiveness of the students is also based upon their capacity for and their record of collective action. During the struggle for independence, when the *ulama* were vacillating and the lawyers were making inspiring speeches, the students provided the vanguard of the Pakistan Movement, flooding the streets, the courts, and the jails. After independence their ranks inflated and their cohesion solidified until they emerged as the largest collection of articulate individuals in Pakistan.

The solidarity of the students has its foundation in their extreme individual insecurity. More than any other group they are at the focal point of the clash and chaos of values. When a young man enters an institution of higher learning, he moves from his rural and ascriptive world to an urban and competitive society. He may still retain his former ties, but now he also has to integrate himself into an entirely new authority pattern. What he learns may conflict with traditional formulas or solutions. Even if it does not, the very process of reexamining traditional customs rather than

accepting them unquestioningly encourages speculation, and speculation leads to alternatives and uncer-
tainty. Moreover, he faces the strains of the confronta-
tion of value structures during the traumatic years of
adolescence, at a time when in Pakistan frustration is
accentuated by a very vigorous segregation between
the sexes.[34] Added to this is the tension of examinations
and worry over future employment. It is not surprising,
therefore, that the students are willing to go to almost
any lengths to fortify their only source of security: their
own solidarity.

This solidarity is supported by organization. Conditions, of course, are very favorable to control. The student body is concentrated in a few universities.[35] There
they live in compact dormitories (halls) which also
serve as foci of social life. Graduation, moreover, is not
a severe threat to the continuity of leadership. Of the
75,310 candidates who appeared for degree examinations in 1959-1960, only 30,303 (40.2 per cent) passed.[36]
Some of the others dropped out, but a sizable number
just lingers on—and on. "Here," complained the Commission on National Education, "is a major cause of in-
discipline."[37]

The formal organization of the students is rather
elaborate with vice presidents, their cabinets and gen-

[34] At the University of Peshawar, for example, a curtain separates
the young men and women in the classrooms. There are separate
reading rooms in the library of the University of Dacca.

[35] Until recently there were only six universities, two in East Pakistan and four in the West Wing.

[36] *Pakistan Statistical Yearbook, 1962* (Karachi: Government of
Pakistan Press, 1962), p. 335.

[37] *Report of the Commission on National Education* (Karachi:
Government of Pakistan Press, 1960), p. 37.

eral secretaries.[38] These are, however, only spokesmen. The real leaders, often called "kingmakers," are far more difficult to identify. Indeed, part of their effectiveness rests on their anonymity. They rarely agitate or lead demonstrations. Yet when a student seeks an elective office in his organization or even employment after graduation, he curries the favor of these men behind the scenes. Similarly, decisions on the tactics used in demonstrations are made not by the elected spokesmen, but by the "kingmakers." In spite of the elusive character of the real leadership, their performance suggests effectiveness. They do deliver the votes in student elections, and their call for a student strike is invariably heeded.

The combination of extreme forms of personal insecurity, effective organization, and a heritage of civil disobedience makes the students volatile. They are ideally suited for mobilizing their own membership and even masses of the population for a big splash: strikes, demonstrations, and riots. They are far less suited for spearheading a quiet and sustained effort supporting government policies or of mobilizing a loyal opposition.

The government appears rather helpless with regard to the students. It obviously cannot permit them to roam around the streets destroying public and private property. Yet there is not much that can be done to prevent this. To fulfill their aspirations and to alleviate their frustration is beyond governmental capacity. To restrain them by compulsion is equally unfeasible. The use of force is resented; the use of force against young

[38] The Vice Chancellor of the University is also President *ex officio* of all student organizations within the University.

men and women, hardly more than children, is perceived as intolerable. The defeat of Nurul Amin is an
eloquent example. Yet beyond this, any government
even moderately interested in the future of Pakistan
must realize that a large share of the leaders of the
country must inevitably come from the students. Surely,
the government can close the University of Dacca or
suspend instruction at the University of the Punjab.
What kind of training can it then expect for its future
political leaders, lawyers, scientists, engineers, even bureaucrats? So the students continue to attract mass support against the government. Through demonstrations,
strikes, and riots they express a measure of power they
never before possessed and are not likely to possess after
graduation. As a bonus they have an opportunity to
release their resentment against authority and their
wide range of frustration.

With this we can turn to the third important group of
articulate men, the members of the legal community.
While the *ulama* meticulously guard Islamic law, the
bar and the bench are custodians of the westernized
secular legal system. The development of this profession
was an early objective of the colonial power. Through
it the new values were introduced and disseminated into
society. Later, perhaps paradoxically, it was this profession that supplied the great leaders of the Pakistan
movement including the father of the country, Mohammad Ali Jinnah. After independence their influence
became formidable. Lawyers accounted for the largest
segment in the legislature.[39] They advised the execu-

[39] Biographies for only 48 of the 106 members of the First Constituent Assembly are available. Of these, 31 held a law degree.
Similarly, 27 of the 80 members of the Second Constituent Assembly
were members of the bar. (Muneer Ahmad, *op.cit.*, pp. 92-94.)

tive on the proper procedure for drafting ordinances and proposed laws. Judges exercised a veto power when such laws were passed or ordinances were promulgated. On issues of national importance they presided over special commissions. Chief Justice Munir headed the Commission of Inquiry on the Lahore riots; former Chief Justice Shahabuddin headed the Constitution Commission; and Chief Justice Cornelius was the chairman of the Pay and Services Commission. When President Ayub Khan gave his country a constitution, his chief adviser was a prominent attorney and later Chief Justice of West Pakistan, Manzur Qadir.

With their wigs and flowing robes the legal community has little prospect of capturing the allegiance of the rural masses for any length of time. They do not even have a well developed organization. Some bar associations, especially those of Lahore and Karachi, on occasion do demonstrate an *esprit de corps*, but their scope is primarily local in character. Since lawyers, unlike the bureaucrats, do not have an assured income, "taking care of number one" is often their prime concern. Their political effectiveness rests upon their influence over the urban population. Within this small but, for political development, crucial group they guide consensus and set the social pattern.

In their western commitments the lawyers are similar to the bureaucracy. There is, however, one substantial difference. The bureaucracy has an all-overriding devotion to order and stratification. The legal profession, while committed to the supremacy of law, is sympathetic to the modern process of lawmaking, a dynamic interaction of interest groups marked by conflict and compromise. Lawyers and judges are extraordinarily

137

sensitive to the civil rights of individuals. They are fearful, suspicious, and even antagonistic to the natural law of the *ulama* or the ordinances of the bureaucracy. These they consider far greater threats to political development (and their own interests) than the violence of the students.

This significant difference tends to place the legal profession in opposition to the bureaucracy. As long as some of their members were conducting their charade of representative institutions, the lawyers individually and the bar associations collectively were fully absorbed in the game. Their enthusiasm waned only when it became apparent that the integrity of the country was at stake and that law and order had broken down. Then they supported martial law. Still, when the immediate danger had passed and the bureaucracy had emerged preeminent, the legal community was the first to register opposition. As early as 1959 during the martial-law-sponsored Union Council elections Foreign Minister Manzur Qadir received considerable mail from lawyers in Lahore and Karachi who threatened to boycott the polls and to expose to ridicule the Basic Democracy system by getting their illiterate peons elected as councilors. Although exact data on the effectiveness of such a campaign is lacking, in informal discussions the members of the Lahore bar exhibited extraordinary pride in the "fact" that the percentage of voters who had exercised their franchise in this city was substantially below the national average. Since then, if anything, opposition to the government has intensified. When the new constitution was announced, prominent lawyers successfully mobilized tens of thousands at mass meetings demanding its repeal. Within a year the courts delivered the first blow at the new political system by declaring *ultra vires* a Presidential ordinance permitting Ministers to retain their seats in the National Assembly. Most recently, in June 1964, the Election Tribunal of East Pakistan issued notices upon two Central Ministers "to show cause why their names should not be referred to as having adopted corrupt practice."[40] A month later the High Court of Dacca declared the government's dissolution of the *Jamā'at-i-Islāmi* illegal.[41]

[40] Dacca, *Pakistan Observer*, June 20, 1964, p. 1.
[41] *Ibid.*, July 14, 1964, p. 1.

PART II

The Program of Political Development

++

Introduction

++

As the year 1958 moved along at its steady, inexorable pace, Pakistan hurtled toward catastrophe with an ever-increasing crescendo. The economy was in chaos. Per capita income dropped. Currency was pouring out of the country. Growth in industrial production slowed to a crawl. Food shortages became acute. By the late summer, hoarding, smuggling, and black-marketing were rampant, and famine began to spread. The government was helpless. Even her minimal controls slipped away. Public order was precarious and rapidly deteriorating. September saw chronic violence in the East Pakistan Assembly. Police had to be called repeatedly into the chamber to sort out rioting factions, and only tear gas could restore a semblance of order. On one frenzied occasion the Speaker was assaulted, the Deputy Speaker killed, and the national flag desecrated. In the meantime, the towns of West Pakistan were being rent by massive agitation for civil disobedience, while dissident tribal chieftains hoisted their own flags and declared their independence.

The headlong rush into chaotic disintegration was checked and reversed on October 7, 1958. The President of the Republic, Iskander Mirza, proclaimed martial law and appointed the Commander-in-Chief of the Pakistan Army, General Mohammad Ayub Khan, to be Supreme Commander and Chief Martial Law Administrator. The Constitution was abrogated, the central and provincial legislatures were abolished, and political parties were prohibited. Regulations appeared in rapid order limiting free speech, free assembly, and the free press. Prices of essential commodities were fixed, strong measures promised against tax evasion. The sentence of death was frequently indicated, and several prominent leaders of the overthrown regime were arrested.

The last uneasy remnant of the old order was President Mirza himself. Whether the generals had any intention of retaining so heavy a political liability remains a state secret. Probably not. It was General Ayub Khan who held the power. He made a whirlwind tour of the provinces to assume personal control of the government. His pictures appeared constantly on the front pages of the newspapers. In two weeks he dropped even the pretense of dual control by substituting the first person singular for the previous "we" in his announcements of government decisions. In any case, President Mirza forced a showdown. In several instances he publicly contradicted the Chief Martial Law Administrator on martial law policy. He approached several prominent leaders, including General Musa, second in command in the army, to solicit their support for dispensing with the Chief Martial Law Administrator. Then on the morning of October 27 he installed General Ayub Khan as his Prime Minister in the hope that this would establish his own supremacy. The response was decisive. That night three senior generals approached President Mirza and demanded his resignation. Faced with a battalion of infantry in his yard and the drawn sidearms of the ultimatum-bearers in his office and finding his telephone wires cut, Iskander Mirza submitted and flew off to England. No question of exile, read the official announcement; it was "merely embarrassing for him to stay." General Ayub promptly abolished the office of Prime Minister and proclaimed himself President. In a final charismatic touch, Miss Fatima Jinnah, sister of *Quaid-i-Azam*, declared that events had brought a "general sense of relief to the people." The Revolution was complete.

The immediate tasks confronting the new martial law government were formidable. There was, for example, a practical matter of armed rebellion inherited from its predecessor. A few days before martial law was proclaimed, the Khan of Kalat had been arrested for secessionist activities. This, however, did not end the matter. Baluchi tribesmen organized a tribal force (*lashkar*) of about 30,000 men and delivered an ultimatum. They demanded the unconditional release of their chief and the return of confiscated arms. The rejection of these terms would bring sabotage, threatened the tribesmen. The new government reacted immediately and with firmness. Troops were dispatched, and after a "regular battle" the tribal force was dispersed. Army casualties amounted to five dead and six wounded. In turn, the troops captured 168 prisoners. Seven leaders, after a summary martial law trial, were executed and their bodies shipped back to Baluchistan.

Somewhat less spectacular was the initial activity seeking to relieve the food shortage. Imports were received from abroad. Canada promptly committed 33,-000 tons of wheat. The United States agreed to supply an additional 850,000 tons, of which 450,000 tons were to be delivered before June 1, 1959. Meanwhile, the government initiated a campaign through the newspapers to convince the population that vast domestic stocks which had been hoarded under the previous regime would now become available for general distribution. Almost daily the front page headlines reported discoveries of hidden food stores: 540,000 maunds of wheat in Rawalpindi, 100,000 maunds in Kalat, 70,000 maunds in Sialkot and Rs 40,000,000 worth of grains in Multan, to cite only a few.

There were other problems also—inflation, smuggling, and blackmarketing among the most prominent. Still, even during these early hectic days, it became apparent that the new regime was not satisfied with short term, makeshift improvisations. From the very first days of martial law, General Ayub Khan concentrated his primary efforts upon a long-range program of political development. He was determined to establish for Pakistan a political system with a capacity to direct social and economic change.

As a matter of fact, in October 1958, the opportunity for substantial progress toward this objective was better than at any time since the death of Mohammad Ali Jinnah. The military leaders who seized the government enjoyed over their predecessors an increment in the capacity to coerce. Revolution did not, as in several other countries, disrupt the chain of command. Instead, its unity simplified decision-making. Advanced technical equipment available to the army facilitated the communication of policies and orders. The rigorous discipline of the troops improved the prospects of implementation. Perhaps more important, the military leaders also enjoyed an increment in the capacity to persuade. The armed forces were genuinely popular. Their past record of protecting Muslim lives and property during the postpartition massacres and in Kashmir inspired confidence. In general, soldiers were exempted from the resentment which had crystallized against the deposed government. Their reputation for integrity was untainted. The army, it was widely hoped, would be more responsive to popular aspirations and more effective in improving the standard of living.

It might have been expected that a political development program initiated under martial law and guided by a general would rely heavily upon coercion. Force, indeed, was not excluded. It was often threatened as a corrective and was even occasionally applied. Nevertheless, from the first days of martial law through the present it has never been used on a massive scale. What is perhaps even more significant, there was no apparent attempt to increase the existing rudimentary capacity of coercion. Instead, the effort to endow the political system with the capacity to direct social and economic change concentrated upon the maximization of the governmental capacity to persuade.

The rejection of the path of massive coercion became evident by October 10, 1958. That day in a clear challenge to the new military regime the members of the East Pakistan High Court, claiming lack of authority, refused to administer the oath of office to the newly appointed governor. In response General Ayub Khan did not order the judges arrested or intimidated. He did not dispense with the oath of office. Instead, he issued the Laws (Continuance in Force) Order, 1958 which directed that "Pakistan shall be governed as nearly as may be in accordance with the late Constitution." The Supreme Court and lower courts were promptly reconstituted. Only special martial law orders were exempted from their jurisdiction. On November 11, 1958, it was announced further that the special military courts in

Karachi would wind up their operations and that the others would follow suit. Prompt concessions to the bureaucracy reflected a similar choice. Their loyalty was enlisted by a major share of power. The generals would rule not through their military command but through the Civil Service. Troops remained in evidence for only three days and within a month were withdrawn altogether. Almost immediately civilian deputies were appointed to the Chief Martial Law Administrator and the Martial Law Administrators. The integrity of the cadres was guaranteed. The drive to eliminate corruption, the officials were assured, would not be permitted to degenerate into a general witch hunt.

The program designed to maximize the governmental capacity to persuade was a three-pronged approach. In an environment where the small-scale units persist as foci of orientation, it necessarily included a massive effort to stimulate national integration. In an environment where the international demonstration effect is a source of increased alienation, a vigorous and effective plan for accelerated economic growth was an equally imperative ingredient. The main effort, however, was directed toward the construction of political institutions which would attract popular commitment.

It had these main features. First, the construction of political institutions was to be a *gradual process*. Every new step was introduced with special reference to the past and to the future, and all the media of communication were concentrated on disseminating this impression. The Revolution was *caused* by the disintegration of the political structure and *brought about* a military interregnum. The system of Basic Democracies was *caused* by the consolidation of the Revolution and would *bring about* the Constitution. The Constitution was *caused* by the successful operation of the Basic Democracies and would *bring about* the lifting of martial law. Permission for political party organization was *caused* by the successful operation of the Constitution and would *bring about* a representative political system.

Furthermore, it was to be a *guided process*. Each major step was accompanied by control mechanisms. In the early days of martial law General Ayub Khan conceded a share in the government of Pakistan to the courts and the bureaucracy. Law would be interpreted by the judges; implementation of policy would remain the function of the administrative hierarchies. It was President Ayub Khan, however, who made the laws and decided policies. It was he, moreover, who appointed the judges and promoted the administrators. Later, under the system of Basic Democracies, village councilors were expected to administer their communities and initiate rural development programs. A centrally appointed bureaucrat, however, served as "Controlling Authority." Then when the Constitution replaced arbitrary rule, the President again retained crucial controls. The power of the legislature was restricted; its members were elected by indirect suffrage. Fundamental rights were carefully circumscribed. Political parties were regulated.

Nevertheless—and this is its third major feature—it was a guided process *toward representative institutions*. Martial law and the Revolution established Mohammad Ayub Khan as the undisputed head of the government. Subsequent months saw the popularization of the new leadership. They also witnessed a gradual expansion of the decision-making process: concessions to the courts and to the bureaucracy. Within a year the system of Basic Democracies offered some popular participation in local government. Against heavy odds and the contrary advice of his advisers, President Ayub Khan pressed on to convert his personal hegemony into a politically responsible leadership. In June 1962 martial law was withdrawn. The Constitution invited elected legislators to share in the formulation of national and provincial policies. Then political parties were legalized.

In short, Pakistan offers for study a rare strategy for development: a *genuine* case of guided democracy.

7

++

The Quest for Nationhood

++

THE APPRECIATION of a link between national integration and political development in Pakistan was not
original with the martial law government. In fact, part
of the program followed previously established paths.
The threat of hostile India, for example, continued to
serve as a significant rallying cry. Newspapers continued to display prominently articles underscoring Indian
aggressive designs. The designation of Bharat for the
Republic of India persisted after the Revolution. Nevertheless, one can discover some clues of greater restraint
on the external enemy agitation. The martial law declaration of President Mirza did include a sneering reference to those who "scream for war, knowing full well
that they will be nowhere near the firing line."[1] Later
President Ayub Khan repeatedly called for "friendly
relations with our neighbors." Even when in April 1959
a series of border incidents occurred and an Indian
bomber was shot down over Pakistan, Ayub Khan coun-
seled moderation.[2] Press reports on Indian aggressions
and aggressive intentions also declined somewhat. During the six months preceding martial law, for example,
on an average of 16 days a month the semiofficial *Dawn*

[1] Dacca, *Morning News*, October 8, 1958, p. 1.
[2] Karachi, *Dawn*, March 25, 1959, p. 1 and April 25, 1959, p. 1.

carried such headlines on page one. This figure dropped to ten in the six months following martial law.[3]

President Ayub Khan also continued the emphasis upon common Islamic bonds. The martial law proclamation of October 7 spoke of a new constitution suitable for Muslim people; among the first acts of the Ayub Cabinet was to pray at Mohammad Ali Jinnah's tomb.[4] Official pronouncements continued to include invocations of the Almighty's blessings and prayers for guidance. Islamic history and ideology, always integral parts of public education, were introduced as compulsory subjects in private schools as well. Still on Islam, as on the issue of the external enemy, martial law imparted restraint. The designation "Islamic Republic" was dropped, and a martial law ordinance declared that the "Republic [was] henceforth known as Pakistan."[5] Characteristic of the government's initial attitude perhaps was a statement of Foreign Minister Manzur Qadir at a press conference. "I did not say at any time whether the future Constitution will be Islamic or not," he admitted to the assembled journalists. It was up to the elected representatives to work out the "details."[6]

A range of more novel approaches was also offered to stimulate national consciousness. There was symbolism. Plans were announced for the construction of a suitable memorial for Mohammad Ali Jinnah, the Great Leader who most eloquently epitomized the common

[3] The monthly breakdown of days with front-page reports on Indian hostility: April 1958—14; May—16; June—13; July—12; August—23; September—13; November—10; December—11; January 1959—7; February—9; March—10; April—14.

[4] Dacca, *Morning News*, November 1, 1958, p. 1.

[5] Karachi, *Dawn*, October 11, 1958, p. 1.

[6] *Ibid.*, March 15, 1959, p. 1.

aspirations of the people of Pakistan.[7] There was action. Convinced that "the general apathy of the rural masses arose principally from institutional defects in our agrarian structure and maladjustments in the terms on which land was being used for agricultural purposes," the President in January 1959 introduced land reforms in West Pakistan.[8] At the core of the program, however, there was the administrative initiative of the Bureau of National Reconstruction and the policy of accommodation toward regional grievances. More recently and perhaps reluctantly, the focus has shifted somewhat to such external incentives as the renewed prominence of the foreign threat and a rising emphasis upon an independent foreign policy.

The Administrative Initiative

It is not exactly unusual for a government to conclude that a problem is best handled through a new government agency. Accordingly, in January 1959 the Bureau of National Reconstruction was established with a substantial budget.[9] Its task was "to coalesce all the divergent linguistic, sectarian and social groups into a single cohesive nation."[10] Its approach promised to differ from the previous pattern in two significant ways. First, although Islamic ideology was not excluded, the Bureau's efforts were directed to a secular national unity. Second, it was apparently prepared to reverse the previous dys-

[7] Mohammad Ayub Khan, *Speeches and Statements* (Karachi: Pakistan Publications, 1961), I, 25.

[8] *Ibid.*, p. 47.

[9] In 1961-1962 the Central Government budget for the Bureau was Rs 18.8 lakhs (Government of Pakistan, *Budget of the Central Government for 1962-63* [Karachi: Government of Pakistan Press, 1962], p. 180).

[10] Karachi, *Dawn*, January 14, 1959, p. 1.

153

functional pressure for cultural assimilation. It encouraged the development of local culture as part of the nation-building process.

Activity soon reached signal proportions. Under its indefatigable director, Brigadier F. R. Khan, the Bureau printed in great abundance books, pamphlets, and articles on the common struggle for independence, the common interests of the population, and the national policies of the government. Color pictures of Mohammad Ali Jinnah and President Ayub Khan were widely distributed and freely supplied. The number of organized tours of citizens (especially students) to other and distant parts of the country was accelerated, while at special seminars the learned presented extensive discourses on national character, national consciousness, and nationhood. Meanwhile, projects focused on regional cultures were heavily subsidized. The Bengali Academy of Dacca, for example, received Rs 15,000 in 1961 for the collection of local folk songs.

No definitive, quantitative evidence is available concerning the results. Nevertheless, it is clear that the Bureau never penetrated the rural areas of the country. It did not, perhaps because it had never even tried. The fact is that in so major an effort, the illiterate masses were tragically ignored. It is my impression, moreover, that even among the more educated, urbanized segments the initial results were on the negative side. Identification with regions and the provinces did not perceptibly decline in favor of national orientation. More often it intensified. Such seemed to be the case with three Bengali student groups I interviewed after their visits to the West Wing. Such indeed was my experience at the All-Pakistan Convention of Basic Democrats in Dacca, February 2-4, 1962. During these three days delegates from West Pakistan participated in discussions, committee deliberations, convention recommendations, and a variety of social and cultural programs with the East Pakistani. At the conclusion of the program, tours were to be arranged for the visitors to see the East Wing. In the course of the convention a number of vigorous references were made to a united commitment to Pakistan including a rather dramatic statement by President Ayub Khan in his opening address. Still, it was clear that there were firm and definite regional groupings. Many delegates made sincere efforts to establish contacts between the "camps," but these took the form of cautious expeditions into undiscovered or unfriendly territory. The East Pakistani seemed to perceive a patronizing attitude in the West Pakistani delegates. The latter, in turn, thought they detected suspicion on the part of their fellow citizens from Bengal. A delegate from Mardan complained: "They treat us like foreigners. I tell them they are our brothers, but they still treat us like foreigners." "Now I know why I never liked the Punjabi," confided another from Sylhet. Almost invariably a discussion during the many social segments of the program would congeal along regional lines. As I strolled along and visited the various gatherings, I was greeted with obvious relief. During the first ten minutes of the tea following the President's opening address, no less than three different delegates walked up with the almost identical opening remark: "You at least are not a Bengali." Incessantly the foreigner was asked whether he detected differences between the people of the two Wings. I made it a point to answer in the negative. Whether the questioner came from East or West Pakistan, my answer *always* caused disappointment and evoked a vigorous presentation of the salient differences. It may be remarked parenthetically that while there was considerable similarity in the exposition of those coming from the same Wing, the descriptions varied both in values and in approach between people who came from different Wings.

As a matter of fact, an adverse initial reaction could have been expected. Even a cosmopolitan traveler experiences a culture-shock when he visits distant lands and in the process accentuates his previous commitments and group identifications. When students and delegates whose psychological security is deeply involved with their own small-scale environment visit another, different region where people are similarly motivated and committed, predictably their perception will focus first upon those features which differentiate and divide, thereby reinforcing previous regional characteristics and loyalties. As if this were not enough, in such exchanges the visitors—especially the Bengali in West Pakistan—invariably became the target of a demonstration effect. As is customary on such tours, the human misery in a number of refugee settlements and the severe privation in some rural areas were meticulously avoided. Instead, the wealthier and more imposing sections were exhibited. While this may have flattered the pride of the hosts, it forced an implicit comparison with the more modest circumstances of their guests. The latter rarely responded by sharing pride in the achievements of Karachi or Lahore; more often envy and antagonism were aroused instead.

The long-run consequences could well have been brighter. It is certainly possible that continued and frequent interchanges would have brought closer ties. While it appeared clear that suspicions and antagonisms existed at the student exchanges and the Basic Democrats Convention, it was also my personal impression that the delegates were concerned about this. Thus, for example, the individual who complained about being treated like a foreigner spent most of his time the next day trying to get acquainted with East Pakistani delegates. In turn, many Bengali invited their West Pakistani colleagues into their homes. Perhaps a good number of the invitations were considered a formality or even a necessary chore, *but certainly not all.*

The Bureau of National Reconstruction, however, did not get a chance to demonstrate its long-range potentialities. Not long after its inception, rumors began to circulate about some of its unpublicized projects. The Bureau was accused of using its funds to buy police spies and informers. In East Pakistan the prominence of police officers in its activities lent credence to such reports.[11] Word spread that the Bureau sought to control the press through weekly meetings between its provincial director and the editors. Then some studies were rather ineptly suppressed. By the fall of 1961 popular suspicion toward the Bureau was rampant. Whether it was entirely justified only secret official documents can reveal. In any case, the hostility became so widespread that shortly before the withdrawal of martial law the government decided to abolish the Bureau as an independent agency. No specific reasons were given.

[11] A Bengali daily pointedly noted that two years after the Bureau's absorption into the Ministry of Information the latter's budget still included a block allocation of Rs 1 lakh for "secret services" (Dacca, *Pakistan Observer*, June 27, 1964, p. 8).

The Policy of Accommodation

While the Bureau of National Reconstruction was subsidizing local cultural efforts, the government also initiated a more direct approach. It addressed itself to the grievances of East Pakistan and those of the former princely states. Through a sympathetic response it hoped to reduce interregional suspicion and to evoke a favorable predisposition to national institutions. As a matter of fact, the President has always been sensitive to Bengali complaints. In his memorandum of October 4, 1954, he urged that the people of East Pakistan be "helped so as to feel equal partners and prove an asset." "That can only be done," he added, "if they are given a considerable measure of partnership." In one dramatic move the Central Government announced the reversal of its previous policy and pledged to post only East Pakistani administrators in the East Wing.[12] The immediate effect of this decision was an acceleration in promotions, an innovation that was received with considerable enthusiasm among the Bengali bureaucratic contingent. Wider implications were also intended. A government administered by the native sons of East Bengal was expected to gain the confidence of the Bengali population. It would remove one source of resentment of the East Pakistani intellectuals and eliminate an obvious scapegoat for the East Pakistani political pressure groups. There were also related initiatives designed to create the impression of provincial *administrative* autonomy through which the martial law regime hoped to deflect aspirations toward provincial *political* autonomy. Additional power was delegated

[12] Dacca, *Morning News*, June 12, 1961, p. 1.

to the provincial government by transferring to it the administration of most development projects; furthermore, the Planning Commission was required to hold a session at least once in three months in Dacca. At the same time, such powerful public and semipublic corporations as the Pakistan Industrial Development Corporation, the Agricultural Development Bank and the railroads were placed under separate and ostensibly independent management in the provinces.[13] Most important, however, were government efforts to allay Bengali fears of economic discrimination. The First Five Year Plan already accepted the principle of economic parity between the Wings. It was not until the Second Plan that some definite progress was made in this direction. Public investment in East Pakistan more than doubled in three years and approached parity with the West Wing.[14] Early in December 1961 a Finance Commission was appointed to arrive at an equitable distribution of central revenue between the two Wings. When the members split along provincial lines, the central government's new formula was closer to the East Pakistani position.[15] A few months later M. Nurul Huda, head of the Department of Economics, University of Dacca, was appointed to the Planning Commission. Dr. Huda's qualifications included not only his articulateness and his previous experience with the Commission, but also the confidence of the faculty and the

[13] *Ibid.*, March 21, 1962, pp. 1, 3 and Dacca, *Pakistan Observer*, June 3, 1962, pp. 1, 5.

[14] Actual expenditures on development projects rose from Rs 26.5 crores in 1957-1958 to Rs 55.2 crores in 1960-1961. The development budget for 1962-1963 exceeded Rs 110 crores.

[15] For details of the formula see: Dacca, *Morning News*, January 29, 1962, pp. 1, 8.

student body of East Pakistan's largest and most significant university.[16] Significantly, Dr. Huda had a reputation for the conviction that parity in income between the Wings could be accomplished only if the trends of the past would be reversed and if for some time to come East Pakistan would receive the lion's share of public investment. After his appointment Dr. Huda toured East Pakistan. One of his main themes: the Third Five Year Plan would start to remove disparity.[17] Two months later the President followed through with a public pledge of parity in foreign aid allocations.[18] Then when the outline of the Third Plan was announced, East Pakistan's share of public investment was set at Rs 1,800 crores—thus exceeding the Rs 1,600 crores projected for the West Wing.[19]

The government was also prepared to accommodate the hierarchies in the former princely states and tribal territories. What these wanted most was to be left alone, and after the initial unpleasantness in Kalat the government obliged. It refrained from intervening in "internal" administrative matters and applied the Frontier Crimes Regulations with considerable latitude. Officials treated visiting princes and tribal maliks with deference, their agents with courtesy. In the spring of 1962 came a dramatic sequence of personal acts by the President. In May his younger daughter Jameela married the brother

[16] The fact that Dr. Huda was related to two most prominent Bengalis, the new Speaker of the National Assembly, Moulvi Tamizuddin Khan, and the former Chief Minister, Nurul Amin, was clearly a further asset.

[17] Dacca, *Pakistan Observer*, January 2, 1963, p. 1.

[18] *Ibid.*, March 7, 1963, p. 1.

[19] *Ibid.*, August 28, 1964, p. 1.

of the Wali of Swat.[20] A few months later by ordinance the President restored the Khan of Kalat to power.[21]

It is still too early to record a definitive evaluation of this policy of accommodation—especially because, unlike the Bureau of National Reconstruction, it survived the withdrawal of martial law. Nevertheless, it may be remarked that, so far at least, no breakthrough can be observed. In tribal areas events continue their turbulent course. In February 1963 Malik Wali Khan Kukikhel, a prominent chieftain and member of the National Assembly, was shot leaving a mosque in Peshawar. Two months later Mir Karam Khan, another pro-government chieftain, was murdered while asleep at his own residence at Wad. Meanwhile, tribal forces continue to raid government posts. When a police detachment was ambushed in Mengal, leaving nine killed and thirteen wounded, the President finally ordered "strict action." Just what happened at this point is not publicly available. By all accounts the military measures were certainly strict. One dramatic version recounted in the National Assembly includes the bombing of a tribal village by the Pakistan Air Force during the Eid festivities.[22] In the East Wing the evidence of centrifugal tendencies in the face of the President's efforts was slightly less spectacular. Newspapers continue to feature information indicating disparity. Politicians never

[20] Karachi, *Dawn*, May 21, 1962, p. 1.

[21] Dacca, *Pakistan Observer*, July 11, 1962, p. 1.

[22] The Home Minister in his denial insisted that "the allegations were not correct as stated." He refused to elaborate, however, and debate was ruled out by the Deputy Speaker on the technical ground that "the earliest opportunity had not been availed of to raise a discussion on this matter" (*ibid.*, December 11, 1962, p. 1; February 23, 1963, p. 1; April 25, 1963, p. 1; February 7, 1964, p. 1; April 1, 1964, p. 1).

cease orating about it. Student slogans and resolutions frequently refer to this topic. When Foreign Minister Manzur Qadir visited the University of Dacca in February 1962, he was greeted by students with raised fists and chants about the exploitation of the province. When General Azam resigned, the popular verdict was clear; he had been victimized by the West Pakistanis because he was too friendly to the Bengalis. Perhaps the clearest indication that the crisis of confidence remains unabated was the reaction of the Bengali press to a series of articles on Indian subversion in the East Wing carried in the *Morning News*, a daily published in Dacca but directed from the West Wing. The series triggered a response which was immediate, violent, and parochial. Front-page headlines screamed: "hate campaign," "East Pakistan will not surrender to them," "real intention on parity revealed," and most extravagant of all: "venom spit from Karachi now."[23] In its defense the *Morning News* devoted many columns to cite favorable reception of its articles. With the exception of the government officials and legislators committed to the government there was a singular absence of accolades from Bengali leaders.[24]

External Incentives

As the massive internal efforts toward national integration proceeded and the full dimensions of the task unfolded, a rising inclination to seek support for cohesion from international stimuli became perceptible. Always in the background—and not far in the background

[23] *Ibid.*, July 13, 1963, p. 1; July 14, 1963, p. 1; July 15, 1963, p. 1; July 20, 1963, p. 1; July 30, 1963, p. 1.

[24] Dacca, *Morning News*, July 16, 1962, pp. 1, 8; July 17, 1962, pp. 1, 8; July 18, 1962, pp. 1, 8.

—there lurked the recently restrained motif of the external enemy. The year 1961 brought trouble with Afghanistan. In August tension between the countries began to be featured in the newspapers. Afghan "lies" about Pakistan were exposed. Pakistani consulates in Kandhar and Jalalabad were closed down because the staffs were being "persistently harassed by Afghans." It was asserted that Afghan Askaris might "launch another invasion" of Pakistan territory.[25] When Pakistan ordered the closing of Afghan consulates and trade offices, Afghanistan in an ultimatum threatened a rupture in diplomatic relations. On September 4, 1961, the border was sealed and the following day the break was complete.[26]

The chief threat, however, remained India. Actually, September 1960 had brought a brief glimmer of hope when Indian Prime Minister Jawaharlal Nehru visited Karachi. He was warmly received both by the President and the public. The oratory on good will flowed profusely; pledges to forget past conflicts were abundant.[27] The Prime Minister personally signed the Indus Waters Treaty, then proceeded to discuss outstanding problems with President Ayub Khan. Negotiations progressed satisfactorily on a variety of subjects: refugee property, payment of pensions, outstanding debts, trade, and passport and visa arrangements. On Kashmir, however, the deadlock was solid. "This," conceded the disappointed President, "can nullify the rest."[28] After a vaguely

[25] Karachi, *Dawn*, August 16, 1961, p. 1; August 24, 1961, p. 1; August 31, 1961, p. 1.

[26] *Ibid.*, September 5, 1961, p. 1; September 6, 1961, p. 1; September 7, 1961, p. 1.

[27] *Ibid.*, September 20, 1960, p. 1; September 21, 1960, p. 1; September 22, 1960, p. 1; September 23, 1960, p. 1.

[28] *Ibid.*, September 24, 1960, p. 1.

worded communiqué the Prime Minister returned to New Delhi. Relations proceeded to deteriorate. Hope that India would honor her pledge for a plebiscite in Kashmir faded. Then in the fall of 1961 student riots broke out at the Muslim University of Aligarh.[29] A few months later Indian troops invaded Goa, demonstrating that in spite of her ringing declarations India had not eschewed recourse to force. The following year brought Prime Minister Nehru's statement that India's policy on Kashmir was clear and firm and that he would hold "fast to it always and ever."[30] These indeed were the facts, disturbing facts to many Pakistanis. In the early days of martial law the government had been a restraining influence. This now changed. Newspaper headlines again focused on Indian threat and aggression. The average days per month when *Dawn* carried such reports on its front page rose to 15.[31] Government-censored editorials veered toward the use of force. The President called upon his countrymen "to unite and prepare . . . to defend their homeland."[32] When a group of Dacca University students were involved in a fight with Indians during their journey home from Calcutta,[33] the government encouraged a mass demonstration. The inexcusable publication of the Holy Prophet's picture in a West Bengal school textbook[34] led to riots in Cal-

[29] *Ibid.*, October 4, 1961, p. 1.

[30] *Ibid.*, January 8, 1962, p. 1.

[31] The monthly breakdown for the period immediately preceding the Constitution is as follows: January—18; February—17; March—13; April—12; May—17.

[32] Karachi, *Dawn*, January 6, 1962, p. 1.

[33] Dacca, *Pakistan Observer*, January 20, 1962, p. 8.

[34] Lahore, *Pakistan Times*, April 10, 1962, p. 1. This was a blatant offense to the large Muslim minority which observes very strict doctrines prohibiting such practice. After the riots the textbook was withdrawn, but by that time the harm had been done.

cutta and communal violence around Malda. There was a perceptible tendency on the part of the government to magnify such occurrences by keeping them alive through public statements. The riot in Malda, for example, was reported over and over again. Later these reports included the Murshidabad district. It was an act of considerable integrity for a Dacca newspaper to send a correspondent to the area and then report that "there has been no communal clash or even a minor incident in Murshidabad preceding, during, or after Malda disturbances."[35] In the meantime, the government decided to bring the Kashmir issue before the United Nations Security Council, a move which was well publicized.[36] The President of Azad Kashmir[37] toured the country and inflamed passions with his oratory.

As the emphasis upon the external threat rose, faint clues for a new stance in international relations became perceptible. Many Pakistanis envied India's foreign policy—not so much because it was neutralist but because it appeared spectacular. While India left her mark on the world councils, Pakistan—a faithful ally—had few opportunities to establish its own identity in the international arena. Preparation of presidential journeys to foreign countries and arrangements for state visits by foreign dignitaries were perhaps the most striking functions of her diplomats. In this they were successful.[38]

[35] Dacca, *Pakistan Observer*, May 2, 1962, p. 5.

[36] Karachi, *Dawn*, January 13, 1962, p. 1.

[37] "Free" Kashmir is that part of the former principality which was "liberated" by Muslim irregulars and under the United Nations-sponsored cease-fire agreement is occupied by Pakistan.

[38] During the last two years of martial law President Ayub Khan visited (in chronological order) Saudi Arabia, the United Arab Republic, Burma, Indonesia, Japan, Hong Kong, Lebanon, Yugoslavia, West Germany, the United Kingdom and the United States. He

Otherwise Pakistan's foreign policy lacked initiative. It was the tail of the American kite. The spring of 1962 brought evidence that the government was growing restless with this role. There were, for example, those elusive charges that "a certain big Western power" was fomenting the unrest in East Pakistan.[39] Other statements by officials deprecated the importance of Pakistan's military alliances. Their value, explained the Secretary of Foreign Affairs, was reduced to nothing.[40] When during the Laos crisis Pakistan, a SEATO member, was approached to send troops to Thailand, she found that she could not oblige with even a token force.[41]

Chinese offensives in Ladakh and the North East Frontier Agency and the subsequent response by the United States and Great Britain had a profound effect upon the external enemy agitation and Pakistan's foreign policy. The Chinese progress toward the Brahmaputra may have caused some anxiety in Pakistani circles. East Pakistan, after all, lay hopelessly exposed. When the Chinese withdrew, however, the focus of concern shifted back to India. Pakistanis recalled with some distress that only a year before when India had suffered similar reverses from China, the former's response had not been a firm stand against the aggressor but a gran-

received as state guests: Prime Minister Nehru of India, President Sukarno of Indonesia, Queen Elizabeth II of Great Britain, Vice President Johnson of the United States, the Prime Minister of Northern Nigeria, King Mahendra of Nepal, Prime Minister Keda of Japan, the Paramount Ruler of Malaya, Crown Prince Akahito of Japan, King Bhumibol Adulyadej of Thailand, and Mrs. Jacqueline Kennedy.

[39] Dacca, *Pakistan Observer*, February 24, 1962, p. 1.
[40] *Ibid.*, May 31, 1962, p. 1.
[41] Karachi, *Dawn*, May 29, 1962, p. 1.

diose attack upon helpless Goa. With her best troops concentrated on Pakistan's borders, it did not seem far-fetched to envisage India's seeking to restore her lost prestige by an adventure directed against the state whose creation India's leaders had fought vigorously but unsuccessfully a decade and a half earlier. The danger seemed all the more real as it soon became apparent, to the consternation of the Government of Pakistan, that her Western allies were prepared to build up India militarily even though it would upset the already pre-carious balance of power in the region.[42]

This rising preoccupation with the external threat was reflected in the press. During the year of 1963 a record of 307 daily issues of *Dawn* each carried at least one front-page item connoting Indian aggressive designs. This monthly average of 26[43] is more than twice the level of the early days of martial law and far exceeds the high point reached in the months preceding martial law. The government, for its part, helped stimulate and consolidate apprehensions about Indian intentions. The Chinese had not yet withdrawn to the cease-fire line when Foreign Minister Mohammad Ali sounded the alarm. The projected Western military aid to New Delhi, he declared, was an "unfriendly act" to Pakistan.[44] The President himself voiced concern publicly,

[42] Mohammad Ayub Khan, "The Pakistan-American Alliance: Stresses and Strains," *Foreign Affairs*, 42, No. 2 (January 1964), pp. 195-209.

[43] These are the specific totals for each month in 1963: January—26; February—23; March—27; April—27; May—26; June—27; July—29; August—28; September—27; October—23; November—24; and December—20.

[44] Dacca, *Pakistan Observer*, October 28, 1962, p. 1; and October 31, 1962, p. 1.

then dramatically called the National Assembly into emergency session.[45]

At this point the Western Powers did respond to Pakistani pressure. After a brisk traffic of American and British diplomats between New Delhi and Rawalpindi, it was announced that direct negotiations between the two states on the issue of Kashmir would be initiated. They would commence at Cabinet level, but "at an appropriate stage" an Ayub-Nehru summit would take place. The announcement and the ensuing negotiations could not possibly have been more ill-timed. The domestic political positions of *both* President Ayub Khan and Prime Minister Nehru were weaker than in the preceding years. This was not the time when either or both could make substantial concessions, and without such concessions there could be no prospect for settlement. In any case the negotiations dragged on for six months through six rounds with no perceptible progress.[46] Then the talks collapsed. Finally, New Delhi announced that it was withdrawing its "concessions to Pakistan on Kashmir."[47]

One result of the Western diplomatic initiative was that the negotiations helped spotlight the friction between the two countries and kept the issue of the Indian threat before the public. It also provided further impetus to Pakistan's earlier fledgling efforts towards a new, more venturesome international identity. Public officials continued to assure Americans of their good will and denied any intention of renouncing treaty

[45] *Ibid.*, November 6, 1962, p. 1; and November 8, 1962, p. 1.

[46] *Ibid.*, December 28, 1962, p. 1; December 31, 1962, p. 1; January 21, 1963, p. 1; February 9, 1963, p. 1; March 13, 1963, p. 1; April 23, 1963, p. 1; and May 17, 1963, p. 1.

[47] *Ibid.*, August 14, 1963, p. 1.

obligations. Nevertheless, it is clear that the government of Pakistan lost much of her interest in alliances with the West. Early in October Foreign Minister Mohammad Ali flew to Washington for the announced purpose of reviewing the utility of the pacts. Upon his return he declared with evident satisfaction that Pakistan did not support the United States during the Cuban missile crisis.[48] Later President Ayub Khan himself observed that the last vestige of preference Pakistan received as an ally from the United States as compared to neutral India disappeared with the Sino-Indian armed clash.[49] It was not without significance that Pakistan sent only a second-string delegation to the SEATO ministerial conference in Manila (1964).[50]

If her new foreign policy course opened a gap to the West, it also steered Pakistan closer to China. "Friendship from any quarter will be welcome," insisted the President while the National Assembly debated the Indian threat in emergency session.[51] To prove his words, in rapid sequence Pakistan's foreign minister visited Peking; Pakistan signed a border agreement, a trade agreement, and a commercial air agreement with China; Pakistan supported China's rather lonely stand on the nuclear test ban treaty; and Pakistan played host to an eight-day state visit by Chou En-Lai.[52]

The rising prominence of foreign affairs did apparently yield a measure of political cohesion at home. The

[48] Ibid., October 10, 1962, p. 1; and October 28, 1962, p. 1.

[49] Mohammad Ayub Khan, "The Pakistan-American Alliance," p. 200.

[50] Dacca, Pakistan Observer, April 15, 1964, p. 1.

[51] Ibid., October 22, 1962, p. 1.

[52] Ibid., January 6, 1963, p. 1; February 24, 1963, p. 1; March 3, 1963, p. 1; August 30, 1963, p. 1; September 21, 1963, p. 1 and February 20, 1964, p. 1.

arms shipments brought demonstrations in every major urban center in Pakistan. In the National Assembly when a Bengali member implied a government ruse to distract legitimate parochial aspirations he found few supporters.[53] Even the politicians of past regimes now in opposition felt compelled to join the anti-Indian campaign and endorse the new foreign policy. The culprit behind the Separatist movement was a "foreign power," explained Khwaja Nazimuddin. Sardar Bahadur Khan blamed the United States for martial law and assured his followers that the Anglo-American bloc was bent upon wiping Pakistan off the map. In turn Sheikh Mujibur Rahman discovered that the new foreign policy followed the pattern set by H. S. Suhrawardy.[54]

The focus on the foreign enemy, however, has its own pitfalls. The Hindu domestic minority is all too easily identified with the Indian external enemy. Agitation against the latter makes convenient scapegoats of the former. Indeed, 1963 saw a deadly upward spiral of communal incidents and retaliations on both sides of East Pakistan's borders. When Indian authorities expelled Muslims from Assam, public agitation reached a crescendo. Then an event in Kashmir ignited the emotional powder keg. Late in December the sacred hair of the Holy Prophet was stolen from Hazrat Bal Shrine in Srinagar. West Pakistan responded with demonstrations and strikes; in East Pakistan the theft triggered an explosion. First, the mill hands in Khulna started

[53] "Pandit Nehru and Chou En-Lai should be given a *Nishan-e-Pakistan* for giving the Government an opportunity to cancel the Dacca Session," declared Major Afsaruddin (*ibid.*, November 23, 1962, p. 1).

[54] *Ibid.*, December 20, 1962, p. 1; December 22, 1962, p. 1; August 31, 1963, p. 1.

170

looting. Then, gaining momentum from its own destructive dynamism and fed by riots in West Bengal, violence engulfed the entire province. Mangla and Jessore saw large-scale murder and arson. Massacres were widespread in the provincial capital of Dacca. Roving bands assaulted and killed people indiscriminately, seized trains, and burned property. Law and order ceased to exist. The army moved in and ordered a curfew from 2:00 P.M. to 8:00 A.M. The President, his ministers, the Governor and public officials all pleaded with the population to help restore order. Even so, it took several days before an uneasy peace returned to East Pakistan. The cost of this emotional rampage was incalculable. It certainly included thousands of innocent persons butchered and a new flood of Muslim refugees from India.[55]

Nor is the new foreign policy free of traps. Pakistan acquired 750 square miles of craggy mountain peaks in her border treaty with China. Predictably, during his visit Chou En-Lai endorsed Pakistan's demand for a plebiscite in Kashmir.[56] These have been gains. In turn, American response so far has been moderate. The State Department expressed its concern about the blossoming new friendship.[57] The Agency for International Development suspended aid for enlarging the Dacca airfield which was to be used in the Pakistan-China air link.[58]

[55] *Ibid.*, January 14, 1964, p. 1; January 15, 1964, p. 1; January 16, 1964, p. 1; January 17, 1964, p. 1; January 18, 1964, p. 1; January 19, 1964, p. 1; January 20, 1964, p. 1; January 21, 1964, p. 1. See also: *Azad's* reply to show cause notice quoted *ibid.*, April 12, 1964, pp. 1, 8.

[56] *Ibid.*, March 3, 1963, p. 1 and February 24, 1964, p. 1.

[57] *Ibid.*, February 25, 1963, p. 1.

[58] A certain amount of mystery, if not confusion, surrounds this decision. An American version was stated by the Deputy Director of

Further deterioration in Pakistani-American relations may well affect foreign aid allocations.

Indeed, recently the Government has shown some appreciation of adverse results of the external stimuli of national integration. Since spring 1964 official emphasis of the theme of Indian hostility has declined, and in June the President offered "a warm hand of friendship to the people of India."[59] Later he called the election of Prime Minister Shastri "a good augury of Indo-Pakistan relations."[60] Azad Kashmir's irreconcilable President was quietly removed. October saw an Ayub-Shastri meeting in Karachi, and a communiqué expressed "the common desire [for] friendly and cooperative relations. . . ."[61] The inaugural address of 1965 included these relevant words: "We are also beset with dangers. The external ones do not worry me so much as the internal ones."[62] Meanwhile, the pro-China venture was toned down; the president's tour of China was balanced by visits to Moscow, London, and Washington and public stress on closer ties with Iran and Turkey.[63] At least formally, Pakistan remained an ally of the West.

In short, the Government apparently reverted to internal incentives for national integration. The most prominent of these were economic development and representative institutions.

AID in Pakistan a year after the fact: "The loan for the Dacca airport project was withdrawn by the Pakistan Government, and not rejected by the United States. This is in the record." Two days later an official Pakistani spokesman said the statement was "absolutely incorrect" (*ibid.*, September 11, 1964, p. 1 and September 13, 1964, p. 1).

[59] Karachi, *Dawn*, June 2, 1964, p. 3.

[60] *Ibid.*, July 8, 1964, p. 1.   [61] *Ibid.*, October 13, 1964, p. 1.

[62] *Ibid.*, March 24, 1965, p. 4.

[63] A Three Nation Alliance for Development (Regional Cooperation for Development) was signed in Istanbul. (Dacca, *Pakistan Observer*, July 24, 1964, p. 1).

8

++

The Plan for Accelerated Economic Growth

++

ECONOMIC PLANNING in Pakistan has been something of a phenomenon. Not until April 1957 did the National Economic Council approve the First Five Year Plan, which was expected to cover the period of 1955-1960. Even then it was consigned to a minor file. "I was staggered to learn," admitted Prime Minister Firoz Khan Noon on April 24, 1958, "that until a few days ago the Five Year Plan had not even been authenticated by the Government for publication. With hardly two more years to go, the Plan continues to be regarded as a routine departmental file, meant only for recording of prolific notes and crossnotes."[1] Eventually on May 12 it was released.

This same rather haphazard manner characterized its provisions. To be sure, its massive 652 pages contained an imposing number of tables and charts. The style was flowing; the theories were recondite. It was rich in ideological assertions and sparked by extravagant visions. With reality, however, the First Five Year Plan had only a superficial acquaintance. Consider the target for per capita income. The Draft Plan (1956) projected an increase of 12.5 per cent by 1960. The achievement of this goal, however, was predicated upon

[1] Quoted in Mushtaq Ahmad, *Government and Politics in Pakistan* (2nd ed.; Karachi: Pakistan Publishing House, 1963), p. 78.

two major factors: an annual population growth of less than 1.5 per cent and a five-year increment of 20 per cent in gross national product. In fact, the population growth rate was above 2 per cent. This is not merely the wisdom of hindsight. The planners themselves at the time they prepared the Plan knew that the rate they projected was illusory. It was felt, the Deputy Chairman of the Planning Commission explained, that this figure had to be understated "to keep despair away."[2] The projection of the national product was so extravagant that in two years even its pretense was abandoned. In the final version of the Plan, therefore, it was revised downward to 15 per cent. Yet even this more moderate estimate relied upon an exaggerated appraisal of resources. During the first three years (1955/56-1957/58), non-development expenditures of the government exceeded public revenues by Rs 46 crores. Nevertheless, even when the final draft appeared in 1958, it still projected a public saving of Rs 100 crores. Similarly, the first three years brought only an annual average of Rs 70 crores of foreign aid.[3] Yet the final draft expected to *utilize* Rs 172 crores from this source during the last two years. A final illustration: At this late date, past the halfway mark of the period, the Plan still included a block allocation of Rs 70 crores to East Pakistan *for which no suitable projects were available.*[4]

The government was not elated by the performance

[2] Albert Waterston, *Planning in Pakistan* (Baltimore: Johns Hopkins Press, 1963), p. 46.

[3] Government of Pakistan, *First Five Year Plan: Preliminary Evaluation Report* (Karachi: Government of Pakistan Press, 1959), pp. 9, 18.

[4] Government of Pakistan, *First Five Year Plan* (Karachi: Government of Pakistan Press, 1958), p. 19. See also: David Bell, "Allocating Development Resources: Some Observations Based on Pakistan Experience," *Public Policy,* IX (1959), 105.

of the First Five Year Plan. "The Planning Commission realized at a very early stage," observed an official chronology, "that, if planned development was to have any perceptible impact on the economy of the country, this experience must not be repeated in the case of the Second Plan."[5] Accordingly preliminary work started on the latter in March 1958. Since this was two years before the commencement of the new plan period and two months before the First Plan was published, it seemed a promising start. By August 5 a Draft Working Paper including the general features of the Plan was completed and sent to the provincial governments and the central ministries for comments.[6] At the same time, the appropriate government agencies were asked to present schemes (projects) for review. In general, however, proceedings dawdled along at their usual pace until the establishment of martial law. Then followed some energetic activity. "The economic . . . status of an overwhelming part of our population must be raised," declared President Ayub Khan, "if an independent Pakistan is to have any meaning for them."[7]

First of all came some structural changes. The Ministry of Economic Affairs was abolished and the Planning Commission was made directly responsible to the President. Sections in charge of the implementation were brought together in the President's Secretariat as a Project Division. Toward the end of the year G.

[5] Government of Pakistan, Planning Commission, "Preparation of the Second Five Year Plan (1960-65)—A Historical Résumé," unpublished document, November 11, 1960.

[6] Secretary, National Planning Board, d.o. letter No. 2 (1)-Cord/ NPB/58.

[7] Mohammad Ayub Khan, *Speeches and Statements* (Karachi: Pakistan Publications, 1961), i, 26.

Ahmed, a senior civil servant, was appointed chairman of the Commission with instructions to expedite the economic program. Then early in 1959 the Economic Council was established to serve as the supreme economic advisory body to the President, with the Deputy Chairman of the Planning Commission named as its *ex officio* secretary[8] of the Council. Finally, the operational effectiveness of the planning apparatus was enhanced by the evident interest of the President. At times President Ayub Khan took a personal hand by issuing special directives to the provincial governments and central ministries. In turn he reserved for himself all the major announcements regarding the Plan: the objectives (July 1959), the outline (December 1959), and the final draft (June 1960). By the summer of 1960 one achievement was assured: the Second Five Year Plan had been completed by the *first day* of the new plan period.

These are some of the main features of the Second Five Year Plan as it finally emerged. Its overall target was an increase of 20 per cent in gross national product. Given the Commission's estimate of 1.8 per cent annual growth in population, per capita income was expected to increase at 10 per cent. In terms of sectoral allocations of public investment agriculture was clearly favored. The Planning Commission and especially President Ayub Khan were convinced that only through a heavy emphasis in this sector would the rural masses participate in economic development.[9] Self-sufficiency in

[8] Its members: the President, Governors of East and West Pakistan, the Deputy Chairman of the Planning Commission, the Chairman of the Pakistan Industrial Development Corporation and the two provincial Water and Power Development authorities and the central ministers for Finance, Industry and Works, Irrigation and Power, Railways and Communications, Commerce and Food and Agriculture.

[9] This proposition, of course, is far from universally accepted, and

176

food, a target the First Plan missed by a wide mark, was again posited as a primary goal. No less than 54 per cent of total public investment was earmarked for items: Agriculture, Village AID, and Water and Power.[10]

In order to sustain these objectives the Plan projected total investment of Rs 1,900 crores, including Rs 1,150 crores to be invested by the government. At constant prices this meant an increase of 50 per cent over the First Plan expectations and nearly 70 per cent over the First Plan performance. The resource structure of the Second Five Year Plan, however, was similar to that of its predecessor. In the light of previous deficits, the estimated public saving was reduced from 13.3 per cent to 10.5 per cent of total projected public investment.[11] The foreign aid and loan component continued to predominate. Even if defense support and the Indus River project were excluded from calculations, it still amounted to 69.5 per cent of total public investment.[12] This time, however, these projections were accompanied by a most determined program to attract foreign private and public capital.

As a matter of fact, Pakistan, unlike India, never expressed a preference for socialism. The First Five Year

---

empirical evidence is mounting that it is altogether erroneous. Nevertheless according to several public officials who did participate in the formulation of the Plan, the President, the members of the Commission, and most senior advisers (including American advisers) supported this line of reasoning.

[10] Government of Pakistan, *Second Five Year Plan* (Karachi: Government of Pakistan Press, 1960), p. 12.

[11] This includes the items "surplus on revenue account" (Rs 80 crores), "additional taxation" (Rs 100 crores), and "resources of local bodies" (Rs 20 crores) (*ibid.*, p. 32).

[12] *Ibid.*

Plan emphasized the importance of the private sector and suggested only timidly the importance of public authority in the development of new resources.[13] The martial law authorities followed and reinforced this example. After the very first Cabinet meeting, General Ayub Khan sought to allay fears and assure the business community of "full support and protection."[14] In another major policy speech a few months later he again reiterated: "It has long been one of the cardinal policies of the Government of Pakistan to allow free enterprise full play in the development of the country."[15] When the Second Five Year Plan was published, it contained a specific pledge: "No industries are reserved for the public sector; public investment is provided only in those activities which are not ordinarily developed with private capital or where, on present indications, private investment will not be forthcoming. Disabilities of the private investor are now being steadily removed. Indigenous and foreign private capital will receive positive encouragement."[16] Early in April 1959 an Investment Promotion Bureau was set up to attract private investors from abroad.

The brunt of the effort, however, was directed to increasing foreign aid. President Ayub was convinced that the western nations would commit their support if they could be convinced that the projects were economically sound and that the government was politically friendly. He set out to have Pakistan qualify on both counts. Within a short time the country witnessed

[13] Government of Pakistan, *First Five Year Plan*, p. 86.

[14] Mohammad Ayub Khan, *Speeches and Statements*, i, 8.

[15] Speech before the Advisory Committee of the Ministry of Commerce on April 29, 1959 (*ibid.*, i, 109).

[16] Government of Pakistan, *Second Five Year Plan*, p. 8.

a veritable burst of scholarly activity. The Planning Commission sponsored nearly two hundred detailed studies. In addition, special commissions were appointed to report on major economic and related problems.[17] Prominent national figures and foreign experts were invited to join the deliberations. Western governments and international banking agencies were showered with data, at times personally presented by the Chairman of the Planning Commission. In the meantime, the government was bent upon demonstrating its political attachment to the Western Powers. Pakistan had already joined the SEATO and CENTO alliances. Now these ties were further reinforced. President Ayub Khan personally attended the CENTO ministerial meetings. He also proposed the reorganization of SEATO after the more efficient NATO pattern. Then on November 12, 1959, Pakistan signed a bilateral treaty of "Friendship and Commerce" with the United States.[18]

The Second Five Year Plan had hardly been signed and published when it was twice revised. The rate of inflation and the cost of some projects, admitted the Planning Commission, had been underestimated.[19] Thus far the tradition remained unbroken. There was, however, one fundamental difference. This time it was a substantial upward revision. The new five-year projection called for Rs 2,300 crores investment. Performance seemed to warrant optimism. By most economic stand-

[17] A few examples of the Commissions: Tax Inquiry, Rural Credit, Education, Agriculture, Land Reform, Transportation, Industrial Survey, Government Reorganization.

[18] United States, Department of State, *Treaties and Other International Acts*, No. 4683 (Washington: Government Printing Office, 1961).

[19] Government of Pakistan, *Second Five Year Plan (Revised Estimates)* (Karachi: Government of Pakistan Press, 1961), pp. 10-11.

ards the first two years of the Second Five Year Plan were among the most successful in Pakistan's history. National income rose by 9.7 per cent, the production of food held at a level 17 per cent above the 1947-1957 average, and the index of industrial production reached 119.2 (1959-1960 = 100).[20]

These accomplishments chiefly reflected the success of the government initiative to attract foreign investment. Stimulated by the activities of the Investment Promotions Bureau, foreign private investment began to show interest in the opportunities in Pakistan. In two years arrangements were completed for new projects amounting to Rs 48.37 crores with a foreign investment component of Rs 22.9 crores.[21] Meanwhile foreign aid and loans rose to a tide. On September 20, 1960, the Indus Basin Development Fund Agreement was signed in Karachi. Its objective was to liberate West Pakistan from the Indian strangle hold over its water. It also meant an $867 million investment (including $632 million in foreign exchange) by the United States, India, the United Kingdom, Australia, Canada, New Zealand, West Germany, and the International Bank of Reconstruction and Development over a ten-year period.[22] The same year the International Bank of Reconstruction and Development, acceded to Pakistan's request and formed a Consortium of foreign-aid-supplying countries. Then at its second meeting (June 1961) the Consortium promptly committed $320 million of aid for 1961-1962.

[20] Government of Pakistan, *Economic Survey of Pakistan 1961-62* (Rawalpindi: Government of Pakistan Press, 1962), Statistical Section, pp. 16-17 and State Bank of Pakistan, *Bulletin*, September 1963, pp. 14, 114.

[21] *Economic Survey of Pakistan 1961-62*, p. 43.

[22] Lahore, *Pakistan Times*, September 20, 1960, p. 7.

A few months later (October 14, 1961) the United States signed an agreement under Public Law 480 to ship $621 million worth of agricultural commodities within four years and accept non-convertible rupees in payment.[23] Finally, during its third meeting (January 24 and 25, 1962) the Consortium agreed to provide an additional $625 million, thus raising the commitment for the second and third years of the Second Five Year Plan to $945 million.[24] Perhaps the best indication of the measure of accomplishment is the fact that this last total to be made available in a span of two years amounts to no less than 86 per cent of the expectations of foreign aid for the entire five-year period.

Response to government initiative was rather more mixed at home. The positive results include an increase in the utilization of allocated and projected funds. Although expenditure in the agricultural sector during these two years reached only 72.2 per cent of funds budgeted, the overall performance left only 9.3 per cent of total allocations unutilized.[25] Improvement was particularly impressive in East Pakistan. There, as Table 7 indicates, the rate of utilization rose quite substantially.

Less encouraging was the performance of saving. The official estimates claim that the average rate of saving rose from 6.6 per cent in 1959-1960 to approximately 8.1 per cent in 1961-1962 and then argue that since the marginal rate was 12.4 per cent for the first year and 21.8 per cent for the second, "by the end of the Plan the rate of saving may well exceed the planned 10 per

---

[23] *Ibid.*, October 15, 1961, pp. 1, 14.

[24] Karachi, *Dawn*, January 27, 1962, p. 1.

[25] John H. Power, "Two Years of Pakistan's Second Plan," *The Pakistan Development Review*, III, No. 1 (Spring 1963), p. 128.

Table 7

Rate of Utilization of Development Allocations in East Pakistan in Selected Years[26]

Year	Budgeted Amount (lakh of rupees)	Actual Expenditure (per cent)
1955-1956	1,493.55	48
1956-1957	2,573.78	62
1957-1958	3,241.40	81
1958-1959	3,424.80	93
1959-1960	4,359.13	67
1960-1961	5,981.44	92
1961-1962	6,810.00	93

cent."[27] Actually the accomplishment is more statistical than real. In contrast to earlier Planning Commission practice, these latest official calculations do not deduct from gross investment that part of foreign aid which directly finances consumption rather than investment. This technique raises the estimate of domestic saving *by the amount of consumption financed abroad!* Adjusted figures indicate that during the first year of the Second Five Year Plan domestic saving reached only 5.7 per cent of the GNP, or scarcely above the average First Plan rate of 5.6 per cent. The next year did bring a sizable jump to 7.4 per cent, representing a marginal saving rate of 38.6 per cent.[28] The performance of a single year, of course, is a very unreliable guide of

[26] Data collected from the official files of the Finance Department, Government of East Pakistan. For the 1961-1962 figures see: Government of East Pakistan, *Economic Survey of East Pakistan 1961-62* (Dacca: East Pakistan Government Press, 1962), pp. 49-51.

[27] Government of Pakistan, Planning Commission, *Mid-Plan Review of Progress in 1960/61-61/62 Under the Second Five Year Plan* (Karachi: Government of Pakistan Press, 1962), p. 7.

[28] John H. Power, *op.cit.*, p. 130.

achievement, but even if it were to be accepted at its full value, it still does not sustain the expectation of reaching the 10 per cent annual rate projected by the Plan for 1965.

Perhaps most disappointing was the apparent waste of all the scholarly effort. Although President Ayub Khan assumed the chairmanship of the Planning Commission in July 1961, the government could not or would not implement the major recommendations of the various "blue ribbon" commissions and groups of experts. Consider the report of the Taxation Enquiry Committee. Among its most prominent recommendations were: (a) the reduction of the income tax exemption limit to Rs 4,200; (b) the imposition of a capital gains tax; and (c) the central taxation of agricultural incomes. None of these was implemented. The recommendations of the Commission on National Education included: (a) five years of compulsory education by 1970; (b) a substantial rise in college admissions standards; (c) an increase from two to three years in the bachelor's degree programs; and (d) a total work load for university faculties of 1,500 hours per academic year. Progress toward compulsory education is difficult to estimate. As for the others: admissions standards remained the same; after a very short trial the two-year B.A. programs were restored, and the chronic student unrest at the universities makes a work load of 1,500 hours pure fiction. The Report by the Food and Agriculture Commission and surveys on rural credit, industry in East Pakistan, and transportation in East Pakistan met with similar fates. They were consigned to remote bureaucratic pigeon holes to be dusted off occasionally for some inquiring scholars.

The pace of economic development slackened markedly at the end of martial law in June 1962. To be sure, foreign aid continued to flow in great abundance. By March 1963, or slightly after the halfway mark, foreign assistance committed to the Second Five Year Plan reached $939 million in addition to $707 million worth of commodity aid under U.S. Public Law 480 and $640 million foreign exchange support for the Indus Basin Replacement Works.[29] For the last two years of the Plan, the Pakistan Consortium pledged $425 million in May 1963, and an additional $431 million in July 1964. The Soviet bloc entered with a $30 million from the Soviet Union for oil exploration and more recently a $40 million loan from Czechoslovakia.[30] At home, however, the setbacks were formidable. The rural areas of East Pakistan were ravaged by devastating cyclones and floods. One cyclone alone in March 1963 killed 9,742 villagers, according to an official count.[31] The elements, however, were only part of the trouble. Rural resentment against industrial projects, especially those which involved relocation, was already seething. In June 1963 villagers attempted to cut a dam at Magura and were foiled only by their lack of technical knowledge. Even so, the hastily assembled police was forced to fire to disperse them. The towns in the meantime were plagued by chronic labor unrest. The final quarter of 1962 brought sporadic strikes by railroad workers, government clerks, and teachers in East Pakistan. In the following spring, in spite of government threats, dissolution of unions, arrests of some 230 employees, and sus-

[29] State Bank of Pakistan, *Bulletin*, September 1963, pp. 23-24.
[30] Dacca, *Pakistan Observer*, March 27, 1963, p. 1.
[31] *Ibid.*, June 20, 1963, p. 1.

pension of 99 railroad workers, the situation deteriorated into a massive walkout. Chittagong police fired into crowds of demonstrators; across the country in Karachi three workers were killed by police bullets. Hardly had these conflicts been settled when textile workers, nurses, and even doctors walked off their jobs.[32] As if all this were not enough, the Planning Commission found that Rs 700 crores worth of projects (nearly 50 per cent of the public sector program) included in the Plan were quite unfeasible, and new schemes had to be substituted.[33]

Faced with such reverses, it is not surprising that the performance of the third year of the Second Five Year Plan fell considerably short of expectations. The rate of utilization of allocated resources declined sharply—in East Pakistan to 76 per cent.[34] The national income increment scarcely exceeded 1 per cent, well below the population growth-rate. Production of rice (the country's major food crop) declined 7.3 per cent, and the exportable surplus of jute (the major export item) was reduced by 12 per cent.[35] The news, however, was not all bad. The index of industrial production continued to register healthy gains—some 13 per cent during the second half of 1962—and wheat crops reached a new high.[36]

The fourth year results are not available at this writ-

[32] *Ibid.*, October 9, 1962, p. 1; November 2, 1962, p. 1; December 2, 1962, p. 1; January 23, 1963, p. 1; February 23, 1963, p. 1; February 24, 1963, p. 1; March 2, 1963, p. 1; May 1, 1963, p. 1; May 15, 1963, p. 1; October 25, 1963, p. 1.

[33] Statement by Said Hasan, Deputy Chairman, Planning Commission, quoted *ibid.*, February 1, 1963, p. 1.

[34] Expenditure amounted to Rs 108.94 crores compared to an allocation of Rs 142.95 crores (data collected from the files of the Finance Department, Government of East Pakistan).

[35] State Bank of Pakistan, *Bulletin*, September 1963, pp. 11-13.

[36] *Ibid.*, pp. 11-12.

ing. The President, however, is optimistic. "The current year," he declared in a broadcast in April 1964, "is likely to show a six per cent increase in the gross national product."[37] His optimism is apparently shared by the Planning Commission. Certainly it is reflected by the outline of the Third Five Year Plan, which proposes no less than a total investment of Rs 5,200 crores in 1966-1970—a sizable jump from the Rs 2,300 crores target of the Second Plan. It also predicts decreased

Table 8

Financing of Government Development Accounts (1960-1965)[38]

	Amount (Rs crores)				
	1960-1961	1961-1962	1962-1963	1963-1964*	1964-1965**
Domestic Resources	100	108	121	94	93
Foreign Aid	98	126	205	223	274
	Percentage of Total				
	1960-1961	1961-1962	1962-1963	1963-1964	1964-1965
Domestic Resources	51	46	37	30	25
Foreign Aid	49	54	63	70	75

* Revised.
** Projected.

[37] Dacca, *Pakistan Observer*, April 2, 1964, p. 5.

[38] Government of Pakistan, Planning Commission, *Mid-Plan Review of Progress*, p. 65 and Dacca, *Pakistan Observer*, June 13, 1964, p. 8. Actually this trend is even more dramatic than the table indicates. "Foreign aid" does not contain substantial sums available under the Indus Basin Development Fund, while "domestic resources" include customs duties levied on commodity aid.

reliance upon foreign aid, which is remarkable since the record of recent years shows quite a contrary trend.[39] Apparently it is hoped that domestic saving will more than double—no mean feat in itself and also a radical departure from previous trends. As Table 9 indicates, for example, non-corporate private saving has showed much fluctuation but no significant increase over the years.

Table 9

Non-Corporate Private Saving in Pakistan[40]
(net saving in thousand rupees)

1955	708,900	1959	498,297
1956	721,707	1960	655,930
1957	482,347	1961	259,555
1958	387,480	1962	629,149

It is too early to tell whether these projections are ambitious or fantastic. Although a breakthrough to self-sustained economic growth has not been accomplished so far, the tempo of the growth rate has accelerated since October 1958. Much will depend upon the continued availability of foreign aid. Even more will depend upon the ability of the government to stimulate and mobilize domestic saving. This in turn will rest in no small measure upon President Ayub Khan's success in constructing an institutional pattern that can attract popular commitment.

[39] Presumably, the Planning Commission is not relying on a statistical sleight of hand, calculating domestic resources in current prices and converting external assistance into rupees at a fixed official rate. Given a steady inflationary trend, this could well give the illusion of a decreasing share of foreign aid.

[40] Stephan R. Lewis, Jr. and Mohammad Irshad Khan, "Estimates of Non-Corporate Private Saving in Pakistan: 1949-62," *The Pakistan Development Review*, IV, No. 1 (Spring 1964), p. 7.

9

++

Martial Law, A New Beginning

++

O<small>N OCTOBER</small> 10, 1958, General Ayub Khan granted an interview to Watson S. Sims, correspondent of the Associated Press. It had been a hectic day for the Chief Martial Law Administrator. He had had news from Dacca on the resistance of the High Court. There had been reports concerning disaffection among the senior bureaucrats. Worse still, the first rumors had begun to arrive about President Iskander Mirza's dubious activities. Nevertheless, General Ayub Khan was self-confident and relaxed during the entire interview. He answered all questions in his crisp military manner. Only the end of his somewhat extended response on the political goals of the new regime offered a clue to the depth of his emotions. "We have got to get back to democracy," he exclaimed. "We must make it work!"

No details of the political strategy were suggested throughout the interview or were specified during subsequent months. From the perspective of hindsight, however, two major approaches emerge as the most prominent ingredients of the initial stage of institutional reconstruction. One approach was directed toward the consolidation of the base of operation. It entailed a liberal use of intimidation and a concurrent effort to popularize the martial law leaders. Another approach had as its aim the establishment of an institutional groundwork upon which the future political structure of Pakistan would be securely founded. It featured the system of Basic Democracies.

The Consolidation of the Base of Operation

The imposition of martial law brought a whole series of repressive measures abolishing all civil liberties, censoring the press, and imposing extraordinary penalties for criminal acts. Special military courts were established and were authorized to pass any sentence "except death, transportation, or imprisonment exceeding one year or whipping exceeding fifteen stripes."[1] Recalcitrants were threatened with the death penalty. Several prominent members of the previous regime were arrested and held without bail; others were confined to their homes.[2] Early in 1959 in rapid succession the Public Conduct Scrutiny Ordinance, 1959 and the Scrutiny Ordinance, 1959 and the Public Offices (Disqualification) Order, 1959 were promulgated.[3] These authorized extraordinary screening procedures defined the scope of "misconduct" and "inefficiency" and specified punishments. Review boards invariably included a military officer whose vote was determining. While the senior bureaucratic cadres in general remained unaffected, by July 1959 some 1,662 officials had been punished, 813 of them by dismissal.[4] Then on August 6, 1959, the Elective Bodies (Disqualification) Ordinance, 1959 was issued. It authorized special tribunals to try

[1] Dacca, *Morning News*, October 9, 1958, p. 3.
[2] *Ibid.*, October 13, 1958, p. 1; October 28, 1958, p. 1; November 9, 1958, p. 1.
[3] *Ibid.*, January 8, 1959, p. 1; March 26, 1959, p. 1.
[4] *Ibid.*, July 4, 1959, p. 1.

189

former political leaders for their "misconduct."[5] Only by accepting an offer of disqualification from "being a member or a candidate for the membership of any elective body" could these men avoid prosecution. A few decided to contest, but most accepted, forced retirement. Approximately seven thousand persons were thus excluded from political life.[6]

As martial law was fading, the measures of coercion were continued—perhaps even intensified. Ex-politicians were warned that they would not be permitted to contest elections and were "sternly" admonished against "fooling the masses." Trade organizations were reprimanded for violating rules and informed that the government would seize them if they were not "managed properly." The same warning was then extended to social welfare bodies. Intermittently the population was reminded that martial law was still in effect. In January 1962 Martial Law Regulation 94 reconstituted a previous regulation (No. 55) prohibiting attendance and address of any meeting or procession. On January 30 ex-Prime Minister Suhrawardy was arrested, unleashing a further flood of threats including the promise of additional arrests. Two weeks later the Security of Pakistan Act was amended to remove writs of habeas corpus in connection with political *détenus* from the jurisdiction of the courts. The sequence continued until on April 2 shortly before the withdrawal of martial law the government threatened to invade the mosques by banning

[5] *Ibid.*, August 8, 1959, p. 1.

[6] In West Pakistan unofficial estimates place EBDO disqualifications at 3,000. In East Pakistan this total (including previous disqualifications by the Security of Pakistan Act, 1952 and PRODA) amounted to 3,978. (*Ibid.*, October 7, 1959, p. 1 and unpublished information collected from official East Pakistan government files.)

meetings and processions "for a religious purpose" if their "nature" was political.[7]

Actions which were intended to intimidate were accompanied by vigorous efforts designed to popularize the military regime. A few days after the proclamation of martial law Ayub Khan himself toured both Wings, addressing not only government officials but also a large number of public gatherings. Although certainly not an excessively gregarious person, the President moved around freely in the cities, visited towns, villages, and even remote mountain communities. During such trips he was easily accessible and with his relaxed manner charmed his audiences. The members of his Cabinet followed this lead, some with hesitation and reluctance, but others like Lieutenant General Mohammad Azam Khan with unbounded enthusiasm. The popular image which the new rulers projected was that of men who were not content to enjoy the trappings of political power in a distant capital but were genuinely fond of the people of Pakistan and honestly cared for the fate of every single individual. It was indeed the image of the benevolent ruler so prevalent in the doctrines and traditions of Islam and which during the last centuries had remained the ethical goal but unhappily was not the practical experience of the Muslims in India.

There was, however, another motif with far-reaching ramifications in the popular appeal of the national leadership. It was the motif which had stirred the masses during the struggle for independence; the kin-

[7] Karachi, *Dawn*, October 15, 1961, p. 12; December 3, 1961, p. 1; December 5, 1961, p. 1; February 16, 1962, p. 1; April 2, 1962, p. 1; and Dacca, *Morning News*, January 21, 1962, p. 1; January 31, 1962, p. 1; February 3, 1962, p. 1.

dling of an optimistic view of the future. The politicians of the past decade had indeed betrayed the interests of the people and exploited the national resources to their personal advantage. Martial law would rectify all this and deliver on the promises of the past. The cost of living would drop; incomes would rise. Workers would receive better wages, traders be assured fair profit. Cheap medical care would be provided for all. There would be better housing and more water for refugee colonies. The population problem would be solved. Kashmir would be liberated. The national pride would be rehabilitated. Such were the promises of the day.

Abruptly in the spring of 1960 the President withdrew from his campaigning and became singularly reticent. He still made regular public pronouncements and occasionally visited remote areas, but his drive for personal exposure waned noticeably. Increasingly, he relied upon his ministers to fashion his image. In contrast to his extensive tour throughout the province in January 1960, the President during the *last two years* of martial law spent only forty-three days in East Pakistan, thirty-seven of them in the provincial capital of Dacca. The President's close adviser, Lieutenant General W. A. Burki, a medical officer who had never been inclined toward informal chitchat with people in the streets, also withdrew from the limelight and ventured forth only occasionally for a statement on public health or birth control. Lieutenant General K. M. Sheikh, another military member of the Cabinet, did make a somewhat perfunctory attempt to capture public attention. He, or perhaps more accurately Begum Sheikh, launched a "Buy Pakistani" movement featuring rejection of imported silks for the ladies' sarees and the substitution of domestic cotton fabrics. The movement did receive attention in the towns of West Pakistan; the ladies were not impressed. Lieutenant General Mohammad Azam Khan, the third military member of the original martial law cabinet, was the only one who persisted in his efforts to gain public support. His record is most instructive.

General Azam had had an illustrious military career. During the Kashmir hostilities he commanded Pakistani regular forces in the area. In 1953 when the religious riots brought chaos to Lahore, he restored order through martial law. In the planning of the military coup in 1958 he played a key role and became Martial Law Administrator for the province of West Pakistan. On the fateful night of October 27 he was one of the generals who called on President Mirza to "request" his resignation. When President Ayub Khan formed his first Cabinet, General Azam joined it as senior member and Minister of Refugee Rehabilitation. He initiated impressive progress in refugee resettlement and traveled throughout the country publicizing martial law. Then on April 12, 1960, he was appointed Governor of East Pakistan.

Bengal, with its record of suspicion—even hostility—to West Pakistan and little enthusiasm for the military, presented General Azam with his greatest challenge. He responded accordingly. His energy appeared boundless, his interest contagious. He seemed ubiquitous—visiting villages, laying foundation stones, inaugurating seminars. He rarely, if ever, prepared a speech. He was never eloquent, but his rambling, often disjointed delivery succeeded remarkably in conveying sincerity and affection. Whether on tour of a village or at a university tea he was always accessible and readily engaged in friendly chats. He never missed a chance to shake a hand or listen attentively to a complaint. At the feast of Eid, the time of Muslim rejoicing, General Azam embraced his fellow countrymen without distinction for class or position. In a case of emergency his word was as good as his deed. The cyclones of 1961 wrought terrible devastation in the province. Promptly he arrived on the scene and personally directed relief. His appearance and his orders and counterorders to the divisional and district commissioners may have caused administrative confusion. Nonetheless the population gained the image of a man who came to the people in their hour of need and did his best to use his powers to help them. He actually saved lives, was the refrain of the popular account. It was indeed a most impressive experience to see General Azam speaking in English or Urdu to a group of villagers who understood hardly a word he said, but who surrounded him in great masses and listened affectionately.

Whenever possible, General Azam would speak in most optimistic, perhaps even extravagant, terms of the people and their glorious future. Our people are the best in the world; our country is the finest in the world. We are already making tremendous strides. We shall learn and develop and become the richest and the happiest. The intellectuals would frown and suspend judgment, but most others responded enthusiastically. Yet all this emphasis on progress was coupled with a strong traditionalist ingredient. General Azam spoke of Islam and the old values as something precious to be cherished. He derided the failures of secularism in the West. He appealed to the *ulama*, the parents or guardians, and the village elders. His symbols were frequently religious; his speeches abounded with appeals to Allah, quotations from the Holy Prophet, and warnings about the devious ways of Satan. Among the recent leaders of Pakistan Mohammad Azam Khan was almost alone in gaining the confidence of the traditionalist elements. In two years the Pathan soldier became the most popular governor East Pakistan had ever had.

General Azam's popularity, as his performance, was a personal one. His constant pressure upon the Civil Service to emulate his own example became counterproductive. The bureaucracy sabotaged his efforts at every turn and even circulated derogatory rumors about him in the President's Secretariat. More important, General Azam's constant harangues about the better future, like those of the Muslim League leaders two decades before, contributed substantially to a very rapid inflation of the level of expectations in the province. Even in areas scarcely touched by the international demonstration effect, expectations far outstripped attainment. Predictably, the ensuing frustration inspired a search for scapegoats. General Azam's personal popularity protected him, but not the more aloof President and his Cabinet.

In fact, by 1962 there was ample evidence that while the campaign of intimidation had neutralized many of the former political leaders of the country, the popularity of the new regime was receding. A member of the presidential Cabinet (Z. A. Bhutto) was the target of an incident at the University of the Punjab, while violence erupted at several colleges. Most dramatic, however, were the developments in the East Wing. In October 1958 and again in January 1960 President Ayub

195

Khan had been welcomed by cheering crowds in Dacca. Triumphantly he had moved through the province. Now, two years later, there was sullen silence as he drove past New Market, and his visit to Rajshahi had to be canceled. Only General Azam Khan's popularity remained on the ascendance, and he resigned in May.

The Basic Democracies

On October 27, 1959, the first anniversary of the Revolution, a system of local councils was introduced. Through them, explained the President, "every village and every inhabitant in every village in our country would become an equal partner with the Administration in conducting the affairs of the state."[8] Through this system Mohammad Ayub Khan hoped to generate a new group of leaders capable of mobilizing mass support, but also amenable to government persuasion. "If this machinery even now does not function effectively— that is, if this type of democracy does not succeed," he declared, "then God help us."[9]

In view of the major importance assigned to these institutions both in Pakistan and abroad, they deserve a more detailed description.[10] The system of Basic Democracies is a five-tier arrangement of councils. At the lowest rung and at the heart of the pattern are the Union Councils.[11] These are local boards composed primarily of representatives popularly called Basic Democrats (BD's) who have been elected through direct

[8] Mohammad Ayub Khan, Speeches and Statements, II, 35.
[9] Ibid.
[10] See "The Basic Democracies Order, 1959," The Gazette of Pakistan (Karachi: Government of Pakistan Press, 1959), pp. 1759-1809.
[11] In the cities and towns their equivalents are called Town or Union Committees.

adult suffrage. The ratio was approximately one representative per one thousand population. The number of elected members organized into one council was left to the discretion of the (Divisional) Commissioners but on the average amounted to ten. In addition to these, the Government, through the Sub-Divisional Officer and Deputy (District) Commissioner was authorized to appoint nominated members, but their number was not to exceed one-half of the elected representatives. The functions of the Union Councils cover a variety of subjects. Many are related to economic development on the local level. With the previous sanction of the (Divisional) Commissioner they can levy taxes and impose rates, tolls, and fees (Article 60). They are also authorized to promote "agricultural, industrial and community development and to adopt measures for increased food production" (Items 31 and 32, Third Schedule). Another group of functions delegated to the Union Councils deals with the administrative and welfare functions of local government. Lighting of public ways, public streets, and public places is an example (Item 3). So is the regulation of the disposal of carcasses of dead animals (Item 12). So also is the organization of the celebration of public festivals (Items 26 and 27). Finally they possess a power of potentially highest significance. It was anticipated that from time to time the Union Councils jointly would provide an electoral college for superior organizations and positions.[12]

The second tier consists of the *Thana* or *Tehsil* Councils.[13] Their jurisdiction extends over an area of about

[12] Statement by Foreign Minister Manzur Qadir (Dacca, *Morning News*, November 21, 1959, p. 1).

[13] They are fundamentally the same bodies except that for historical

ten Union Councils. They too are composed of elected and appointed members. Chairmen of Union Councils within the *Thana* (*Tehsil*) make up the first category. The government may (and does) add by appointment members not exceeding the number of "representatives." The Chairman of the *Thana* (*Tehsil*) Council is by definition the Sub-Divisional Officer, and in his absence the Circle Officer—an *ex officio* member of the Council—presides. The powers of these councils are left rather vague.[14] It appears that they are primarily coordinating bodies and a communications link through which public policy is channeled to the Union Councils and hopefully to the people.

More important is the next tier—the District Councils. The districts, which were the core areas of colonial administration, continue to play a predominant role. Civil servants holding posts specified by the (Divisional) Commissioner are "official" members of the District Council. They are augmented by an equal number of appointed "unofficial" members. At least one-half of this second category, however, must be selected from the chairmen of Union Councils of Town and Union Committees. The chairman of the District Council is by definition the Deputy (District) Commissioner. The Basic Democracies Order, 1959 divides the powers of the District Councils into "compulsory" and "optional" functions. Compulsory functions include among others the "provision and maintenance" of primary schools, libraries, hospitals, public roads, and playgrounds, as

reasons they are called "thana" councils in East Pakistan while in West Pakistan they are called "tehsil" councils.

[14] Unlike those of the Union and District Councils, the powers of the *Thana* (*Tehsil*) Councils are not specified in a separate schedule.

well as "protection of foodstuffs," "regulation of traffic," and the "adoption of measures for increased agricultural production." Under optional functions the District Councils enjoy wide jurisdiction over education, culture, social welfare, economic welfare, public health, and public works.

The Divisional Councils—the fourth tier—are coordinating and advisory bodies. The formula for membership is similar to the District Councils, including official members and appointed non-official members, at least half of which must be selected from the chairman of the Union Councils or Town and Union committees. The chairman, by definition, is the (Divisional) Commissioner.

The order establishing Basic Democracies also specified a Provincial Development Advisory Council for each Wing. Its composition followed the pattern of the Divisional Council except that only one-third of the appointed members had to be selected from Union Council chairmen. The Council's powers were purely advisory and limited to "development." Interestingly, the first announcement about the detailed plans for Basic Democracies after the Governors' Conference at Nathiagali (June 13, 1959) did not indicate the establishment of this body.[15] It was only after the next Governors' Conference at Karachi (July 1, 1959) that provisions for these Provincial Councils were revealed. Evidently they were established almost as an afterthought as temporary substitute provincial legislatures in order to appease parochial sentiment. They never did have any power, not even in the area of economic development. Later these councils were the first to go.

[15] Dacca, *Morning News*, June 14, 1959, p. 1.

Arrangements for the election of Basic Democrats proceeded rapidly after the promulgation of the ordinance. The Sub-Divisional Officers, Deputy (District) Commissioners and (Divisional) Commissioners were in effect placed in charge. The Commissioner was authorized to delimit the constituencies, the Deputy Commissioner to dispose of disputed petitions and the Sub-Divisional Officer to adjust and rearrange the electoral rolls.[16] Broadly based suffrage was assured by the use of the prerevolutionary Electoral Rolls Act, 1957 which provided for universal adult suffrage. Nomination procedures were simple. The only requirements were two eligible voters, one willing to nominate, the other to second. Qualifications for holding office, however, were more restrictive. There were significant disqualifications under the Elective Bodies (Disqualification) Ordinance, 1959 either through court action or through voluntary retirement inspired by an EBDO notice. In addition, some 9,215 candidates including 30 per cent of the contestants in Karachi were rejected by official scrutiny.[17]

Elections were scheduled to run during the end of December 1959 and early January 1960. On December 1, 1959, Martial Law Regulation No. 55 was amended to permit meetings in connection with the elections,[18] and the President himself undertook a "whistle-stop"

[16] "Basic Democracies (Conduct of Election) Rules, 1959," *A Handbook of Basic Democracies*, Part I (Dacca: East Pakistan Government Press, 1960), pp. 55, 56, 72.

[17] Government of Pakistan, Ministry of National Reconstruction and Information, *Scope and Functions of Basic Democracies and Their Contribution to Development* (Karachi: Government of Pakistan Press, 1960), Appendix.

[18] Discussions of national political or economic issues were still prohibited.

tour in both Wings. A certain reluctance or inertia was exhibited by the population, however. About 25 per cent of the seats were uncontested, and there were some seats for which either no nominee could be found or none remained after withdrawals and official "scrutiny."[19] Voting turnout was uneven (35 per cent in Karachi, 52 per cent in East Pakistan), but according to official estimates it averaged an imposing 60 per cent of the eligible voters.[20]

The candidates who were successful had this in common. They were mostly literate. More than 84 per cent of all Basic Democrats and 98 per cent of those from the East Wing claimed ability to read and write.[21] They were mostly agriculturally employed—some 50,000 of them. Their number included at a conservative estimate 400 large landlords in West Pakistan. Basic Democrats are relatively well-to-do. In the East Wing where the per capita income is not much over Rs 200, their average income is close to Rs 4,000.[22] Finally most Basic Democrats have had little political experience. Only 7 per cent of those in East Pakistan and 12.5 per cent of those in West Pakistan had previous party affiliation.[23] A

[19] Dacca, *Morning News*, December 6, 1959, p. 1; December 8, 1959, pp. 1, 6; December 29, 1959, p. 1; December 31, 1959, p. 1; January 11, 1960, p. 1; March 2, 1960, p. 1.

[20] *Ibid.*, January 11, 1960, p. 1. If this estimate is correct, it represents an impressive achievement. By comparison, in India's third general election 54 per cent of the eligible voters cast valid ballots (Calcutta, *The Statesman*, March 9, 1962, p. 6).

[21] *Annual Report on Basic Democracies*, October 27, 1959, to October 27, 1960 (Karachi: Bureau of National Reconstruction, n.d.), p. 11.

[22] Government of East Pakistan, *Basic Democracy in East Pakistan* (Dacca: Bureau of National Reconstruction, 1962), p. 41.

[23] Government of East Pakistan, *Comprehensive Report on Basic Democracies in East Pakistan* (Dacca: Government of East Pakistan

higher proportion (roughly 30 per cent), however, participated in previous local government such as the Union Boards of East Pakistan.

The first function of the Basic Democracies was to legitimize the martial law government. On January 13, 1960, the votes scarcely having been counted, the Presidential (Election and Constitution) Order, 1960 was promulgated. It called for a referendum by the Basic Democrats "to make known their confidence in [the President]" and to authorize him to formulate a constitution. To assure continuity an affirmative majority also entitled him to serve as President for the first term under the new constitution.[24] On February 14, 1960, the Basic Democrats were polled. Ballots were so printed as to permit only a yes vote. In addition, each was numbered and registered against a specific voter so that the government could identify those who spoiled their ballots. The results: 75,282 out of a total of 78,720 votes cast were affirmative.[25] Three days after the "election," to the accompaniment of a thirty-one gun salute, General Mohammad Ayub Khan was sworn in as President of Pakistan.

The main function of the system of Basic Democracies, however, was to win long-range popular commitment through popular participation. Gradually the five-tier structure was established. Some chairmen and secretaries of Union Councils were given special training

---

Press, 1960), p. 3 and Government of West Pakistan, *West Pakistan Basic Democracies Election Report, 1959-1960* (Lahore: West Pakistan Government Press, 1960), Annex.

[24] "Presidential (Election and Constitution) Order, 1960," *The Gazette of Pakistan*, January 13, 1960.

[25] Dacca, *Morning News*, February 16, 1960, p. 1.

lasting fifteen days in East Pakistan and three months in the West Wing.[26] The impact must not have been spectacular, as a 1962 report found that more than half of the members in the East Wing remained unacquainted with the functions of their council.[27] Meetings were held in some areas regularly, in others (especially in West Pakistan) rather sporadically. Local disputes were "settled"; routine tasks delegated by the officials were performed. New taxes were levied and some were collected.[28] Some irrigation schemes were undertaken and some roads were built by Union Councils.

As the implementation of the system proceeded, the limitations upon popular participation became increasingly apparent. There are, first of all, the severe restrictions placed upon the numerical share of the elected elements in the various councils. In the Union Councils appointed members could and usually did account for one-third of the total membership. With each higher tier, however, their share increased: from one-half in the *Thana* (*Tehsil*) Councils through three-quarters of the District and Divisional Councils to five-sixths of the Provincial Development Advisory Council. The representative ingredient is further weakened by the fact that it is the government, not any popular constituency, that decides just which of the elected councilors do, in fact, have the opportunity to "represent" on the district, divisional, and, till June 1962, provincial level. It should be kept in mind that there are 8,355 Union Council

[26] *Annual Report on Basic Democracies*, p. 2.

[27] *Basic Democracy in East Pakistan*, p. 120.

[28] In East Pakistan 61 per cent of the families paid less than Rs 3 annually in an "average" Union Council. (*Ibid.*, pp. 70-71. See also A. T. Rafiqur Rahman, *Basic Democracies at Grass Roots* [Comilla: Pakistan Academy for Village Development, 1962], p. 45.)

chairmen[29] from which to choose appointees for 76 District and Agency Councils, 15 Divisional Councils and two Provincial Councils. This is a better than one-out-of-ten choice. Thus it is highly unrealistic to assume that the power base of the "representative" member in the District or Divisional Council is his own constituency rather than the appointing authority—and it would be naïve to assume that these "representatives" of the people do not realize this.

Restrictions placed upon the power of these bodies, of course, further impair popular participation. There is no separation of power between the government's administrative agents and the Councils. The Councils, in fact, do not have any independent authority. As far as their share in executive authority is concerned, even in theory there is very little: some allocation of funds for development projects on the district level and a limited jurisdiction over local disputes. As a matter of practice, these grants of authority mean very little, and the "Controlling Authority" is in full command. In Union Councils where the "representative" members hold a majority, the Sub-Divisional Officer retains remarkable powers.[30] He may: "(a) quash the proceedings; (b) suspend the execution of any resolution passed or order made by the local council; (c) prohibit the doing of anything proposed to be done; and (d) require the local council to take such action as may be specified" (Article 74). The question hardly arises above this level. In fact, we find a practical voting situation in which at least one-half of the membership

[29] Including chairmen of Town Committees, Union Committees, Municipal Committees, and Cantonment Boards.

[30] In West Pakistan the Controlling Authority is the Deputy (District) Commissioner.

are administrative subordinates of the chairman and the rest are appointed on the recommendation of the chairman. When the Council advises the Controlling Authority (chairman), in theory and in practice the latter can take this or leave it; but when the chairman advises the Council, at least in practice the latter invariably takes it.

These restrictions built into the system, moreover, are aggravated by the attitude of the bureaucracy. One hears frequent and laudatory remarks by the upper echelons; the intermediate and lower level officials have not yet been caught up in the enthusiasm. To most of them the Basic Democrats are "inefficient and irresponsible"[31] and deserve to be treated accordingly. In the spring of 1962 the Sub-Divisional Officer in Dinajpur called in the Basic Democrats of his jurisdiction and in his office formally warned and threatened them. He did not even ask these "representatives" to sit down during his reprimand. "Complaints were often heard," reports Mushtaq Ahmad, "and they were also voiced from the platform of the Basic Democracies Conventions held in Dacca and Lahore that the officials were reluctant to change their methods and were not agreeable to take the Councillors into their confidence."[32] In an exercise of restraint, the East Pakistan report observes "that a number of departments have yet to establish a real relationship with the members and chairmen of Union Councils."[33]

Against the background of these limitations upon popular participation, it is perhaps not surprising that

[31] *Basic Democracy in East Pakistan*, p. 85.

[32] Mushtaq Ahmad, *Government and Politics in Pakistan* (Karachi: Pakistan Publishing House, 1963), p. 204.

[33] *Basic Democracy in East Pakistan*, p. 55.

the system of Basic Democracies has so far neither attracted appreciable popular commitment nor produced leaders capable of mobilizing the masses. The "intellectuals" remain aloof or are antagonistic. In a singular speech to Basic Democrats, Pakistan's Minister of National Reconstruction declared: "The entire intelligentsia is against you."[34] More important, the rural masses also remain skeptical. A report on the operations of the Basic Democracies in East Pakistan published by the Village Aid Academy in Comilla but supervised by the Director, Bureau of National Reconstruction, Government of East Pakistan, complains that even in the District Council the "non-official members do not feel that membership . . . enhances their status in public esteem."[35]

If the President was disappointed with the initial performance of the Basic Democracies, he showed no signs of it. On the contrary, he expressed his confidence in these institutions by expanding the ingredient of popular participation. Early in 1962 the decision was announced that no government appointments to the Union Councils would be made in the future. Thus they would become entirely elected bodies.[36] The President also expressed his confidence in these institutions by expanding their authority. On March 2, 1961, in a most dramatic intrusion into the jurisdiction of the *ulama* and other traditional leaders the Muslim Family Laws Ordinance was promulgated.[37] Under it the chairmen of

[34] Lahore, *Civil and Military Gazette*, March 12, 1962, p. 1.

[35] *Basic Democracy in East Pakistan*, p. 134. It is perhaps not surprising that the provincial director of the Bureau of National Reconstruction promptly restricted the circulation of this report.

[36] Dacca, *Pakistan Observer*, January 16, 1962, p. 1.

[37] *The Gazette of Pakistan*, Ordinance No. vɪɪɪ of 1961, March 2, 1961.

the Union Councils were granted wide powers in the regulation of polygamy, in the conciliation of marriage conflicts, and in the settlement of property after divorce. Later in the same year serious discussions were initiated to transfer control over primary education from the bureaucracy to the Union Councils.[38] Most important, the President expressed his confidence in the Basic Democracies by proceeding to build the next stage of institutional reconstruction, the framing of the Constitution of Pakistan.

[38] Government of East Pakistan, *Proceedings of the 7th Meeting of the Provincial Development Advisory Council*, November 6-11, 1961, pp. 5-6.

10

++

The Genesis of a Constitution

++

PRESIDENT AYUB KHAN was convinced that if he was to convert his personal hegemony into national and provincial institutions which would attract popular commitment, it was essential that he play a decisive role in the formulation of the new Constitution. His March 15, 1959, memorandum included this revealing passage: ". . . the situation is not irremediable if tackled with resolution and courage, and that has to be provided by the top leadership—ME. I feel it is my moral and spiritual duty to guide thinking so that we have a constitution that will cover our weaknesses, will not allow political instability to arise, [and] will take care of local and regional prejudices. . . ." Later, in his radio address introducing the Constitution, he referred to it as "my system."[1] The preamble of the document closes with the words: "NOW, THEREFORE, I, FIELD MARSHAL MOHAMMAD AYUB KHAN . . . do hereby enact this Constitution."[2] The country would be expected to recognize the preeminent role of the President. Yet the motivation here, so far as it can be ascertained, was not primarily personal vanity. More likely it was an effort to impress the population that the Presi-

[1] *The Constitution: The President Addresses the Nation* (Karachi: Inter Services Press, 1962), p. 11.

[2] Government of Pakistan, *The Constitution of the Republic of Pakistan* (Karachi: Government of Pakistan Press, 1962), p. 2.

dent and through him the armed forces were committed to the Constitution and would not permit trifling with it. "The people," explained the President at one point, "must be convinced that we are serious, otherwise any good we do would come to nothing."[3]

The President apparently was equally resolved to enlist as broad a support for the Constitution as possible.[4] Ostensibly at least, the masses would be invited to participate. Hence the referendum by Basic Democrats to authorize him to proceed. In addition, prominent citizens, political groups, and the bureaucracy would be "involved." Few would be given the opportunity to complain that they had not been consulted. Accordingly, on the day he was sworn in as President (February 17, 1960) he appointed a Constitution Commission. It was composed of eleven "constitutionalists," including two retired judges, a lawyer, and two prominent businessmen and was presided over by a retired Chief Justice of Pakistan, Mohammad Shahabuddin.[5] Thus commenced the first stage of constitution-making.

The Constitution Commission

Chief Justice Shahabuddin is a man of great integrity. He is also a highly experienced administrator and jurist. One pitfall he was determined to avoid. He was not going to be a rubber stamp. Thus, while conceding that

[3] Dacca, *Morning News*, October 31, 1958, p. 1.

[4] On August 4, 1959, at a special top-level meeting in Karachi the President for the first time spelled out his plans for the procedure by which the country would receive its new constitution.

[5] Other members: Azizuddin Ahmad, D. N. Barori, Abu Sayeed Chowdhury, Aftabuddin Ahmed, Obeidur Rahman Nizam from East Pakistan, and Mohammad Sharif, Tufailali A. Rahman, Arbab Ahmad Ali Jan, Sardar Habibullah Khan and Mian Naseer A. Shaikh from West Pakistan.

the task of giving a constitution rested with the President and that his own role was merely advisory, as a condition for his acceptance he insisted on a promise that along with the constitution the report of his commission would also be published. It should be added in all fairness that he received such a pledge from the President without delay or hesitation and that when the time came the pledge was in fact carried out.

The first meeting of the Commission was held in Lahore on March 19, 1960.[6] The terms of reference included two major categories. The Commission was instructed to identify the causes for the failure in 1958 and to consider future remedies. Secondly, it was given the task of presenting constitutional proposals for democratic institutions that would be "adaptable to changing circumstances," were founded on Islamic principles, and would contribute to national unity and stable government. The Commission was also advised to take into account "the genius of the people, the general standard of education and of political judgment in the country, the present sense of nationhood, and the prime need for sustained development." In June 1960 an additional term of reference was added, requesting the Commission's opinion on the timetable for implementation of its proposals.[7]

A few words about procedure may be helpful. Early in its deliberations the Commission decided to use as the basis of its judgment the views of opinion leaders. This they proposed to ascertain by widely circulating a questionnaire and by inviting through the press "any-

[6] Karachi, *Dawn*, March 20, 1960, p. 1.
[7] Government of Pakistan, *Report of the Constitution Commission* (Karachi: Government of Pakistan Press, 1961), p. 1.

one interested" to complete the forms or to request an interview with the Commission. In total, 20,892 forms were sent out. Some 6,269 completed questionnaires were returned, and 565 persons were interviewed at length. There was, of course, an "official delegation" expressing the views of the government, or, more specifically, those of the President. A wide range of political leaders of the deposed regime, including Chaudhri Mohammad Ali, ex-Prime Minister of Pakistan, also responded. In general, those interviewed were literate and most articulate. They were also mostly "modernists." The traditional hierarchies were rarely heard from. Consequently, an almost inescapable bias was built into the sample, with the westernized segment represented many times its actual proportion in the country. As the interviews proceeded, they attracted considerable attention and excitement, so much so that the government felt compelled to issue a warning that martial law would intervene if "playing politics" with the questionnaire continued.[8] When Chief Justice Shahabuddin protested, the President overruled the more aggressive members of his Cabinet[9] and the warnings were toned down. After tabulating the results, the Commission held a number of meetings during which the recommendations were agreed upon. Chief Justice Shahabuddin wrote out the draft in longhand, which after approval by the majority was printed. One member, Sardar Habibullah Khan, strongly dissented and his opinion was appended at the end of the document. The work of the Commission was completed on April 29, 1961.

The *Report* is a rather extensive document. It contains

[8] Dacca, *Morning News,* July 3, 1960, p. 1.
[9] Notably Lieutenant General Sheikh and Manzur Qadir.

ideological assertions, theoretical arguments, and a compilation of the opinions of those interviewed. It covers many aspects of Pakistani history and British legal tradition. It also offers an abundance of recommendations. To catalogue them all is not our purpose. Instead we shall concentrate upon five key categories of proposals. There are, first of all, the recommendations on the distribution of power on the national level, involving as they do the legitimization of the powers and the tenure of the President. Secondly, in a country where the small-scale social and economic units predominate, the relationship between the national and local levels of government is no less important. Thirdly, the recommendations concerning the electorate and the extent of suffrage become significant in case of any effort designed to enlist public support through public participation. Closely related is the fourth category: the legality and the role of political parties that have a direct bearing upon the fundamental problem of evolving a national leadership structure with a capacity to mobilize the masses. Finally, the amendment procedure is noteworthy, as it regulates the rate of modification of the Constitution.

Let us first turn to the distribution of power on the national level. It was clear from the beginning that the President would insist on the presidential form.[10] Interestingly, the Commission found its own sample to favor a similar course,[11] and after some discussion of the weaknesses of the parliamentary system the Commission

[10] On the day the Commission started its work, President Ayub Khan publicly stated that the presidential system was "essential" (Dacca, *Morning News*, March 20, 1960, p. 1).

[11] Of the opinions expressed, 21.3 per cent supported a parliamentary form, 47.4 per cent favored a presidential system, 29.3 per cent preferred a mixed system, while 2 per cent recommended a dictatorship.

broadly endorsed the presidential system. When we turn to the details, the matter becomes somewhat more involved. The President, of course, would be granted the security of a fixed term and the control of the executive branch. Ministers would be appointed by the President and be responsible only to him. To exercise some minimal control, the legislature (upper house) would be required to confirm such appointments. It was also recommended that the Ministers attend legislative sessions as frequently as possible. To prevent too much interference, however, the legislature would not be granted the right to summon ministers. If, moreover, any member of the legislature should accept a position in the Cabinet, he would first have to resign from the legislature.

The President would also be given legislative powers. The Commission recommended a veto power and, in the single instance of appropriations, even the item veto. In case of emergencies he would also enjoy the power of issuing ordinances with effect until the legislature could assemble. A restraint, however, was added here. The President would not have the power to suspend the Constitution except in the emergency of a war.

Undoubtedly, the executive proposed by the Commission was a powerful one. It was balanced by a legislature which would also enjoy enhanced power. What it gave up in control of the executive, the legislature in turn would have gained in independence. The traditional power of dissolving the legislature which the Viceroy had enjoyed and which hung over that body as a sword of Damocles was greatly weakened. To be sure, the President could still dissolve the legislature, but if he did so, he himself would have to stand for reelection. Hence the jeopardy was no longer one-sided. The legislature was to enjoy all the traditional powers including appropriations. To avoid frequent direct confrontations between the legislative and executive branches, a built-in restraint on the power was added. A second house was to be added composed of senior and successful members of society partially selected by an electoral college (lower house plus provincial legislatures) and partially appointed by the President.

The third branch of government was to be a powerful and independent judiciary. Their appointments were to be for life and they were to be guaranteed substantial remuneration. They would enjoy the power of judicial review over acts of the legislature. By including a bill of rights in the constitution the courts could also restrain the executive. In short, the relationship between the branches was, in general, to follow the American pattern.

The second group of recommendations related to the question of unitary versus federal government. The Commission views here were split, and Sardar Habibullah Khan continued his support for a unitary government to the end. Actually even among the other members there appears to have been much sympathy for the unitary form, and only the concern for Bengali regionalism persuaded them to favor a federal system. The American pattern, however, was considered too weak and the Canadian and Indian examples were preferred. Political powers were to be divided according to three lists (federal, concurrent, provincial), but in an emergency the national legislature would be authorized to legislate in all matters. Government on the provincial level would be a facsimile of the national government except that the provincial legislature would be unicameral. One more relevant recommendation must be noted. The provincial governor was to be appointed by the President rather than elected by the province. The total effect of these recommendations was that the proposed government was federal more in name than in substance.

The third category of recommendations dealt with the electorate. It was here that the influence of the modernized segment of society on the Commission was most glaring. On this issue, moreover, the Commission defied the President. Even after the not too veiled hint in June 1960, when the terms of reference were amended and the existence of the Basic Democracies was specifically pointed out, the Commission continued to reject their use as an electoral college. Instead, it rigorously supported direct suffrage limited to literates and property owners. It was convinced, apparently, that those disenfranchised—and most people in the villages would be disenfranchised—would not resent this. During the previous elections, the Commission suggested rather cavalierly, many voluntarily stayed away from the polls.[12] It argued further that the alternatives would be hazardous. Universal direct suffrage was unthinkable at the existing level of literacy and communication. The indirect method was equally unsuitable. The voter (presumably the educated voter), the Commission contended, would not be satisfied "with the right of select-

[12] As contrary evidence, in the elections of Basic Democrats in 1960 conducted on the basis of universal suffrage some 60 per cent of the eligible voters exercised their privilege. This is about the average of American presidential elections and higher than the average in local elections.

ing persons who are to select the representatives instead of himself making the selection."[13]

On the issue of political parties, the *Report* records the apprehensions of the "official delegation" about any national organization which might emerge in competition to the Government. People should not be prevented from associating with each other. There should be no objection against informal groups of "like-minded" persons. However, political parties that demand the loyalty of their members, the delegation argued, must be prohibited. The Commission was not convinced. It concluded that parties are a "necessity" and recommended that a favorable environment for their emergence should be encouraged. "The legislators hereafter will not be like their predecessors," assured the Constitution Commission in a burst of optimism, "coming into the political field soley [sic] to exploit their positions to their personal advantage.[14]

The final proposal to be mentioned here is the amendment process. The Commission recommended a two-thirds vote in the legislature plus presidential assent or a three-fourths vote without it. The provinces, theoretically partners in government, were to have no vote at all in the proceedings.

Presidential Committees

On May 1, 1961, the Constitution Commission formally presented its report to the President. During the interview Chief Justice Shahabuddin broadly hinted that he was prepared to be of further assistance. President Ayub Khan was friendly but did not avail himself

[13] Government of Pakistan, *Report of the Constitution Commission*, p. 68.
[14] *Ibid.*, p. 80.

of the implied offer. Perhaps this reveals his opinion of the work. It is also possible that in line with his original intentions he planned to avoid overlap among the advisory bodies on the Constitution. In any case, the President initiated the second stage of constitution-making when he appointed two special committees and directed them to examine the *Report* in great detail and to make their recommendations to the Governors' Conference. One committee, chaired by Cabinet Secretary N. A. Faruqui, reflected the vested interests of the bureaucracy.[15] The other, over which Foreign Minister Manzur Qadir presided and which was composed of seven cabinet ministers,[16] presumably claimed special expertise or more likely the special confidence of the President. Neither committee made any attempt to consult the population. The only non-member whose opinion was asked and who at times volunteered his views was President Ayub Khan. The emphasis clearly shifted from "what the people want" to "what is best for the people." A series of extended sessions marked the deliberations. Twice they were interrupted, first by the visit of President Ayub Khan to Washington and second by the heart attack of Finance Minister Mohammad Shoaib. There was general agreement on all issues in the Administrators' Committee. Not so in the Cabinet Committee. On several questions, including such critical ones as presidential versus parliamentary or federal versus unitary forms of government, the jurisdiction of

[15] The Chief Secretary of East Pakistan, Kazi Anwarul Haque, and the Additional Chief Secretary of West Pakistan, Muzzafar Ahmed, were the other members.

[16] In addition to its chairman, the Committee also included: Mohammad Ibrahim, Mohammad Shoaib, Abul Kasem Khan, Zulfikar Bhutto, Akhter Hussain, and Habibur Rahman.

the courts, political parties, the electorate and fundamental rights, there was spirited debate and vigorous dissent. The position taken by three members, Manzur Qadir, Zulfikar Bhutto and Mohammad Shoaib, ran consistently parallel with the President's views. In most instances they were opposed resolutely though less vocally by Mohammad Ibrahim, the Law Minister and a Bengali. Conflict became so sharp and irreconcilable that the latter refused to attend further meetings, left the capital, and withdrew to his home in Dacca.[17] Mr. Ibrahim was generally supported by his Bengali colleagues Habibur Rahman and A. K. Khan. Several 4:3 votes indicate a genuine difference of views. Yet, significantly, on only one major issue—the justiciability of fundamental rights—did the majority hold to a position which was in direct conflict with the views of President Ayub Khan.

While the Committees deliberated, the government kept the population informed of the progress and the expected target date. In late September the President launched a most singular trial balloon. In an address he informed the Karachi Bar Association that the broad features of the Constitution would be published in November and the public would be asked to comment on it. Only after such a public debate would the final

[17] Although the Law Minister no longer attended to his duties he nevertheless refused to resign his office. The President, anxious to avoid publicly demonstrating a severe split among his advisers, made several attempts to conciliate him. The situation remained unsettled until April 15, 1962, when, according to the official announcement, Mohammad Ibrahim was "allowed to relinquish his ministership." Health problems were given as the reason, whereupon the former Law Minister conspicuously attended public meetings to demonstrate his vigor.

draft be promulgated, in the spring of 1962.[18] It makes interesting speculation just why such an announcement was made, inasmuch as it went contrary to the President's previous intentions of presenting the finished document as a take-it-or-leave-it proposition. There was no framework prepared for such a public discussion, as in the case of the questionnaires of the Constitution Commission. Above all, the work was too far advanced to introduce the new dimension of public opinion.

The Committees concluded their work in October. The results were presented in the form of comments on the Constitution Commission's recommendations. The document is concise and most revealing. There was general consensus that the presidential system was preferable.[19] The Committees also agreed with the Constitution Commission on the power of the Courts. They all favored judicial review and the justiciability of civil rights. There were sharp differences, however, on the legislative branch. First, the Cabinet Committee recommended that for the sake of political stability and economic development the legislature should not be permitted to cut the budget below a certain minimum, and this minimum should be the level of appropriation in the current year. Second, the legislature should be restrained from introducing bills regarding the armed forces or preventive detention without the consent of the President. One disagreement between the two Committees may be mentioned here marginally. The Cabinet Committee proposed a unicameral system on the

[18] Dacca, *Morning News*, September 26, 1961, p. 1.

[19] There was only one dissent. Presumably Law Minister Ibrahim supported the parliamentary form.

219

national level, while the Administrators' Committee supported the Constitution Commission's recommendation for a senate.

On the issue of federalism there was little disagreement in the recommendations. The Administrators' Committee on the whole accepted the pattern of the Constitution Commission. The majority of the Cabinet group wanted to strengthen the national government further by eliminating any exclusive jurisdiction of the provincial government. There would be only two lists: one federal and the other concurrent. Behind the scenes, however, there was strong conflict over this issue. *Within* the Cabinet Committee a powerful minority pressed in the opposite direction. They demanded a short federal list and a statement that all other areas be under the exclusive jurisdiction of the provinces.

The issue of franchise united the Committees against the Commission. They supported indirect elections with the elected Basic Democrats forming an electoral college. Political parties remained a rather thorny question, as both groups were aware of the President's opposition to them. The majority of the Cabinet Committee suggested that during the first election parties should continue to remain prohibited, but that later a new determination could be made. The Administrators, however, were more emphatic. They contended that, for several reasons—including protection against parochialism, assistance in presidential elections, and a smoother relationship between the executive and legislative branches—political parties should not only be permitted, but also encouraged. On the final issue of constitutional amendments the committees were again united. They accepted in general the Commission's suggestion of two-thirds and three-fourths formulas. Yet they sought to fortify the President's position even further by authorizing him to refer the question to the electoral college (Basic Democrats) in case of an adverse three-fourths vote.

The Final Draft

The last stage in the genesis of the Constitution was reached when the Governors' Conference opened on October 23, 1961. If there had ever been an intention to publish the outlines of the document, this was now formally reversed. Instead, the complete Constitution was promised for March 1962.[20] The President, of course, was in the advantageous position of having before him a wide range of recommendations from which he could choose at will, and finding his own views advocated by his articulate and persuasive Foreign Minister, Chairman of the Cabinet Committee. He could therefore remain aloof from the debate and intervene only at some crucial points.

The Conference demonstrated clearly that he was not surrounded by yes-men. By all indications it was a rather stormy affair with personal recriminations given a free rein. At the focal point of the discussion, it seems, was not so much the specific institutional arrangement, although the proposed relationship between the central and provincial governments loomed large, but the post-Constitutional reconstruction of political life, with such key questions as suffrage and political parties. The President, who tended to support the more liberal element on the institutional structure, appears to have been fully committed to his system of Basic Democrats serving as

[20] Dacca, *Morning News*, October 25, 1961, p. 1.

an electoral college, and continued to remain suspicious of political parties. Although some items remained unsettled, at the end of the Conference a drafting committee composed of Manzur Qadir and the Law Secretary Abdul Hamid was appointed. Three months later at the next Governors' Conference at Dacca the final problems were resolved by the President. Editing and printing required another eight weeks. Then on March 1, 1962, in a radio address, the President announced the details.

If it is necessary to categorize the document which emerged from the Dacca Conference, it probably can be described as embodying the presidential system. The President is assured a fixed term of five years. As Chief Executive he is Supreme Commander of the Defense Services. He appoints and removes ministers. He grants "pardons, reprieves and respites." He also enjoys the privilege of addressing the legislature and has the power of veto. In this his powers are similar to the American pattern.

The Chief Executive of Pakistan, however, is granted some very significant additional powers which are more in line with a parliamentary system. To begin with, he is authorized to appoint a number of parliamentary secretaries who shall "perform such functions . . . as the President may direct." He also controls the term of legislative sessions. Unlike the Congress of the United States the National Assembly, which incidentally is unicameral, does not meet at regular intervals. The Speaker may convene it at the written request of one-third of the total membership. Routinely it is dependent upon the President's call. The only limitation on this power is the stipulation that there must be at least two sessions each year. Moreover, as long as this condition is met the President may prorogue the Assembly at any time, even after a single day's or single hour's session. Thirdly, the President may dissolve the Assembly. This he may do at any time for any reason with the following two exceptions. He may not dissolve the National Assembly if its unexpired term is less than 120 days. Nor can he dissolve the Assembly after a formal notice of impeachment or removal from office due to incapacity. There is a further stipulation, namely that in a case of dissolution the President himself would have to stand for reelection within 120 days.

The President also has the power to issue ordinances while the Assembly is not in session which "have the same force of law as an Act of the Central Legislature" for a period of six months. Such ordinances will have to be placed before the National Assembly for approval "as soon as is practicable." In case of a grave emergency, which by definition exists not only in case of war or threat of war but also when internal disturbances cannot be controlled by the provincial government, the President may issue ordinances and also be free from a reversal by the National Assembly.

The President's power was further fortified. First, there are two specific limitations on the Assembly. It cannot accept the introduction of any bill relating to preventive detention, thus leaving the definition of subversion entirely to the discretion of the President. In fact, there is no constitutional bar to the arrest of any citizen, even a legislator, and if the President or Governor so directs the citizen can be held without being informed of the charge. Equally restraining is the rather complex budgetary procedure. The Annual Budget Statement submitted by the President distinguishes between expenditure charged upon the Central Consolidated Fund and other expenditure. The former may be discussed by, "but shall not be submitted to the vote of, the National Assembly." In the latter category most expenditure is similarly beyond legislative changes unless the President himself consents. The only items upon which the National Assembly can act are those clearly marked as "new expenditure." Just how serious this limitation is appears from the following fact. Total "new expenditure" in the Central Government's Budget for 1962-1963 amounted to slightly more than one per cent of the demands for grants and appropriations.[21]

Another method limiting the power of the legislature is the right of the President to appeal directly to the electoral college. If a law is vetoed by the chief executive and the legislature musters a two-thirds majority, this does not override the veto but merely creates a "difference of opinion." The President then may submit the issue to the Basic Democrats in a form which is suitable for a yes or no answer. The same process applies to amendments to the constitution, except that the required vote in the face of a presidential veto is three-fourths.

If the legislature cannot effectively challenge the President, neither can the courts. The Constitution of 1962, unlike its predecessor, does not contain a Bill of Rights. Some civil rights are listed under "principles of law-making," but for each there are special clauses authorizing departure from them under various circumstances, ranging from the interest of the security of

[21] Rs 17.6 crores out of Rs 1430 crores (Government of Pakistan, *Budget of the Central Government for 1962-63* [Karachi: Government of Pakistan Press, 1962]).

Pakistan to the interest of proper discharge of public functions. Under "Freedom of Expression," for example, no less than eight legitimate departures are authorized. Moreover, the courts are specifically denied the power to question the validity of a law on the ground that it "disregards, violates or is otherwise not in accordance with the Principles of Law-making." A similar provision prohibits review of any law as to its constitutionality. These restrictions appear to have the effect of strengthening the legislature, and it was officially explained that "the scheme adopted in the Constitution brings our position on the same lines as the position existing in England."[22] Actually, with the legislature meeting only for a short period each year—less than six weeks in 1962—and the President holding the power to issue ordinances, the courts posed a potential threat to the executive. This threat was removed by the Constitution.

The President was fortified even against impeachment. A minimum of one-third of the National Assembly must give written notice that they intend to initiate procedure to remove the President for willfully violating the Constitution or for gross misconduct. The resolution itself cannot be moved for fourteen days after this declaration. Then, after debate in the National Assembly, if three-fourths of the members held him guilty, the President would then be removed. If, however, the motion should fail, all those who initiated the proceedings would forfeit their seats in the Assembly.

There remains only one threat to the President. His candidacy for a second five-year term needs no legislature approval, but if he seeks a third term his candidature requires endorsement through secret ballot of a

[22] *The Constitution: The President Addresses the Nation*, p. 9.

225

joint session of the National Assembly and the provincial legislatures. This restraint, however, is somewhat remote as it can be applied only after a record of almost ten years of presidency. In the meantime a lot of water may flow down the Indus and the Meghna.

In summary then, it should be observed that the presidential system adopted by the Constitution is fundamentally different from that recommended by the Constitution Commission. The latter, following the American pattern, had proposed a strong executive to be sure, but also a strong legislature and a strong judiciary. It is closer to the English model to accept the supremacy of one branch over another. The difference is that in Great Britain Parliament is supreme; in Pakistan, for all practical purposes, it is the President.

Having settled the distribution of power within the central government, the document approved in Dacca proceeds to define the framework of federalism. It establishes two provincial governments that, like American states, have residual powers. Still, here again there is a difference. In Pakistan the central government *shares* in the residual powers. The latter may in fact legislate on any issue which involves the national interest, a concept which is broad and vague to say the least. Moreover when the central government legislates (even in the area of the residual powers) all contrary provincial laws become void.

Reflecting the arrangement on the national level the provincial governments are divided into three branches. The Governor (executive), of course, controls the predominant share of power. His opposition in practice makes any effort by the legislature futile. If such conflict should actually arise, the procedure prescribed would

226

follow this pattern: In the first round the bill is passed, and the Governor vetoes it. Then if the legislature again passes it, this time by a two-thirds vote, the Governor may veto it again. The third round would start with another passage by a two-thirds margin. At this point the Governor may request the President to refer the matter to the National Assembly. Only if the latter also approves the bill could it then become law.

The power of the Governor is especially noteworthy as he, unlike the President, is not an elected official. He is not responsible to any constituency or elected body. The Courts cannot remove him. His sole commitment is to the President who appoints him. This commitment, however, is total. The Governor has to implement presidential directives. His ministers and parliamentary secretaries require prior presidential approval.

Proceeding to the process of selection of representative officials, we find not unexpectedly that the President and legislators are elected by the electoral college of Basic Democrats. In his radio speech introducing the Constitution the President acknowledged the probability of resentment by intellectuals and promised future adjustments.[23] Political parties remained banned, but the National Assembly was authorized to legalize them. In their absence the government was to assume the responsibility to provide exposure for all candidates by sponsoring public meetings and discussions.

The specific political arrangements are materially of greatest importance. Yet beyond these details, in terms of the overall program of political development, one additional, most striking feature must be noted. For Table 10, I compiled the recommendations of the Con-

[23] *Ibid.*, p. 11.

Table 10

Comparison of the Constitutional Recommendations
of Various Advisory Groups with the
Views of the President

	Constitutional Commission	Cabinet Committee	Administrators' Committee	President Ayub Khan	Constitution
A. Parliamentary System					
Presidential System	X	X	X	X	X
1. (a) Presidential veto	X				
(b) Veto plus referendum		X	X	X	X
2. (a) Unicameral legislature		X		X	X
(b) Bicameral legislature	X		X		
3. (a) Judicial review	X	X	X		
(b) No judicial review				X	X
4. (a) Civil rights justiciable	X	X	X		
(b) Civil rights not justiciable				X	X
B. Unitary System					
Federal System	X	X	X	X	X
(a) Only federal and concurrent lists		X			X
(b) Also exclusive provincial powers	X			X	*
C. Universal-indirect		X		X	X
Limited-direct	X		X		
D. Political Parties	X		X		
No Political Parties		X		X	X
E. Amendment					
(a) 2/3 and 3/4	X				
(b) 2/3, 3/4, and referendum		X	X	X	X

* No clear record available.

stitution Committee, the Administrative Committee,
and the Cabinet Committee and compared them in the
Table with the views of the President as indicated by

his memoranda of October 4, 1954, and March 15, 1959, as well as his other public pronouncements. The conclusion is abundantly clear. In spite of the elaborate machinery involved in the formulation of the Constitution, in spite of the many hours of deliberations, and in spite of the wide variety of recommendations, the final version agrees in every major detail with the political pattern desired by the President. Mohammad Ayub Khan legitimized his order; Pakistan now had a new Constitution.

11

✦✦

A Guided Democracy in Action:
Building Influence

✦✦

PRESIDENT AYUB KHAN's radio address announcing the new Constitution was the signal for a publicity campaign whose dimensions were almost unprecedented in South Asia. Newspapers reported the event in banner headlines. Within a few days they proceeded to publish the entire document accompanied by extensive reports of favorable comment by prominent citizens and "the man in the street."[1] Editorials hailed the event. "The important thing for all patriotic people to realize," declared *Dawn*, "is that it is a sincere fulfillment of the pledge given by the architect of the Revolution when he took power in October, 1958."[2] The *Pakistan Times* was even more unrestrained. "This is an occasion of rejoicing and thanksgiving," its editor concluded.[3] The Bureau of National Reconstruction flooded the streets with handy sets of the presidential address plus an outline of the new Constitution in Urdu, Bengali, or English. Newsstands and bookstores, which were given almost inexhaustible supplies, prominently featured the complete document. In the meantime, the Cabinet bestowed upon Field Marshal Mohammad Ayub Khan

[1] In its issues of March 4-7, 1962, *Dawn* devoted 1,950 column lines, and the *Pakistan Times* 1,170 column lines to such reports.

[2] Karachi, *Dawn*, March 2, 1962, p. 1.

[3] Lahore, *Pakistan Times*, March 5, 1962, p. 4.

the highest order of the land, *Nishan-i-Pakistan*.[4] Union Councils, District Councils, and a variety of other bodies called special meetings to pass unanimously resolutions congratulating the President on his achievement. Delegations vied for the honor of presenting "felicitations" personally; others sought the favor of the President's visit to their meetings. At one such occasion the adulation of the speakers was so gross and flowed with such abundance that the President exclaimed: "I seek *touba*—forgiveness—from Almighty God. Such praises are enough to upset one's mental equilibrium."[5] No less zealous were the activities of some cabinet members. The Home Minister, Zakir Husain, and the Governor of West Pakistan, Malik Amir Mohammad Khan, hailed the brilliance of the document and the wisdom of its author. Foreign Minister Manzur Qadir held almost daily sessions to explain the Constitution to the press, to Basic Democrats, and to the bureaucracy.[6]

Approval, however, was not universal. The bar associations of Karachi and Lahore had little difficulty restraining their enthusiasm. Chief Justice Shahabuddin's rather less than glowing evaluation was promptly suppressed.[7] In Dacca the Nawab, Major Askari, was sympathetic. Given existing conditions, he explained, it was the best that could be achieved. In general in East Pakistan, however, there was sullen silence. The Governor

---

[4] Lahore, *Pakistan Times*, March 23, 1962, p. 1.

[5] *Ibid.*, March 28, 1962, p. 1.

[6] *Ibid.*, March 6, 1962, p. 1; March 7, 1962, p. 1; March 8, 1962, p. 1; March 13, 1962, p. 1; March 15, 1962, p. 1; March 16, 1962, p. 1; March 26, 1962, p. 1; March 21, 1962, p. 1.

[7] In his radio address the President paid tribute to Chief Justice Shahabuddin's contributions, whereupon the latter was deluged with complaints from his colleagues concerning his assumed support for the Constitution.

231

was not available for comment. The professors at the University, in order to avoid being interviewed, refused to answer their phones. After some pursuit the head of the Geography Department submitted to giving a favorable statement. Later his colleague in the Political Science Department joined him. The more senior members of the faculty, however, remained silent. Most conspicuously, the *Pakistan Observer* and the Bengali language dailies refrained from editorial comment and refused to devote space to the reporting of accolades. "If I cannot report unfavorable reaction, I shall not report anything," explained the editor of the *Observer*.[8]

The preparations for the selection of the legislators meanwhile moved into high gear. The day after the President announced the Constitution, Akhter Husain was sworn in as Chief Election Commissioner.[9] Promptly thereafter the procedures were published.[10] Nominations required an eligible candidate and his endorsement by two eligible voters. A voter and a candidate were eligible if local authorities certified that he was a citizen of Pakistan, "not of unsound mind," and met the residence requirement.[11] Political disqualifications of EBDO remained in force, although others, such as the disqualification of retired judges, dismissed or retired bureaucrats, and those who before the Revolution had been detained for less than sixty days under the Security of Pakistan Act, 1952, were now lifted. Then followed

[8] At one point he was officially informed by the Director, Bureau of National Reconstruction, that the offense of "propaganda" against the Constitution was interpreted to include remaining silent.

[9] Lahore, *Pakistan Times*, March 3, 1962, p. 1.

[10] *Ibid.*, March 7, 1962, p. 1.

[11] For the National Assembly this was satisfied by residence anywhere in Pakistan; for the provincial assemblies residence in the particular province was required.

a brisk schedule of deadlines (for nominations, official scrutiny, withdrawal) and the date of election for the National Assembly and the provincial assemblies. The whole process would run less than two months.[12]

All in all some 2,700 candidates were nominated. Official scrutiny removed 21 in East Pakistan and six in the West Wing. Later the Election Commission reinstated all but five of them. On their own initiative a total of 250 candidates withdrew, leaving the field to 595 contestants for 150 National Assembly seats and 1,862 candidates for the 300 provincial assembly seats. Such names as Khuhro, Daultana, Qayyum Khan, Maulana Bhashani, Nurul Amin, and Sheikh Mujibur Rahman, who had dominated the political life of the first decade were now missing from the lists. Some were under arrest; some had been disqualified. Still others chose to remain aloof. Nevertheless, there were candidates of national reputation. From the central cabinet, Z. A. Bhutto, Habibur Rahman, and A. K. Khan entered the contest. Zakir Husain, another minister, avoided a test only after a quick survey in his constituency at Chittagong. Former Prime Minister Mohammad Ali (Bogra), Ambassador to Japan, rushed home to campaign. Former central ministers seeking election included Sardar Bahadur Khan, Lutfur Rahman, Ghulam Ali Talpur, Ramizuddin Ahmad, Raja Ghazanfar Ali Khan, and Mahfuzul Huq. Perhaps the most prominent of all candidates, however, was Moulvi Tamizzudin Khan, Chairman of the first Constituent Assembly.

The setting of the elections had these two distinctive features. First, the constituencies were small. In the past some electoral districts had included tens of thou-

[12] Lahore, *Pakistan Times*, April 1, 1962, p. 1.

sands of voters. Now an average of five hundred Basic Democrats would determine each National Assembly contest, and half as many would choose each provincial legislator. Second, political parties were banned. Consequently there were no organizations to mobilize support or formulate issues. Each individual had to rely primarily upon his own resources or, as in the case of aging Moulvi Tamizuddin Khan and a few others, upon an informal grouping of followers.

The campaign itself was definitely a drab affair. As the Constitution provided, the government did sponsor meetings of Basic Democrats at which all candidates were invited to express their views and were given an opportunity to meet their electors. Newspapers were encouraged to report the proceedings. In West Pakistan the response was moderate. Among the candidates for National Assembly, 146 (47 per cent) of the total but only 27 (18 per cent) of the winners had published views on political issues. I tabulated the major themes in this sample, with the result shown in Table 11.

Some of these figures are certainly interesting. It is, of course, not especially surprising that few advocated the repeal of the Constitution and universal suffrage. Perhaps more noteworthy is the frequency of public commitment at government-sponsored sessions to the parliamentary system (separation of powers) and political parties. Also unexpected is the relatively moderate role of the foreign policy theme and the small percentage of winners who raised the Kashmir question. Yet beyond these data far more significant is the fact that the majority of candidates and the predominant majority of winning candidates did not participate in such publicly reported meetings. Instead they relied upon ascriptive identifications. In Hyderabad two *pirs*, a *qazi*, and a *mir* were the chief contenders. D. I. Khan Division saw the "nawab's descendants" locked in the struggle. In Quetta and Kalat tribal affiliations played a dominant role. In Lahore *biradris* held the balance of power.[13]

Table 11

Major Campaign Themes of National
Assembly Candidates in West Pakistan
at Government-Sponsored Meetings
as Reported in the Public Press

	Percentage of Sample		Percentage of Winners	
1. Constitution		59.5		51.8
Endorsement	7.5		11.1	
Repeal	0.6		—	
Amendment	19.1		14.8	
a. Political Parties		30.0		22.2
For	28.7		18.5	
Against	1.3		3.7	
b. Suffrage		23.2		18.5
Universal-direct	10.2		—	
Basic Democrats	13.0		18.5	
c. Separation of powers		23.2		22.2
d. Federalism		2.7		—
2. National Integrity		56.8		51.8
3. Economic Aspirations		52.7		51.8
4. Islamic Ideology		45.2		33.3
5. Foreign Policy		36.3		22.2
Kashmir	19.8		7.4	
6. Fundamental Rights		15.7		7.4
7. Social Welfare		14.3		18.5

A major exception in this pattern was cosmopolitan Karachi. In Constituency Number 2, H. M. Habibullah

[13] *Ibid.*, April 18, 1962, p. 1; April 22, 1962, p. 1; April 23, 1962, p. 1; April 27, 1962, p. 1.

reportedly had the support of the Punjabi and Pathan Basic Democrats. His strength, however, disintegrated in the face of the appeal of a wealthy textile family formerly from India when the latter, it is alleged, outbid Habibullah in the purchase of votes. Bribery was also charged *and admitted* in Constituency Number 1.[14]

In East Pakistan the campaign was thoroughly individualistic. The government-sponsored meetings were only sparsely attended, and the press, with the exception of the Karachi-controlled *Morning News,* ignored them altogether. The Bengali language *Azad* ran a series of biographical sketches of former Muslim League members. The *Pakistan Observer* called upon candidates to answer three specific questions and offered space for this purpose. Only a handful responded. Bengali candidates evidently preferred a less public performance. Four separate campaigns that I personally observed from close quarters suggest the following pattern. First, claims of associations with the defunct parties were frequent themes. Second, political problems, especially the issue of universal suffrage, regularly entered the discussions between candidate and elector. There were also formal negotiations for votes, either in terms of money or future favors. Finally, although to a somewhat lesser extent than in West Pakistan, ascriptive identifications were ever-present and remained of critical importance.

The elections were conducted in an orderly manner. No disturbances were reported. The country was quiet, some say sullen. These were the statistics. Electors cast ballots in record number: 96.6 per cent for the National

[14] Herbert Mark Kagi, "Administrative Responses to Urban Growth: Karachi, Pakistan," unpublished Ph.D. dissertation (University of Syracuse, 1964), pp. 163-165.

Assembly and 97.8 per cent in provincial assembly races. Eighteen candidates (seven for the National Assembly, eleven for the provincial assemblies) were elected uncontested. One hundred fifty (64 in the National Assembly, 86 in provincial assembly contests) received a majority of votes. Most won by a plurality, ten winning provincial candidates polling less than 20 per cent of the votes. Voting pattern comparisons between the two Wings reveal closer contests in East Pakistan. There only three candidates won unopposed and another 48 won by majority. In the West Wing 15 were unopposed and 102 won by a clear majority.

The returns brought few surprises as far as the nationally prominent candidates were concerned. The three members of the Ayub Cabinet were elected. So were Moulvi Tamizuddin Khan, Mohammad Ali (Bogra), Sardar Bahadur Khan, Lutfur Rahman, Ghulam Ali Talpur, and Ramizuddin Ahmad. Former Central Ministers Raja Ghazanfar Ali Khan and Mahfuzul Huq were defeated. Abdul Wahab Khan, former Speaker of the National Assembly, was upset by Major Mohammad Afsaruddin Ahmad. The latter, a relative unknown on the national scale, received 253 votes to Abdul Wahab Khan's 20.[15]

The composition of the new assemblies had these identifiable characteristics worth noting. To begin with, the electors apparently showed no special preference for their fellow Basic Democrats. This was especially true in the National Assembly race where among the winners the Basic Democrats are in a distinct minority. In this respect, most dramatic was the resound-

[15] Karachi, *Dawn*, April 29, 1962, p. 1; April 30, 1962, p. 1; Dacca, *Pakistan Observer*, April 30, 1962, p. 1.

ing defeat of A. H. M. S. Doha, retired Inspector-General of Police and chairman of the showcase Union Council at Tejgaon.[16] In spite of this, however, the evidence does not support a contention that Basic Democrats were rejected. In East Pakistan, for example, 25 of the 57 Basic Democrats who contested won seats.

Second, the electors demonstrated no aversion for the politicians of past regimes. Although political parties had been prohibited, the vast majority of successful candidates had a clear record of political affiliations. Most impressive was the performance of the Muslim League. In East Pakistan, for example, where the party had been practically wiped out in 1954, no less than 43 out of 76 National Assembly members from the province had been actively associated with the League in the past.[17]

The third distinctive feature of the Assembly is the predominance of three economic and professional groups: the landlords, the lawyers, and the businessmen. Together they account for 136 members out of a total of 156.[18] The balance are teachers, doctors, and retired bureaucrats. Farmers and industrial labor remain almost totally unrepresented. The final group

[16] This was one contest I personally observed. Apparently Mr. Doha sought to capitalize on my presence by proclaiming to his audiences that "this foreign professor" supported his candidacy, which incidentally was not accurate. His gambit, however, was far from successful. In fact, it alienated some electors.

[17] Dacca, *Pakistan Observer*, May 3, 1962, p. 1 and May 7, 1962, p. 1. In the Mymensingh District, the largest and most populous in the country and the home of Nurul Amin, Muslim League members won 9 out of 11 seats.

[18] The Constitution provides for the election of six women legislators on the national and five each on the provincial levels.

characteristics to be noted are—as Table 12 indicates—youth and advanced education.[19]

Table 12

Age Distribution of the Members
National Assembly, 1962[20]

	East Pakistan	West Pakistan
40 and below	25	35
41 to 49	12	22
50 and over	36	19

Educational Level of the Members
National Assembly, 1962[21]

	East Pakistan	West Pakistan
Graduation and above	55	36
Matric and above	4	15
Below matric	10	14

Just what President Ayub Khan thought of the newly elected legislators is difficult to tell. He said that he was satisfied and then assured his "whole-hearted support to those who would be motivated by patriotic spirit."[22] Then on June 7, 1962, at Ayub Hall in Rawalpindi the National Assembly convened and the Constitution came into force. Thus began the most crucial phase of political development in Pakistan.

When martial law was lifted, its contributions to political control were withdrawn. The President lost his ability to control decision-making through the obedience of military commanders, civil servants, or even judges—men whom he himself had appointed. The gov-

[19] Data tabulated by Mushtaq Ahmad, *Government and Politics in Pakistan* (Karachi: Pakistan Publishing House, 1963), pp. 272-273.
[20] Ages of the remaining seven members not available.
[21] Educational level of the remaining sixteen members not available.
[22] Karachi, *Dawn*, April 30, 1962, p. 1.

239

ernment lost its ability to control the population by the threat if not the policy of massive coercion. The contributions of martial law to political control may not have been substantial. They were withdrawn, however, at the time when compensatory capacities were not yet available. The President had yet to establish his influence which could guide legislative deliberations. The government had yet to offer a leadership pattern which could mobilize mass support.

The Constitution was a gamble. President Ayub Khan staked his reputation upon his conviction that these compensatory capacities would be promptly acquired and that the Constitution itself would serve as a catalytic agent. He was prepared to make almost any sacrifice to assure success. Soon he was required to do just that.

Building Influence in the Legislatures

Evidently President Ayub Khan was determined to leave the selection of the legislators to the electors. He was, of course, engaged in the massive publicity campaign in support of the Constitution. He toured the West Wing, even issued a manifesto appealing for support from the traditionalist (Islamic) hierarchies. He cautioned against disruptionist elements and urged the election of God-fearing and patriotic candidates. Still he never became sufficiently specific to endorse or disown any candidate. He would not even commit himself in favor of his ministers and directed them not to trade on their official positions.[23] Other members of the Cabinet were warned not to interfere in the contests.

The President also remained aloof from the race for

[23] Dacca, *Pakistan Observer*, March 27, 1962, p. 1.

the second highest office in Pakistan, that of Speaker of the National Assembly. Intervention would have meant manipulation of an election by so unstructured a group as the new legislators—no mean feat in itself. Since by general agreement the position was to be filled by an East Pakistani, it would also have required involvement in turbulent Bengali politics—a precarious undertaking. Intervention moreover was not necessary, as the candidates were not unfriendly to his program.

The two major contenders were Moulvi Tamizuddin Khan and Mohammad Ali of Bogra. Both were prominent sons of Bengal. Neither was identified with martial law or with the government which had collapsed in 1958. Moulvi Tamizuddin Khan was closely associated with the independence movement in Bengal, was a prominent Muslim League leader and the chairman of the first Constituent Assembly. Politically a progressive man, he was dedicated to democratic processes. When in 1953 Governor-General Ghulam Mohammad dissolved the Assembly, all the legislators—disgruntled perhaps but meek—accepted the decision. All, that is, but Moulvi Tamizuddin Khan. He fought back with the only weapon at his command: the law. He brought suit in court and pressed his case most vigorously. Ultimately he lost, but in the process he won the admiration of many of his fellow citizens and the confidence of party workers. Yet he also possessed the support of the traditional element. They saw in his beard and simple Bengali garments the symbols of his commitment to the values and customs of his ancestors. His close association with the rural masses and his considerate manner earned him respect. I interviewed a random sample of villagers in his home district. He is a good man, was the most frequent characterization.

Mohammad Ali of Bogra was quite a different person. He was younger, more westernized. He was clean shaven and wore western suits. He was far less accessible. Most of his adult life had been spent abroad. Even when he was home he was too busy and let everyone know it. A random sample in his birthplace indicates he created the image of an "important man." Traditional leaders tended to shy away from him. Politicians distrusted him. They did not forget that in 1954 he had accepted the commission to replace the summarily dismissed Prime Minister, Khwaja Nazimuddin, former Bengali lieutenant of *Quaid-i-Azam* Jinnah.

Mohammad Ali never had much of a chance. The officially defunct but nevertheless active political organization of the Muslim League fully supported his opponent. So did the other political groups. In January 1962[24] in an event of considerable political significance, Moulvi Tamizuddin Khan's younger daughter married the son of Nurul Amin, last Muslim League Chief Minister of the Province. The most prominent participant in the negotiations and ceremony was former Prime Minister and Awami League leader, H. S. Suhrawardy. After his election to the National Assembly, Moulvi Tamizuddin Khan further consolidated his position by supporting the revival of old parties and the creation of "new ones as well, if needed." A healthy opposition, he declared, was needed even under a presidential form of government.[25] At the same time he also assured the benevolent neutrality of the President with a series of

[24] The exact date was kept a secret.
[25] Karachi, *Dawn*, June 5, 1962, p. 1.

informal statements counseling a fair trial for the new Constitution.

Mohammad Ali had an early warning of his position among his Bengali colleagues when they refused to support his wife for a National Assembly seat reserved for women. His only hope was to gain an edge by rallying support in West Pakistan. He flew off to Lahore to initiate negotiations. Somewhat to his surprise he found that on President Ayub Khan's advice—and partially on their own inclination—the West Pakistani legislators refused to turn the vote against the candidate who was supported by the majority of East Pakistani members of the National Assembly. Mohammad Ali conceded defeat. Moulvi Tamizuddin Khan was unanimously elected first Speaker of the National Assembly under the Constitution of 1962.

President Ayub Khan preferred legislators elected without the guidance of the government. He was content with a Speaker who was not committed to him. He was prepared to rest his influence in the legislature upon his control of patronage. The Cabinet that had served him through martial law, the President announced, would resign the day the new Constitution went into effect. Except for a few specialists, most new ministers would be recruited from the assemblies.[26] In addition, the posts of parliamentary secretaries authorized by the Constitution were open, waiting to be filled by him. "To those of you who share my views on these fundamental matters," declared the President, "I extend an invitation to come forward and collaborate with me in my difficult task. . . . I shall be happy to guide you and to assign

[26] Dacca, *Pakistan Observer*, May 19, 1962, p. 1.

you functions in the programme of national build-up which I have chalked out for myself."[27]

Admittedly, such appointments did not carry much power. Parliamentary secretaries, even ministers, would have no control over the administrative structure. This was made abundantly clear. At most they would be advisers to the President. The prestige to be gained was no more impressive. Nevertheless, such appointments carried rather attractive perquisites: bungalows, cars, offices, and travel at government expense, to mention only a few. Such rewards have their own efficacy. "In Pakistan," President Ayub Khan noted, "people thought it fit to aspire to become ministers the very day they were elected to the Assemblies."[28]

His estimate proved correct. Some legislators, including his younger brother Sardar Bahadur Khan, announced that they would not accept appointed office. Most others promptly after their election began maneuvering for the President's favor. Interpreting various clues, these legislators decided that in order to be successful they would have to meet two criteria. First, they would have to demonstrate their popularity. Those few who had won by impressive majorities constantly referred to their electoral success. Others who had carried the election only by a plurality sponsored post-election meetings. All were busily seeking to enlist the support of their fellow legislators. To prove such support, the most prominent (or aggressive) aspirants collected signed pledges.[29] The other requirement for presidential favor, it appeared, was personal loyalty. Few legislators were prepared to make a public commitment, but fewer

[27] *Ibid.*, June 10, 1962, p. 1.   [28] *Ibid.*, July 17, 1962, p. 8.
[29] *Ibid.*, June 4, 1962, p. 1.

still voiced outright opposition. Privately and at audiences their position was less equivocal. They pledged to support the President and the Constitution faithfully. One practical demonstration of such devotion: when it became clear that a predominant majority of the National Assembly were former members of the Muslim League, some observers expected a caucus of these individuals and the formation of a bloc of "like-minded" persons. Structuring of this kind, especially before the legislature had even met, would have created a severe barrier to the presidential guidance of this body and was unlikely to receive accolades from Rawalpindi. Yet without any overt initiative from President Ayub Khan the ex-Leaguers themselves scuttled all organizational activity.

In spite of all the feverish activity, President Ayub Khan showed no inclination to auction off ministerial appointments to the highest bidders. The first two appointments to the new Cabinet were "specialists." For the finance portfolio the President needed a man with international reputation and one who would assure continuity in fiscal policy. He selected Abdul Qadir, Mohammad Shoaib's successor, in the spring of 1962. The other post filled was that of Law Minister. In view of the widespread opposition of lawyers to the Constitution, the President needed a man of highest reputation in the legal community. His choice fell on the former Chief Justice of Pakistan, Mohammad Munir. Significantly, neither had ever sought elective public office.

As the legislators gathered in Rawalpindi for the first session, the problem of asserting influence over the Assembly became more and more pressing. The President, according to an estimate at the time, could count upon a core of nearly fifty West Pakistani legislators who were sympathetic to his views.[30] From them he selected Zulfikar Ali Bhutto, a staunch and articulate minister in the martial law cabinet, and Khan Habibullah Khan, a lawyer and judge and vigorous supporter of the President's ideas in the Constitution Commission. There was a problem, however, with the latter. Habibullah Khan had only recently retired from the Peshawar Bench of the High Court of West Pakistan, and Article 126 (2) of the new Constitution specifically prohibited a former judge of the Supreme Court or of the High Court from holding "any office of profit in the service of Pakistan before the expiration of two years after he ceased to hold that [his judicial] office." The difficulty was promptly resolved. The Constitution (Article 224 [3]) also authorized the President to "remove any difficulties that may arise in bringing this Constitution . . . into operation." He now used this clause to amend the Constitution and thus enable Habibullah Khan to join the Cabinet.[31] Fifty supporters in the National Assembly, however, were quite inadequate. For a majority the President needed at least another thirty. For some semblance of a national government he needed East Pakistani support. Thus, as the recruitment for the Cabinet intensified, the spotlight shifted to the Bengali contingent.

The newly elected assemblymen from East Pakistan were no less anxious to share in patronage than their colleagues in the West Wing. They were quite aware, however, of the cool reception the Constitution had received in the province and did not at all relish the prospect of being greeted by boos and black flags at Dacca

[30] *Ibid.*, June 10, 1962, p. 1.   [31] *Ibid.*, p. 5.

Airport upon their return. Their problem was somewhat complicated by four specific demands circulated by the "younger element" as a minimum legitimate price for Bengal cooperation.[32] The more senior members therefore urged the President to make at least some token concessions, otherwise their position in the province would be extremely precarious. Their insecurity, they noted pointedly, was further aggravated by the constitutional provision requiring ministers to resign their Assembly seats.[33] Against this background, acceptance of a Cabinet post might well mean being totally at the mercy of the President.

President Ayub Khan was sympathetic to the East Pakistani position, and he needed their support. It was a difficult situation. To make substantial concessions on policy and especially to announce these dramatically would have been tantamount to a public admission of presidential weakness, hardly a hopeful base from which to gain influence in the National Assembly. To amend the Constitution for the second time in its first week in order to accommodate the personal apprehensions of suitable candidates would have inspired little confidence in the stability of the system. Yet some allowances were clearly indicated. In the end the President made his first major sacrifice for the viability of his Constitution by amending it, again under Article

[32] The demands included: "1) Release of all political prisoners in both wings; 2) Democratisation of the Constitution including justiciability of fundamental rights; 3) Power of determining the *vires* of laws framed and executive actions taken in relation to the Constitution to vest in the High Courts and finally in the Supreme Court; and 4) Balanced economic development of the country, in particular, of East Pakistan" (*ibid.*, June 11, 1962, p. 1).

[33] Article 104 (1).

247

224 (3), to enable his ministers to retain their Assembly seats. Then, sensing that Mohammad Ali (Bogra) was the weak link in East Pakistani solidarity, the President endorsed him as Leader of the National Assembly. Gratefully Mohammad Ali pledged his loyalty. He entered the Cabinet, his statement read, with "a spirit of dedication and service of our people."[34]

Joining Mohammad Ali were four other East Pakistani ministers. Abdul Monem Khan, a longtime politician and protégé of Nurul Amin, became Minister of Health, Labour and Social Welfare. A. K. M. Fazlul Quader Choudhury, leader of the bicycle rickshaw operators in Chittagong, received the Agriculture and Works plus the Education and Information portfolios. Wahiduzzaman, a Faridpur industrialist, was named Commerce Minister. Finally, Abdus Sabur Khan, another businessman and former chairman of the Khulna Chamber of Commerce assumed the office of Minister of Communications.

Mohammad Ali and his four allies brought another twenty-eight East Pakistani legislators into the presidential fold, thereby assuring a clear majority. It was, however, a rather slim majority. Just how slim became apparent when early in July the government arrested Khan Abdul Quayyum Khan. When in protest the "opposition" in the Assembly staged its first walkout, only sixty-one legislators (including the Speaker) remained in the chamber.[35] It was a remarkable experience to observe cabinet ministers rushing to the doors, trying to drag in members from the corridors. Even then it was some time before order could be restored. Clearly,

[34] Dacca, *Pakistan Observer*, June 14, 1962, p. 1.
[35] *Ibid.*, July 7, 1962, p. 1.

there could be no further delay for the appointment of parliamentary secretaries. Within ten days a list of seventeen such appointments was announced.

The President's influence was further consolidated by his firm discouragement of intrigues. He was not grateful when Mohammad Ali "defended" him by calling former Foreign Minister Manzur Qadir a Rasputin.[36] Nor did he encourage Z. A. Bhutto's periodic maneuvers to replace Mohammad Ali (preferably by Bhutto) as Leader of the National Assembly and Foreign Minister.[36a] Gradually a hierarchy emerged among his followers, contributing substantially to their cohesion. His influence was firmly established when in August 1963 the National Assembly lost its non-committed Speaker. Moulvi Tamizuddin Khan died. He was succeeded by Fazlul Quader Choudhury, a member of the original post-Constitution Cabinet and a man clearly indebted to the President.

The course of events in the provincial assemblies followed a similar path. At first there was a little trouble in West Pakistan. The presentation of the Railway Budget occasioned some unkind words about the operation of the railroads. Then a cut-motion[37] reducing a Rs 2,300,-000 demand by Rs 1,614,000 was introduced and carried by a voice vote.[38] This, however (in my opinion), reflected more the unfamiliarity of the members with

[36] A few weeks later, during the visit of the Shah of Iran, the President took his guest over rough mountain roads to visit Manzur Qadir in Nathiagali.

[36a] When Mohammad Ali died, Bhutto in fact succeeded him.

[37] Under a parliamentary system a successful cut-motion is equivalent to an expression of no confidence in the government.

[38] Lahore, *Civil and Military Gazette*, June 19, 1962, pp. 1, 3, 5; and June 20, 1962, pp. 1, 3, 4, and 9.

the seriousness of such a motion and the Speaker's personal convictions than opposition to the government. For many months the West Pakistan government was able to guide the provincial assembly through its nine ministers and five parliamentary secretaries.

In East Pakistan the position was less secure. The new governor, Ghulam Faruque, was an able administrator and had had a distinguished record in the economic development program of West Pakistan. He did not, however, have political support, and as the successor of General Azam Khan he was roundly abused.[39] Unfortunately, neither did he have political acumen. The summer of 1962 again brought floods to the Chittagong area. Azam Khan had gained much popularity from visiting such areas in previous years. The Governor saw no purpose in this. His Finance Minister repeatedly asked him to tour the disaster area, then begged him to permit at least some member of the cabinet to do so. Ghulam Faruque remained adamant. His presence, he argued, would only confuse the efforts of the local bureaucracy. He had his officials down there; they could take care of it, he explained. In the provincial assembly the Ministers of Finance and Law fought a desperate and hopeless battle. The "lively debates," one correspondent reported, "occasioned repartees between nearly the whole House on one side and the two lone occupiers of the Treasury Bench."[40] The situation did not improve until the Nawab of Dacca, Major Khwajah Hassan Askari, joined the provincial cabinet. Then, in addition to other ministerial openings being

[39] When he tried to visit the University of Dacca, the students blocked his way and screamed into his face: "Go home, you stooge."
[40] Dacca, *Pakistan Observer*, June 13, 1962, p. 1.

filled, a full contingent of thirty parliamentary secretaries was appointed. In an assembly of 155 members, 39 were directly under executive control, and since in these instances proven support (signatures) was the prime criteria for appointment, the President established some measure of influence.

Governor Ghulam Faruque became the first prominent casualty of the Constitution. He had come to the province and had labored hard. Yet for the want of political skill all his efforts went for naught. His letter of resignation spelled out his problem. "I have been all my life a government official. My experience is therefore confined wholly to matters connected with economic development and I am afraid I cannot lay a claim to any ability to organize or lead a party."[41] Agreeing with the Governor's analysis, the President accepted the resignation and appointed as his successor Abdul Monem Khan, Central Minister of Health, Labour and Social Welfare and a member of the National Assembly from East Pakistan.

The emergent presidential influence in the assemblies soon suffered two major, although temporary, setbacks. The first challenge came from the courts. On April 5, 1963, after a month's deliberation the Special Bench of Dacca High Court declared void, inoperative *in toto*, and *ultra vires* of the Constitution the presidential order removing the provision requiring ministers to resign their seats in the National Assembly.[42] On May 13 the Supreme Court of Pakistan dismissed the appeal, declaring that ministers ceased to be members of the legislature on the day of their appointment, but that laws

[41] *Ibid.*, October 26, 1962, p. 8.
[42] Karachi, *Dawn*, April 6, 1963, p. 1.

which they helped formulate would remain in force.[43] There was no question of further resistance. Arbitrary action at this stage, less than a year after the promulgation of the Constitution, would have meant a total rupture of the President's political program. He accepted the decision, and the ministers vacated their seats.

The other setback occurred in the West Pakistan Legislature. Speaker Mobinul Haq Siddiqui was not one of President Ayub's supporters. The conflict may have been one of principle. It certainly included personal hostility between the Speaker and the Governor of West Pakistan. In any case, by the summer of 1963 the ministers detected a most definite bias in his rulings, permitting and encouraging remarks which were considered offensive to the President and the Governor. After some rather perfunctory efforts to conciliate, the issue came to a head on July 4, when the government majority requested the Speaker's resignation. Mobinul Haq Siddiqui refused, and when the motion of no confidence was introduced he promptly adjourned the assembly "for lack of quorum." Such action, however, was rather futile. The assembly reconvened under the chairmanship of the Deputy Speaker, and the no-confidence motion carried 104 to 2. The same evening the Governor issued the order for the Speaker's removal. When it was all over, the West Pakistan Assembly had a pro-government Speaker.[44]

Yet despite some disappointments the President did succeed in gaining decisive influence in the assemblies. His budgets were approved. His Political Parties Act,

[43] *Ibid.*, May 14, 1963, p. 1.

[44] *Ibid.*, July 5, 1963, pp. 1, 9; July 6, 1963, pp. 1, 9; July 7, 1963, p. 1; and July 10, 1963, p. 1.

1962 passed with only minor modifications. The main Opposition amendments were defeated by 66 to 43 and 62 to 30 votes.[45] His ordinance (January 7, 1963) amending this act carried in the National Assembly, 71 to 62.[46] His constitutional amendment on fundamental rights required a two-thirds majority or 104 votes. On its third and final reading it received 109, including 17 from one segment of the Opposition.[47] A few weeks later the East Pakistan Assembly approved the restrictive press ordinances of the Governor. Since the Opposition walked out before the final vote, no exact tabulation was reported. During the debate the key challenge lost, 61 to 21.[48] Then, in two crucial tests of influence, the National Assembly first passed, 78 to 38, the President's Franchise Bill and then approved, 106 to 26, the government-sponsored second amendment to the Constitution.[49]

Pursuing a New Pattern of Leadership

The President's success in building influence in the legislatures assured the short term stability of the political system. Its long-term persistence, i.e., its capacity to outlive Mohammad Ayub Khan's presidency, however, cannot be purchased by patronage. That requires a leadership pattern that is capable of mobilizing mass support behind national institutions and objectives. The

[45] The Opposition came closest with a 52:48 vote on an amendment dealing with the definition of the term "officebearers" of a political party (*ibid.*, July 12, 1962, p. 1; July 13, 1962, p. 1; July 14, 1962, p. 1; and July 15, 1962, p. 1).

[46] Dacca, *Pakistan Observer*, April 18, 1963, p. 1.

[47] *Ibid.*, December 25, 1963, p. 1.

[48] *Ibid.*, January 29, 1964, p. 1.

[49] *Ibid.*, April 15, 1964, p. 1 and June 12, 1964, p. 1.

problem of constructing such a leadership pattern is not a new one. British viceroys, then *Quaid-i-Azam* Mohammad Ali Jinnah struggled with it. Now it was President Ayub Khan's turn.

The Revolution offered a simple pattern of leadership: the government was firmly planted upon a single column of bureaucrats supported by the armed forces. It might be recalled, however, that even in the initial months the President was concerned about developing a broader leadership structure, one that could not only compel obedience, but also attract consent. Accordingly, it became his task to construct an additional column of national hierarchy, a hierarchy based upon popular representation. Indeed the system of Basic Democracies was an attempt to build such a structure from the "grass roots" up. Later the President continued to reinforce the Union Councils, but after the Constitution he concentrated upon the upper end of the projected second column. He set out to organize representative leadership from the national level down. In this purpose the National Assembly was to play the crucial part. Hence the President offered to share his power with the legislators. Hence he kept aloof from the campaign, hoping that the polls would reveal popular favor with some accuracy. Hence he was prepared to make substantial concessions in the selection of his ministers. The foremost obligation of the National Assembly, he told the inaugural session, was "to work and defend" the Constitution.[50] Similarly, it was the "first task" of parliamentary secretaries "to go to the people at all levels and explain to them the spirit and salient features

[50] Lahore, *Pakistan Times*, June 9, 1962, p. 6.

of the Constitution and in doing so to educate them about the *bona fides* of the Government policies."[51]

Apparently, at first President Ayub Khan assumed that a new and effective national hierarchy headed by the legislators could be accomplished without a special political organization. Having demonstrated their confidence by electing them, the population ought to support their representatives. It soon became clear that it was not as simple as that. Since the "representatives" were elected by the Basic Democrats, victory at the polls did not necessarily reflect popular favor. Moreover, the very fact that they had accepted presidential appointments dissipated in some parts of the country whatever credit they may have had. Within a week, a majority of the members from East Pakistan denounced the "ministerialists."[52] Within a month, mass meetings in Karachi, Lahore, and Peshawar under the leadership of Khan Abdul Qayyum Khan demanded a new constitution, while in Dacca nine prominent leaders in a public statement insisted on the same.

As late as June 21, 1962, the President found political parties repugnant. "Let us try," he advised, "to avoid reverting to the same old system which had done us no good."[53] At Cabinet meetings the new ministers, especially Mohammad Ali and Zulfikar Bhutto, however, pressed him to change his mind. Political parties regulated by law, they argued, would provide an organizational framework for mass mobilization on behalf of the government. They might further aid such development by clearly demarcating the difference between those groups which were opposed to some government

[51] Dacca, *Pakistan Observer*, July 17, 1962, p. 1.
[52] *Ibid.*, June 15, 1962, p. 1.   [53] *Ibid.*, June 22, 1962, p. 1.

policies and others which advocated the repeal of the entire constitutional structure. Finally, political parties could fragment the leadership of the Opposition. Reluctantly, President Ayub Khan agreed and sacrificed his fond hope of leadership through personal excellence to leadership through organization. The statement of the objects and reasons of the bill includes the admission: "Today healthy political organizations are needed to channelize public opinion for preserving the ideology and integrity of Pakistan."[54] It was the President's second major concession in support of his Constitution. On June 30 some three weeks after the return of constitutional government Law Minister Munir introduced the appropriate bill in the National Assembly. For good measure, Khan Abdul Qayyum Khan was arrested in Lahore.[55]

The debate was vigorous. The consensus clearly favored revival. At issue was the control of the revived political parties. The President's supporters as second echelon Muslim Leaguers could hardly arrogate control of the defunct and now renascent party machinery. The "first team," though disqualified under EBDO, still retained much of its popular appeal and could, it was feared, easily isolate the Ministerialists. This prospect clearly did not elate the latter and certainly was not in line with the President's objectives. Hence they argued with some zeal for the complete disqualification of a wide segment of the politicians of the past. The other members of the National Assembly, those who did not share in presidential patronage, faced similar problems. They too were from the second team. Any embarrass-

[54] Karachi, *Dawn*, June 21, 1962, p. 11.
[55] Lahore, *Pakistan Times*, July 7, 1962, p. 1.

ment of the government, however, was their gain. So, through eloquent speeches in defense of democracy, they opposed any limitation upon participation by anyone in party leadership or activity. After a temporary deadlock the Ministerialists had their way. The final version of the bill authorized the organization of political parties on two main conditions. First, they must be founded on Islamic ideology. Anti-Islam bias was unlawful. Second, they must not admit among their membership those convicted of moral turpitude, dismissed government servants or public officials *or* politicians disqualified under EBDO in 1959.[56] Incidentally, Mohammad Ali, the Leader of the Assembly, was in the hospital during most of the debates. In his place the Ministerialists were led by Z. A. Bhutto and Fazlul Quader Choudhury. It was the first time that the tall Bengali distinguished himself as a presidential stalwart.

The immediate response to the new law did not seem to bear out the hopes of its sponsors. Mass meetings and demonstrations demanding the repeal of the Constitution continued. Dacca University students burned copies almost as soon as the government press printed them. One after another, former politicians pledged their solidarity to each other and assured their audiences that they would not collaborate in any attempt to revive political parties before "the restoration of full democracy."[57] When H. S. Suhrawardy was released from detention, he promptly organized the National Democratic Front, a loose alliance of the entire range of oppositional elements. It included most major political leaders of East Pakistan and such prominent politicians

[56] Karachi, *Dawn*, July 15, 1962, p. 6.
[57] Dacca, *Pakistan Observer*, July 19, 1962, p. 1.

from the West Wing as Maulana Maududi, Sardar Bahadur Khan, M. Daultana, Z. H. Lari, and M. A. Khuhro.[58] At this point the NDF seemed to be a popular mass movement, spearheaded by a phalanx of national leaders and dedicated to the total destruction of the President's political system.

Meanwhile, the Ministerialists were having their troubles. Those from East Pakistan were greeted with black flags, rotten eggs, angry slogans, and massive demonstrations upon their return to the province. In Chittagong and later in Comilla police had to intervene to extricate Fazlul Quader Choudhury.[59] Khulna greeted A. Sabur in a similar manner.[60] No less vexing was the reluctance encountered by any suggestion that a new party be formed under the leadership of the President's supporters in the National Assembly. The strenuous efforts of Z. A. Bhutto, Khan Habibullah Khan, and even Mohammad Ali made little progress.[61] The program to build a new column of leadership from the top was getting nowhere fast.

President Ayub Khan was still loath to become involved in party politics. Yet clearly he could not tolerate so dramatic a demonstration of the political impotence of his legislative supporters. He decided to intervene and endorse the calling of a Muslim Leaguers' Convention. That the conveners chose this title rather than the designation Muslim League Convention reflected their very real appreciation of the fact that they did not have the support of the men who had led the party before its

[58] *Ibid.*, October 5, 1962, p. 1.
[59] *Ibid.*, July 15, 1962, p. 1 and August 1, 1962, p. 1.
[60] *Ibid.*, August 1, 1962, p. 1.
[61] *Ibid.*, July 30, 1962, p. 1 and August 1, 1962, p. 1.

dissolution in 1958. On the whole it must have been a rather discouraging affair for the ministers. They could well serve as lieutenants in the presidential cabinet. None really had the stature to assume a general's control of a party machine. So in the end after repeated emphasis upon building the party "from the bottom up" they elected aging Choudhury Kaliquzzaman as chief organizer and then amidst sighs adjourned.[62]

If the Ministerialists suffered from a scarcity of men with national reputation, the elements opposing the Constitution had a surfeit of them. The National Democratic Front with its loose organizational pattern served as a temporary cover for very *un*like-minded persons, and the strain soon began to show. Gradually, distinct deviational trends became apparent. First, in West Pakistan two smaller parties—the *Nizam-i-Islām* and the *Jamā'at-i-Islāmi*—were reconstituted. Then a month after the Karachi convention a segment of the "first team" felt compelled to revive its own Muslim League. They called the former party's Council, its governing body, into session at Dacca. Khwaja Nazimuddin abandoned his political retirement and the writing of his memoirs and was elected party president. Sardar Bahadur Khan accepted the post of general secretary. The *Nizam-i-Islām, Jamā'at-i-Islāmi* and the Muslim League (Councillist) all emphasized their opposition to the new Constitution and pledged their support to the National Democratic Front. "As long as I remain President of the Muslim League," declared Khwaja Nazimuddin, "the party will not be interested in joining the present Government because I feel under the Constitution it is not

[62] Karachi, *Dawn*, September 5, 1962, p. 1.

possible to give effect to all the policies enunciated in the Muslim League resolutions."[63]

Nevertheless, the revival of these parties did make a difference. It reinforced polycentric diffusion of the groups within the National Democratic Front. By more clearly demarcating differences in leadership and separation in organization *within* the opposition, it diverted some attention from the conflicts *between* the opposition and the President. More important perhaps, when these parties were reconstituted, their locus of power moved into the legislature. Admittedly, Maulana Maududi and Khwaja Nazimuddin were not members of the National Assembly. They sought to mobilize popular support behind their organizations by calling mass meetings. These efforts, however, were not especially successful and were regularly disrupted by violence.[64] Policy-making was influenced primarily by the contingencies of the party members in the National Assembly, *not* by the aspirations of constituents. In view of this and in spite of all the eloquent orations to the contrary, the effect of their parties' revival meant at least their ostensible acceptance of the institutional framework. Their opposition narrowed its base substantially to specific policies or particular office holders. The net result was a major gain for the President, a far greater gain, in fact, than the Karachi convention of Muslim Leaguers.

The remnant of the National Democrat Front with its total resistance to the President's system still retained the support of the EBDO'd politicians. They at least had no other place to go. It also retained much of its

---

[63] Dacca, *Pakistan Observer*, October 28, 1962, p. 1.
[64] *Ibid.*, October 11, 1962, p. 1 and May 4, 1963, p. 1.

ability to mobilize the masses. This was particularly true in the East Wing. H. S. Suhrawardy and later Maulana Bhashani toured the province and addressed giant public rallies.[65] In their wake a "cross-section of intellectuals" called for a federal type *parliamentary* government. Student demonstrations became chronic. The Dacca University Convocation had to be canceled. President Ayub's visit to Rajshahi triggered clashes with the police in which eleven students were injured.[66] When Suhrawardy moved to West Pakistan, he still attracted sizable audiences but on the whole fared little better than Maulana Maududi or Khwaja Nazimuddin. Most of his meetings were disrupted by organized, presumably pro-government gangs. At one point in Karachi his assistant, Abdul Majid Khamgavi, was knifed in the back.[67] The real blow against the National Democratic Front came in January. Maulana Bhashani became ill, then H. S. Suhrawardy suffered a heart attack.

Having apparently divided his opponents, the President was now ready to demarcate the limits of permissible dissent. Khwaja Nazimuddin and his supporters apparently qualified. The President regretted that the former had joined hands with the disruptionists, but he did not go beyond such verbal criticism. He considered that Khwaja Sahib was a personal friend and a good pious man.[68] In contrast, total attack upon the Constitution or incitement to violence was clearly non-permissi-

[65] *Ibid.*, October 13, 1962, p. 1; October 15, 1962, p. 1; October 19, 1962, p. 1; October 20, 1962, p. 1; October 21, 1962, p. 1; October 22, 1962, p. 1; and October 25, 1962, p. 1.
[66] *Ibid.*, December 17, 1962, p. 1; December 22, 1962, p. 1; December 23, 1962, p. 1.
[67] *Ibid.*, December 3, 1962, p. 1.
[68] *Ibid.*, December 11, 1962, p. 1.

ble behavior and invited coercive countermeasures. Government advertisements were withdrawn from East Pakistani newspapers. One daily, the *Ittefaq*, was charged with contributing to the unrest and was financially penalized. Students in Dacca and Karachi were arrested.[69] On January 8, 1963, the President promulgated two ordinances amending the Political Parties Act, 1962. The first sought to impose this act upon the National Democratic Front (which at times claimed non-party status) by redefining the term "political party" to include any group "operating for the purpose of propagating a political opinion." It also authorized the government to direct disqualified (EBDO) politicians to refrain from "making statements of a political nature, addressing press conferences or public meetings." The second ordinance empowered the President to reduce or remove altogether the period of disqualification of former political leaders.[70] The National Democratic Front was to be deprived of many of its senior (mostly West Pakistani) members one way or another. Following through with the new ordinance the government arrested Masihur Rahman, Member of the National Assembly and deputy leader of the Opposition, together with several of his supporters. Obeidur Rahman, Dacca University student leader, suffered the same fate. In February Mahmud Ali Qasuri, member of the NDF, was taken into custody when he refused to submit to police interrogation.[71] Early in May further prom-

[69] *Ibid.*, October 3, 1962, p. 1; October 7, 1962, p. 1; and December 13, 1962, p. 1.

[70] *Ibid.*, January 8, 1963, p. 1.

[71] The High Court of West Pakistan, presided over by Manzur Qadir held the order invalid (*ibid.*, March 23, 1963, p. 1).

inent NDF leaders were arrested in West Pakistan under charges of sedition.[72]

Still the Ministerialists and their Muslim League (Conventionist) continued to have difficulties in their task of building a political structure with a capacity of control by mass persuasion. The East Pakistan Governor's visit to Rangpur was marked by disorders in which twenty-nine persons were injured. Madrassah students[73] demonstrated in Dacca and Feni. Chittagong's schools felt it prudent to remain closed during the Governor's visit. The formation of an East Pakistan NDF Committee including Nurul Amin was announced at a mass meeting in Dacca, which again declared the Constitution unacceptable. West Pakistani NDF leaders now in jail refused to come out on bail offered conditionally by the Chief Justice of the province.[74]

The vulnerability of the Muslim League (Conventionist) became especially acute when the Supreme Court stripped the ministers of their Assembly seats, thus necessitating by-elections to fill the vacancies. If the effort of building another column of the pattern of leadership capable of mobilizing mass support was to continue at all, the time had come for the President to take a direct hand. On May 23, 1963, less than a year after he had declared the Constitution to be in force and had castigated political parties as a "bane of the past," President Mohammad Ayub Khan joined the party of his ministers. This indeed was his third sacrifice for his Constitution. Predictably before the end of the

[72] *Ibid.*, May 8, 1963, p. 1.
[73] Young men following a curriculum concentrating on Islamic doctrine and culture.
[74] Dacca, *Pakistan Observer*, May 10, 1963, p. 1.

year he was first elected Muslim League Councillor,[75] then Muslim League (Conventionist) President.

President Ayub Khan's assumption of direct control over a political party had several immediate and dramatic consequences. First of all, it put the President back on the campaign trail. Ever since his whistle-stop tour during the Basic Democracies election in December 1959 and January 1960, he had remained somewhat aloof, limiting his public contacts to official sessions with government officials or prominent citizens and to occasional rural excursions in West Pakistan. Even the publicity campaign on behalf of the new Constitution did not occasion his greater exposure in East Pakistan. Now after exchanging his western suits and military uniforms for more traditional costumes the President appeared in the rural areas of both Wings discoursing freely with the villagers. This time when a cyclone again hit the East Wing, he promptly visited the affected areas and personally donated funds for relief.[76]

Second, the presidential decision tied the government to a political party. Abdul Waheed Khan was appointed to the Cabinet, then named general secretary of the Muslim League (Conventionist) in charge of the organizational program. More important, in marked contrast to the general elections for the legislatures in 1962, the Cabinet members, the Governors (especially Governor Monem Khan of East Pakistan) and even some civil service personnel actively participated in the by-elections a year later. The small number of electors and the staggered election dates improved the prospects of influencing the votes. The use of official vehi-

[75] Significantly, he was elected Councillor from Mymensingh, East Pakistan, Governor Monem Khan's home district.
[76] Dacca, *Pakistan Observer*, June 4, 1963, p. 1.

cles for campaign purposes was widely observed. Some allegations voiced by the opposition and denied by the government included outright intimidation and an order to subdivisional officers to authorize the expenditure of "any amount" in the areas where elections were being held.[77] In a petition filed by Asghar Husain, an unsuccessful candidate, he formally charged "undue influence, coercion, intimidation and all other sorts of corrupt practices." More specifically, the complainant testified that the provincial governor, a central minister, a provincial minister, the subdivisional officer, circle officers, and police officials "threatened the voters that if they did not vote for Mr. Bhuiya [the Muslim League (Conventionist) candidate], it would be treated [sic] that their actions were anti-state and everyone would have to face the consequences."[78] Whatever the truth of the specific allegations, government machinery including civil service cadres did become involved in the campaign. The results in turn were decisive. All but one of the Muslim League (Conventionist) candidates won by secure margins.[79]

Closely related was an apparent acceleration of the use of coercion against the anticonstitutionalist forces. In January 1964, the *Jamā'at-i-Islāmi* was banned; Maulana Maududi and eighteen other officers of the party were arrested. A month later the West Pakistan National Democratic Front Council meeting was postponed when the government insisted that a CID officer be admitted to the deliberations. Then the police regis-

[77] *Ibid.*, September 11, 1963, p. 1; September 28, 1963, p. 1; September 30, 1963, p. 1; and October 10, 1963, p. 1.
[78] *Ibid.*, May 1, 1964, p. 8.
[79] Karachi, *Dawn*, September 6, 1963, p. 1.

tered a case against the entire Council.[80] The press continued to be harassed. Newspapers announcing anti-Constitution agitation or reporting on it were penalized. In West Pakistan the *Daily Kohistan* was seized and its editor arrested. In the East Wing the *Azad* was ordered to show cause why it should not be required to make a security deposit of Rs 30,000.[81] Finally, a new press ordinance was issued authorizing censorship for thirty days but renewable for another thirty days.[82]

Coincidental with the President's assumption of a direct leadership of the Muslim League (Conventionist) there was a perceptible further deterioration of the anti-Constitutionist leadership. The day the President joined his party, the competitive Muslim League (Councillist) announced it would no longer cooperate with the National Democratic Front. Khwaja Nazimuddin ordered his supporters in the National Assembly to vote with the government on the constitutional amendment on fundamental rights. This action, in fact, mobilized the key votes necessary for the required two-thirds majority. It also made the position of Sardar Bahadur Khan as leader of the Opposition in the National Assembly quite untenable, and thus forced the latter's resignation.[83] Earlier in August Maulana Bhashani, reversing his previous stand, called on the President for political discussions.[84] In December Husain Shahid Suhrawardy, the preeminent leader of the National

---

[80] Dacca, *Pakistan Observer*, January 17, 1964, p. 1; February 10, 1964, p. 1; and February 11, 1964, p. 1.

[81] *Ibid.*, October 11, 1963, p. 1. [82] *Ibid.*, April 3, 1964, p. 1.

[83] *Ibid.*, December 20, 1963, p. 1; and December 21, 1963, p. 1.

[84] On August 12, 1963, Maulana Bhashani denied any intention of meeting the President except on an "all-party basis." Ten days later he was the guest of the President. (*Ibid.*, August 13, 1963, p. 1; and August 23, 1963, p. 1.)

Democratic Front died in Beirut, Lebanon. Within a month Sheikh Mujibur Rahman announced the revival of the Awami League. He was followed closely by Maulana Bhashani's reactivation of the National Awami Party.[85] In the spring of 1964 Miss Fatima Jinnah, sister of *Quaid-i-Azam*, expressed publicly some anti-Constitutionist views, but the mass meetings in Dacca or Chittagong demanding the repeal of the Constitution or the smaller sessions in the West Wing saw few if any of the prominent men of the premartial law days.[86] In less than two years the solid phalanx of politicians was no longer solid at all, and their "unending" opposition proved ephemeral indeed.

The President may have been satisfied with his success of fragmenting his political opposition and guiding their leaders away from an overt anti-Constitutionist position. His accomplishment, however, was primarily negative in character. As yet his party had not—at least not apparently—augmented the bureaucracy in the leadership pattern successfully enough to stimulate commitment to the Constitution or to mobilize mass support for the government. Insofar as the President's party made any progress at all, this was limited to West Pakistan. In the East Wing it encountered decided organizational difficulties. Originally the President hoped to recruit a Bengali as the secretary general of his Muslim League to "balance" the top leadership.[87] In the end he had to be satisfied with a resident of West Pakistan, Abdul Waheed Khan. Meanwhile provincial party organization was plagued by periodic resignations. In May 1964 its Dacca meeting erupted in a riot with leaders and

[85] *Ibid.*, January 25, 1964, p. 1.   [86] *Ibid.*, March 20, 1964, p. 1.
[87] "We prefer to appoint a person from East Pakistan," declared the President. (*Ibid.*, December 27, 1963, p. 1.)

members as full participants. In consequence, thirteen of its prominent members, including Shamsul Huda, president of the Dacca City Muslim League (Conventionist), were expelled.[88] Governor Monem Khan and his ministers labored hard to mobilize public support. It remained an uphill battle. The National Democratic Front remained the most potent political force in the province. When it chose, as it did during the National Assembly debates on the Franchise Bill, it could still effect a general strike (*hartal*).[89] The Governor's visits outside the capital continued to occasion violence. Police had to fire in Chandpur to quell disturbances during Monem Khan's visit. Three men were killed.[90] The Convocation at Rajshahi University was marked by demonstrations and arrests. The university had to be closed. At Dacca University ceremonies were conducted under the protection of 2,000 troops, and still the Governor's speech was inaudible over the noise of demonstrations. The same evening the police fired on students. In addition, twenty-four students were expelled, and in a most extraordinary action two M.A. degrees were withdrawn. This university too had to be closed.[91]

Hence, in spite of the confusion in the opposition leadership, the President found it necessary to retrench himself. With a dramatic announcement substantial and retroactive[92] salary raises were authorized for the military and civil service personnel.

[88] *Ibid.*, May 10, 1964, p. 1.   [89] *Ibid.*, March 19, 1964, p. 1.
[90] *Ibid.*, November 23, 1963, p. 1.
[91] *Ibid.*, March 17, 1964, p. 1; March 23, 1964, p. 1; March 24, 1964, p. 1; April 4, 1964, p. 1.
[92] According to the original announcement, the raises were to be retroactive to December 1, 1962. As it turned out, the effective date was advanced to July 1, 1963. (*Ibid.*, April 22, 1964, p. 1, and April 26, 1964, p. 1.)

12

✦✦✦

A Guided Democracy in Action:
Managing Reelection

✦✦✦

THE time for further advance in the political development program was rapidly approaching. The Constitution promised a presidential election in three years. It
was a promise the President meant to keep. Admittedly
conditions were not exactly ideal. The showdown forced
on the students certainly had not yielded the desired
results. In August 1964 the Supreme Court voided puni-
tive measures in Dacca; in September the University of
the Punjab rescinded its expulsion orders. In Karachi
student unrest continued unabated. Before the end of
the month widespread rioting forced the closure of all
educational institutions in East Pakistan. The Vice
Chancellor of the University of Dacca now required
police protection. Worse still, the government was
rapidly losing its cherished reputation for honesty and
integrity. For a year rumors had been current about the
privileged treatment of the President's son. Gauhar
Ayub Khan resigned his army captaincy and suddenly
emerged as managing director of Ghandara Industries.
The corporation, it so happened, had just acquired a mil-
lion-dollar General Motors assembly plant. There had
also been persistent allegations about legislative support
being mobilized through foreign exchange permits, import licenses and appointments to semipublic corpora-

tions. Formal charges of bribing and intimidating electors had been filed against ministers. Then on September 4, 1964, at a public meeting former Prime Minister Chaudhri Mohammad Ali pointed an accusing finger. The present regime in Pakistan, he asserted, had surpassed all records of political corruption.[1] Storm signals notwithstanding, the President remained undeterred. Elections would be held as scheduled.

It was scarcely a case of personal stubbornness. The continued progress of the political development program was sufficient reason for the realization of this promise. Surely an early and successful presidential election could symbolize popular ratification of the Constitution and thus reinforce the still frail political institutions. It could demonstrate popular endorsement of the President and thus reconfirm the stability of the source of political guidance. No less important, a successful presidential election could help develop the organizational structure of the President's political party and thus help build it into a vehicle of mass mobilization.

The gains could be substantial; the risks were commensurate. An election campaign was bound to focus attention on criticism against the government. It could, as in the past, unify the opposition. Worse still, it could bring defeat. As political conditions remained unsettled, the President moved to reduce the risks to more manageable proportions. He interposed the Electoral College of Pakistan between his office and the citizen.

He had, of course, always preferred indirect elections. In the days of great expectation back in the spring of 1962, however, the President had held out the prospect

[1] Dacca, *Pakistan Observer*, September 5, 1964, p. 1.

of adjustments in the electoral system of Basic Democrats. The inaugural address had promised a Franchise Commission to recommend "more workable modifications."[2] Then the Commission, composed of two judges and two members of the National Assembly[3] and chaired by Chief Election Commissioner Akhter Husain, had been promptly appointed.

In its procedure the Franchise Commission followed the pattern set by the Constitution Commission. It sent out questionnaires and held hearings. It reached some five thousand persons, mostly westernized professionals and "intellectuals."[4] When the responses were tabulated, they revealed that only a minority considered the indirect method of elections "suitable and efficacious."[5] The Franchise Commission, however, was more cautious than the Constitution Commission. It would not challenge the President outright but offered a compromise. After lengthy deliberations it recommended an electoral college for presidential elections and universal direct suffrage for the selection of legislators.[6] By this time, however, the earlier optimism had receded substantially. The Franchise Bill introduced by the government, and after an acrimonious debate passed by the National Assembly, did not respond to the Commission's offer. It merely reiterated the indirect system for all national

[2] Lahore, *Pakistan Times*, June 9, 1962, p. 10.

[3] Justices M. R. Khan and Masud Ahmad; Members of the National Assembly Hasan Ali and Chaudhary Salahuddin.

[4] Altogether 4,407 written replies were received. In addition, 273 witnesses testified.

[5] Less than 40 per cent (1,762) favored the selection of the President by an electoral college composed of Basic Democrats. Just 37 per cent (1,655) preferred such a process for legislative elections (Government of Pakistan, *Gazette of Pakistan Extraordinary*, August 23, 1963, pp. 637bd-637be).

[6] *Ibid.*, pp. 637ab-637ay.

271

and provincial elections. As in 1960 and 1962 the Basic Democrats were to serve as an electoral college.[7]

Actually a presidential election—even though channeled through an electoral college composed of Basic Democrats—was an advance toward representative institutions. No head of state or head of government had previously been elected by universal suffrage in Pakistan. Governors-General had been appointed by the Queen on the advice of the Cabinet; Prime Ministers had been sustained by parliamentary majority or at times by the favor of the Governor-General. A constituency of eighty thousand electors was certainly a massive expansion over a few hundred legislators or a few dozen ministers. The mobilization of their support required an entirely new dimension of organization. For each legislator of the pre-martial law regime now 250-300 Basic Democrats had to be persuaded in order to accomplish a comparable advantage. Eighty thousand electors, moreover, offered a more representative base than the pre-martial law legislators and cabinet ministers. To be sure, they included a goodly share of lawyers, landlords, and tribal chiefs, but for the first time a major proportion of those casting ballots in an election contest for the Chief Executive were villagers who, like the majority of the citizens of Pakistan, had little experience outside the traditional rural life of their own small-scale societies.

The decision to channel presidential elections through an electoral college also had another effect. It divided the campaign into two major components: the election of Basic Democrats by universal suffrage and the election of the President by Basic Democrats forming an

[7] Dacca, *Pakistan Observer*, March 22, 1964, p. 1.

electoral college. First, however, the candidates had to be nominated.

The Nomination of Presidential Candidates

In the summer of 1964 political opposition may have been disrupted; it certainly was not eliminated. A disarray of inchoate organizational fragments, it still could attract massive popular support. A medley of diverse, often contradictory, programs, it still shared the predominant theme of hostility to the government. As the elections approached, its very impotence—it could not even block a two-thirds vote in the National Assembly[8] —militated for cohesion.

The *Jamā'at-i-Islāmi*, of course, was dissolved. The National Awami Party was still making overtures to the government. Maulana Bhashani, it was reported, now offered "to strengthen the hands of President Ayub provided the President adopted an independent foreign policy for the country."[9] The National Democratic Front, however, never ceased to preach unity among those opposed to the President, his regime, and his institutions. It punctuated its position with regular mass meetings and demonstrations. By early July, moreover, the spokesman of the Awami League, *Nizam-i-Islām*, and the Muslim League (Councillist) publicly advocated joint action.[10] Within a week Khwaja Nazimuddin was persuaded to call a meeting. The NDF was carefully excluded, but otherwise it was a most comprehen-

[8] In August 1964 party strengths in the National Assembly were the following: Pakistan Muslim League (formerly Muslim League [Conventionist])—105; Pakistan Peoples Group—25; Muslim League (Councillors)—10; Islamic Democratic Front—6; Independent Group —2; Independent Members—7.

[9] Dacca, *Pakistan Observer*, July 15, 1964, p. 1.

[10] *Ibid.*, July 7, 1964, p. 1.

sive gathering. All four of the revived opposition parties sent delegates. Even the dissolved *Jamā'at* was represented. The sessions started on July 21 in Dacca. Four days later a joint statement announced the unity of purpose of all participants. The parties agreed to nominate a single opposition candidate for the presidency. They also offered a common platform. In a nine-point program they promised a "democratic Constitution" which would provide direct universal suffrage, the primacy of the legislature, independence of the judiciary, and unrestrained political activity. They promised economic and administrative reforms, solution of the Kashmir problem, and an independent foreign policy.[11]

Though a significant accord, it was only for a temporary alliance, not a merger. There remained sharp disagreements on many major issues, including One Unit and the Muslim Family Laws Ordinance. These were glossed over but could not be eliminated. More important, each party retained its organizational integrity. Candidates would be endorsed jointly by the Combined Opposition Parties (COP), but "for the record" each would state his own party affiliation.

The Dacca meeting opened the search for a presidential candidate. There were several suitable alternatives. None, however, seemed ideal. The EBDO'd politicians of the pre-martial law era were still ineligible. Among the others Khwaja Nazimuddin's lack-luster leadership left many uninspired. In any case, his age posed a formidable barrier.[12] Chaudhri Mohammad Ali was more vigorous, but his popularity was confined mostly to West Pakistan. Lieutenant General Azam Khan could

[11] *Ibid.*, July 25, 1964, p. 8.
[12] A few months later (October 22) Khwaja Nazimuddin died.

count on massive support in both Wings, but his close association with the martial law regime and his personal popularity made him suspect to politicians. The path narrowed and by early September led to *Madar-i-Millat* Fatima Jinnah.

Her qualifications were exceptional. The sister of *Quaid-i-Azam* Mohammad Ali Jinnah, she had personally participated in the Pakistan Movement. Seventeen years after independence she still evoked fond memories of the successful struggle for a Muslim homeland. Through the years her reputation remained untarnished. She kept aloof from the bizarre politics of the fifties, and after an initial endorsement of the Revolution (1958) she became a determined critic of the regime and a vocal advocate for democratic institutions. Her most significant qualification, however, was this: Miss Jinnah was the only one considered for nomination who was convinced that she could win.

Nevertheless, her credentials were not flawless. She was a lady of great presence, but still she was a woman. The very idea of a woman as Chief Executive was distressing to the martial tribesmen of the frontier. Worse still, it offended the traditionalist Muslims. The selection of a female candidate to run the administration of the State, declared Maulana Shamsul Huq, the chairman of an Ulama Conference in Dacca, would amount to ignoring the laws of Islam.[13] This handicap was only partially alleviated when the *Majlis-i-Shura* of the *Jamā'at-i-Islāmi* assured the country that "in the present unusual situation the candidature of a woman as head of the State is not against the *Shariat*."[14]

[13] Karachi, *Dawn*, September 25, 1964, p. 1.
[14] Dacca, *Pakistan Observer*, October 3, 1964, p. 1.

Rallying opposition forces did not perceptibly affect the confidence of President Ayub Khan. "I have served the people," he remarked with evident satisfaction. If that was not enough, he wanted to know what else was needed. He welcomed a contest, he said. Then, perhaps as an afterthought, he added, "only by a deserving person."[15] He had little doubt about his own success. It was my impression that he viewed the campaign not so much as a personal contest than as an opportunity to link the Basic Democrats, his lower echelon leaders, with the national hierarchy of his political party. He saw in the campaign an opportunity to accomplish his plan of developing the second pillar—the bureaucracy being the other—in the leadership pattern of Pakistan. He expected to reserve most of his personal appearances for groups of party workers who in turn would carry his message to the voters.[16]

Confident as he may have been, the President did not abandon caution. The Working Committee of his party, now renamed the Pakistan Muslim League, declined to endorse candidates for the Electoral College (Basic Councillors). It would not enter contests decided by universal suffrage. The President's party preferred to await the results and then recruit the winners.[17] On August 19, 1964, the same Working Committee nominated the party's presidential candidate by acclamation: Field Marshal Mohammad Ayub Khan. Then the campaign began.

[15] *Ibid.*, August 26, 1964, p. 1.
[16] I gained this impression in a personal conversation with Abdul Waheed Khan, General Secretary, Pakistan Muslim League, in Rawalpindi late in July 1964.
[17] Karachi, *Dawn*, August 21, 1964, p. 11.

Election of Basic Democrats

There is no more dramatic evidence of the rate and direction of Pakistan's political development than the sharp contrast between her two elections of Basic Democrats. In 1959 the program was in its infancy. The country was under martial law. Political activity was at a standstill. Parties were defunct. Contests for national offices were not permitted; discussion of national issues was prohibited. In contrast, by 1964 the Constitution had already been in operation for two years. Political recruiting and organizing were in full swing. In September all five opposition parties were again in the field. (The Supreme Court had declared null and void the official ban on the *Jamā'at-i-Islāmi*.) There were four candidates for the presidency, and there was a genuine contest between two of them.[18]

The campaign indeed was anything but a façade. To be sure, at first the government did try its hand at some coercion. Students and party workers were jailed. Farid Ahmad, a most articulate Bengali leader of the *Nizam-i-Islām*, was arrested in Lahore.[19] Ataur Rahman, A. S. M. Abdul Jalil, and some forty others met the same fate in Khulna and Rajshahi. In an exhibition of singular determination the government seized Rs 4,000 of Abu Mohammad Ferdous' property to force his surrender to the police.[20] It was all a short and, it seems to me, futile venture. On September 29 East Pakistan observed a general strike (*hartal*) in protest. It was peaceful,[21] but

[18] The two minor candidates were K. M. Kamal and Mian Bashir Ahmad.

[19] Dacca, *Pakistan Observer*, September 14, 1964, p. 1.

[20] *Ibid.*, September 24, 1964, p. 1; September 25, 1964, p. 1; September 26, 1964, p. 1.

[21] The sole exception was Chittagong, where 162 were injured in a clash.

277

it was total. In Dacca, reported the *Pakistan Observer*, even the clocks stopped ticking.[22] Farid Ahmad and most others were released soon enough to participate in the campaign.[23] After that the government was less disposed to intervene forcibly in the Opposition's activities. It bore with restraint mass meetings designed to discredit the regime. It tolerated Chaudhri Mohammad Ali's verbal broadsides. Above all, it permitted Lieutenant General Azam to tour East Pakistan and contribute his enormous popular influence and political talents to the cause of the Opposition.

By any test it was a vigorous campaign. In the towns and villages there was the usual amount of personal controversy and intrigue. There were intense ascriptive loyalties and rivalries. There was, I think, considerable bribery. Although the President ordered public officials to keep out of the contest, reports of official intimidation were rampant. In any case, governors, ministers, and parliamentary secretaries flooded the countryside with oratory. So did the Opposition leaders, ex-governors and ex-ministers. Meanwhile, legions of party workers fanned out into the provinces to direct organization, arrange favors, and contribute to polemics. Above all this feverish activity, however, the population was treated to an unparalleled personal exposure of the presidential candidates. From September until the conclusion of the BD elections[24] the President made fifty-six and Miss Jinnah twenty-five major campaign

[22] Dacca, *Pakistan Observer*, September 30, 1964, p. 1.
[23] Maulana Maududi had been released earlier in response to the Supreme Court's *Jamā'at-i-Islāmi* ruling.
[24] November 9 in the West Wing and November 19 in East Pakistan.

278

addresses and statements which were extensively reported in the press.

These were the main features of the dialogue. First of all, both candidates concentrated upon West Pakistan. The East Wing's share was less than a third of this effort. Second, both candidates relied heavily on mass audiences. Miss Jinnah did so consistently. The President at first held to his plan of reserving appearances primarily for party workers and other select groups. The spectacle of tens, evens hundreds, of thousands of enthusiastic citizens greeting his opponent, however, must have been wearing on the nerves. Each day brought fresh demonstration that in popular appeal his party leaders and workers could not approximate, let alone match, *Madar-i-Millat* Fatima Jinnah. By October the President again had to come to the aid of his party. A brisk schedule of public rallies was added to his already crowded campaign program.

Table 13

Distribution by region and audience of major campaign addresses and statements of President Ayub Khan and Miss Jinnah from September 1, 1964, until the end of BD elections

	Region			*Mass Audience*				*Special Groups*							
	Total	E.P.	W.P.	Total	1	2	3	Total	4	5	6	7	8	9	10
Ayub Khan	56	17	39	33	26	3	4	23	7	6	1	2	3	2	2
Miss Jinnah	25	9	16	22	17	–	5	3	3	–	–	–	–	–	–

1—Public rally
2—Radio address
3—Press conference or release

4—Intellectuals and professionals
5—Basic Democrats
6—Ulama

7—Tribal chiefs
8—Party workers
9—Students
10—Military

279

Another salient feature of the dialogue was the independence of the presidential candidates. Both were politically stronger than the political parties which nominated them. The President, of course, was in complete control of the Pakistan Muslim League, which was still a rather tenuous organizational entity whose main, if not only, appeal was the President's personal support. Miss Jinnah's position was quite different. She did not control any party organization. Her supporters included the full spectrum of antigovernment groups from the traditionalist Islamic elements to the avant-garde advocates of a secular state. Yet she too ran her own campaign, relying less on party hierarchy than on the personal support of prominent intellectuals and that of Lieutenant General Azam Khan.

Here is one striking example of the independence of the presidential candidates. A simple count of column lines identifies four major categories of issues and the relative preeminence of economic and social themes in party manifestoes. An analysis of the dialogue reflects the same categories of issues but reveals a dramatic shift of focus.

Table 14

Comparison of relative weights of issues in party manifestoes and in major addresses and statements of President Ayub Khan and Miss Jinnah from September 1, 1964, until the end of BD elections (in percentages)

	Political System	Economic and Social Problems	Islamic Ideology	Foreign Policy	Misc.
PML Manifesto	21.7	51.0	5.4	11.0	11.9
Ayub Khan	58.0	9.1	11.9	11.0	10.0
COP Manifesto	35.6	36.9	3.7	16.1	7.1
Miss Jinnah	75.8	9.1	7.6	3.0	4.5

Personal acrimony, rampant in exchanges of lower level leaders, at times also infected the national candidates. Miss Jinnah refused to honor the President with his title. She insisted on referring to him as *Mister* Ayub Khan. The latter in turn could not resist the remark that if a bottom standard was set (for presidential qualifications) even then Miss Fatima Jinnah would not make the grade. She was old, a recluse, weak-minded, and lacked experience in statecraft.[25] Still, on the whole, the dialogue remained on a high level and focused on the political system.

This indeed was the most significant feature of the campaign dialogue between President Ayub Khan and Miss Fatima Jinnah. All other problems—independent foreign policy, Islamic principles of law, economic growth, even Kashmir and regional disparities—were reduced to minor roles or were integrated into a single, overriding issue: the political development program. Persistently the President reemphasized political stability, the gradually broadening political base, general progress, and accomplishments of his regime. Just as persistently he recited the contention of pre-martial law confusion and charged his opponents with disruption. Miss Jinnah, in turn, never ceased to indict the regime for arbitrariness and corruption. She raised the alternative of the restoration of democracy, including a parliamentary system, civil liberties, and universal direct suffrage, and then invoked the memory of *Quaid-i-Azam.*

The polling lasted nearly three weeks. It was a somewhat turbulent affair. In several areas proceedings had to be suspended before order could be restored. At

25 Karachi, *Dawn*, October 24, 1964, p. 9.

Table 15

Main political themes and their relative frequency in the major addresses and statements of President Ayub Khan and Miss Jinnah from September 1, 1964, until the end of BD elections

Political Themes		% of total
I. PRESIDENT AYUB KHAN		
A. Record of regime		
General Accomplishments		11.8
Political Stability		18.9
Guided Democracy		34.6
firm leadership	4.7	
democratic direction	20.5	
indirect elections	9.4	
B. Alternative program		
Pre-martial law confusion		9.4
Disruptive activities of Opposition		22.9
C. Other themes		2.4
II. MISS JINNAH		
A. Record of regime		
Dictatorship		4.0
Corruption		6.0
B. Alternative program		
Moral regeneration		14.0
Quaid-i-Azam's heritage		18.0
Restoration of democracy		50.0
democratic institutions	26.0	
direct universal suffrage	16.0	
civil rights	8.0	
C. Other themes		8.0

least one successful candidate was shot; an indeterminate number were wounded.[26] Balloting was heavy throughout the country. The outcome, however, was rather indefinite. We know the names of those elected and those defeated. We also know that some ten thou-

[26] See, for example, Dacca, *Pakistan Observer*, November 2, 1964, p. 1.

sand candidates (by one unofficial count—9,668) were returned uncontested. What we do not know is the party loyalty of those elected *on the day they were elected*. There were, of course, claims. Shaikh Masud Sadiq, Acting President of the West Pakistan PML announced that 83.1 per cent of the successful candidates in West Pakistan were supporters of his party.[27] In turn, Manzoorul Haq, the COP chairman, claimed 65 per cent for the Opposition.[28] The contradictions were even more glaring in the East Wing. At one point the PML claimed 85 per cent and so did the Opposition.[29] It is probable, however, that *at this time* a substantial number, if not most, successful candidates simply did not have party commitment. They were open to persuasion. That came in the final stage of the campaign.

Election of the President

By the middle of November there could be little doubt of Miss Fatima Jinnah's broad popular appeal. Wherever she went—and she traveled tirelessly—solid crowds waited often many hours and greeted her affectionately. Most appeared spontaneously; she had no elaborate organization of advance agents. Undoubtedly, some came only because they were curious, many others because they sought to honor the memory of *Quaid-i-Azam*. Yet whatever their reason for coming, most people left deeply impressed by her personality and sincerity. She demonstrated an extraordinary capacity to mobilize masses.

The President too was popular. His appeal to the Basic Democrats, however, had other potent ingredients

[27] Karachi, *Dawn*, November 12, 1964, p. 4.
[28] *Ibid.*, November 11, 1964, p. 5.
[29] *Ibid.*, November 17, 1964, pp. 11, 14.

as well. It was he, after all, who was their source of political power. Miss Jinnah as president may not have restricted their role in the Union Councils, but she would surely have denied them the opportunity to serve in an electoral college. It was the President moreover who was responsible for their access to substantial public funds. Under his system Union Councils were not only authorized to levy taxes but since 1962, when the old idea of village development was disinterred and a program of public works introduced, they received a major share of allocations[30] and were also authorized to make disbursements at their own discretion. Whether the funds were spent on development or otherwise, they certainly boosted the morale of Basic Democrats—and presumably increased their commitment to the regime.

The most important ingredient of the President's appeal to his electors, however, was the widespread conclusion that his rule was inevitable. Few believed that he could be defeated at the polls. Fewer still thought he would accept defeat. The Basic Democrats may have listened when he declared that he would bow before the verdict of the people, whatever it might be, but they remembered that the same speech contained a warning that the Revolution of 1958 would be considered mild compared to the one which would follow if the people acted in a "stupid" way.[31] Indeed, it seemed futile as well as injudicious to vote against the President.

[30] The allocation for 1963-1964 to East Pakistan *Thana* Councils and Union Councils was Rs 8.75 crores (Government of East Pakistan, *Works Programme through Basic Democracies 1963-64*, Dacca, East Pakistan Government Press, 1963, p. 4). See also: Pakistan Academy for Rural Development, *An Evaluation of the Rural Public Works Programme East Pakistan, 1962-63* (Comilla: Pakistan Academy for Rural Development, 1963).

[31] Karachi, *Dawn*, November 9, 1964, p. 1.

The campaign in the meantime moved into its final stretch. The date for the presidential election was set for January 2, scarcely more than a month away.[32] The focus narrowed to eighty thousand electors, who now had to bear up under the most intense pressures. It is my impression that most votes were decided through direct and local "persuasion." Still the dialogue between the two major presidential candidates did not abate. On the contrary, it intensified. Between the BD and the presidential elections the President made twenty-seven and Miss Jinnah thirty-six additional major speeches and statements. Again West Pakistan was heavily favored, the East Wing's share being less than 10 per cent. Again Miss Jinnah relied chiefly on mass rallies. This time, however, the President clearly concentrated on selective audiences.

Table 16

Distribution by region and audience of major campaign addresses and statements of President Ayub Khan and Miss Jinnah from the conclusion of BD elections to December 31, 1964

	Region			Mass Audience				Special Groups							
	Total	E.P.	W.P.	Total	1	2	3	Total	4	5	6	7	8	9	10
Ayub Khan	27	2	25	8	2	1	5	19	4	11	1	—	—	3	—
Miss Jinnah	36	3	33	27	26	—	1	9	4	4	—	—	—	1	—

1—Public rally
2—Radio address
3—Press conference or release

4—Intellectuals and professionals
5—Basic Democrats
6—Ulama and other religious groups

7—Tribal chiefs
8—Party workers
9—Students
10—Military

[32] Dacca, *Pakistan Observer*, December 1, 1964, p. 1.

As though these presentations did not provide sufficient exposure, the government arranged ten "Projection Meetings," at which presidential candidates were
invited to address the assembled Basic Democrats (who
were brought there at public expense) and to respond
to questions. The issues may have had little to do with
electoral choices, but no citizen in Pakistan, whether in
a large city or distant village—certainly no Basic Democrat—would be permitted to remain ignorant of them.

The issues indeed were remarkably consistent throughout this gigantic effort. The dialogue continued to focus
on the political system.

Table 17

Comparison of the relative frequency of major
categories of issues in the addresses and statements plus
"projection speeches" of President Ayub Khan and
Miss Jinnah from the conclusion of BD elections
to December 31, 1964 (in percentages)

	Political System		Economic and Social Problems		Islamic Ideology		Foreign Relations		Misc.	
	1	2	1	2	1	2	1	2	1	2
Ayub Kahn	62.9	57.3	8.2	11.0	4.1	3.7	12.4	7.3	12.4	20.7
Miss Jinnah	66.0	68.8	7.4	8.2	3.2	1.6	6.4	6.6	17.0	14.8

1—Major addresses and statements
2—Projection speeches

The themes, too, followed the earlier pattern, with the
President defending his political development program
and warning dire consequences if it were rejected and
Miss Jinnah demanding the "restoration of democracy"
and dwelling heavily on the deficiencies of the system.

Table 18

Main political themes and their relative frequency in the major addresses and statements plus "projection speeches" of President Ayub Khan and Miss Jinnah from the conclusion of BD elections to December 31, 1964 (in percentages)

	Addresses and Statements		Projection Speeches
PRESIDENT AYUB KHAN			
A. Record of Regime			
General accomplishments		14.8	17.0
Political stability		14.8	8.5
Guided democracy		34.4	40.5
firm leadership	8.2		—
democratic trends	13.1		19.2
indirect elections	13.1		21.3
B. Alternative Programs			
Pre-martial law confusion		6.5	10.6
Disruption of opposition			
(including internal enemies)		27.9	21.3
C. Other Political Themes		1.6	2.1
MISS JINNAH			
A. Record of Regime			
Dictatorship		21.0	19.0
Corruption		6.5	16.7
B. Alternative Programs			
Moral regeneration		—	—
Quaid-i-Azam's tradition		4.8	9.5
Restoration of democracy		56.5	40.5
democratic institutions	38.7		16.7
universal suffrage	13.0		19.0
civil rights	4.8		4.8
C. Other Political Themes		11.2	14.3

"Mister Ayub Khan" was a dictator, she repeated incessantly. This, I think, was a mistake. Whatever the theo-

287

retical merits of the dictatorship charge, its practical effect was to reinforce the President's most potent appeal: his inevitability. Only in the very last days did the Opposition attack this problem and then through the rather dubious method of a false rumor. The report was circulated that the President was packing his bags; he was preparing to leave the country.[33]

This time the polling was short and relatively orderly. The results were anything but indefinite. The President received 49,951 votes or 62.6 per cent of the total cast. He had a majority in both Wings and in thirteen of the sixteen administrative divisions. Miss Jinnah captured the metropolis of Karachi and the legislative capital of Dacca. She had massive support throughout East Pakistan and lost the province by a margin of only 2,578. She was least successful in the tribal areas where she received only 77 out of 2,512 votes.[34]

The President's supporters celebrated victory with extravagance. They showered their leader with congratulatory telegrams. They organized processions and torchlight parades. Some, including reportedly the President's son, carried their exuberance to the Opposition strongholds of Karachi. The predictable violence cost twenty lives, and the army had to restore order.[35]

[33] Karachi, *Dawn*, December 28, 1964, p. 11.

[34] *Ibid.*, January 9, 1965, p. 1.

[35] Dacca, *Pakistan Observer*, January 5, 1965, p. 1; January 6, 1965, p. 1; January 7, 1965, p. 1. In a sequel Shamsuddin, an alleged witness, charged that Gauhar Ayub Khan had been guilty of murder during the disturbances. The latter remained free while the *New York Times* correspondent and the complainant Shamsuddin were placed under arrest. Later a journalist who may have been mistaken for another witness was shot dead by "unknown assailants." (*Ibid.*, January 19, 1965, p. 1; January 30, 1965, p. 1; February 2, 1965, p. 1.)

Miss Jinnah withdrew from active political life. She had earned a rest. Indeed her vigorous efforts made the election meaningful, raising it from a ritualistic formality to a democratic contest. Her determined leadership made the election a constructive contest. Though the pressures on her to resort to demagogy and to set region against region, class against class, must have been intense, she conducted a dignified campaign focused on the interest of all citizens of Pakistan. Though she advocated fundamental changes in the political system, she had no part in subversion. Her campaign reinforced order—order even in change. Her contributions to the political development program were massive.

The President wished her well.[36] He could afford to be satisfied. One more stage of his program was now completed. Even so, his task was far from finished. In the immediate future he would have to direct his party's campaigns for the National Assembly and the provincial assemblies.[37] In the not too distant future he still had to convert his personal hegemony into institutional control. He still had to establish a viable party organiza-

[36] Karachi, *Dawn*, January 3, 1965, p. 8.

[37] Elections for the National Assembly were held on March 21, 1965. The results (not including the seats reserved for women) were the following: Pakistan Muslim League—115; Combined Opposition Parties—9; National Democratic Front—4; Independents—18. In each of four constituencies there was a tie. Interestingly, Gauhar Ayub Khan was elected by the constituency which had previously been represented by his uncle and the President's political opponent, Sardar Bahadur Khan. In all of West Pakistan only one Opposition candidate was successful (Karachi, *Dawn*, March 22, 1965, p. 1). Two features of this campaign should be noted here. First, early in January a large number of intermediate level Opposition leaders were arrested. Second, for the first time the Combined Opposition Parties formally aligned themselves with the National Democratic Front.

tion reaching into the villages. He still had to enlist popular commitment behind the political system. If the democratic direction of his program was to continue, he still had to fashion a loyal opposition with significant political power. If his program was to survive him, he still had to groom a successor. In this spirit the President celebrated his victory:

> Let us make the fullest use of the opportunity which Allah has given us. Let us complete the task assigned to us so that generations that come after us inherit durable institutions enshrined in the hearts of the people and sustained by an abiding faith in Pakistan.
>
> Pakistan Paindabad.[38]

[38] Karachi, *Dawn*, January 3, 1965, p. 8.

Conclusion

++

Conclusion

++

JUST SIX YEARS AGO Mohammad Ayub Khan took the helm of the State of Pakistan. Since then he has many accomplishments to his credit. The disintegration of the country, an acute threat in 1958, seems rather remote now. Economic growth has been steady and may be gaining momentum. In the industrial sector expansion has been impressive. The government gained cohesion when control over the machinery was consolidated. Its image gained coherence when the cacophony of contradictory statements by President, Prime Minister, cabinet members, provincial chief ministers and sundry other officials was replaced by clear policies uniformly enunciated. The government gained stability when the President stayed in office for over five years and remained secure.

The political system of Pakistan has not as yet acquired the capacity to direct the course and rate of social and economic change. This is not surprising. The time elapsed has been too brief for that. More bothersome is the observation that there is no clear evidence that the political system is making progress in this direction. Significantly, the major achievements of the President's regime in general have been confined to programs requiring control only over a very narrow base. Efforts involving an expanded measure of popular commitment have not been similarly rewarded. Thus, for example, the economic development program has been sustained by massive foreign aid, not by a marked rise in domestic saving. Certainly private subscription to government bonds or yields from broadly based taxes have not kept pace with the growth in national income. Similarly, mass support for national integration has remained tenuous. From the Frontier to Bengal fellow citizens from other regions remain favored targets of scapegoating. The Bureau of National Reconstruction seemed to make little headway toward a national focus of orientation. In any case its efforts were soon curtailed. Sympathetic response by the government toward regional grievances has yet to yield positive results. Only the threat of an external enemy and a dramatically independent foreign policy have so far evoked a measure of national identification. Unhappily, these are treacherous enticements. They may set a course which would not only imperil the prospects of future advance, but also destroy the accomplishments of the past. Cohesion stimulated by agitation against the most plausible external enemy exposes to persecutions some fifty million Muslims in India. Worse still, it incites riots and public disorders in Pakistan. Meanwhile, an independent foreign policy, especially one bordering on eccentricity, risks a substantial deceleration in the inflow of foreign aid. Pakistan's strategic importance is considerable, but it is hardly sufficient to support profitably a policy of playing off over an extended period her Western allies against the Communists. Finally, the massive efforts to construct representative institutions have not been rewarded by a rally of mass support behind the political system. That the system of Basic Democracies, even after it was reinforced by the delegation of additional political, legal and economic functions, together with the new Constitution, should produce so narrow a margin of popular commitment (if indeed there was a positive margin) must have been disappointing to President Ayub Khan. He accepted the need to bolster his political system through a political party organization with pronounced distaste; he himself became party president with evident reluctance. The revived Pakistan Muslim League has since demonstrated its ability to hold mass meetings at regular intervals and to manage elections through the Basic Democrats. It has had considerably less success in maintaining discipline within the organization or in controlling its primary units. If, moreover, its preference for non-party contests in the Union Council elections in November 1964 and for indirect national elections in January and March 1965 are an indication, the President's party still has no confidence in winning a popular contest.

The difficulties encountered in the conversion of acknowledged accomplishments into an increment in the political system's capacity to control may only be symptoms of the recent origin of the program. Even so, they are suggestive at least for a preliminary evaluation of guided democracy as a vehicle for political development. Consider first the claim that this pattern, by consolidating the decision-making process, offers an increment in its effectiveness.

Pakistan's experience confirms the expectation that a military commander supported by disciplined armed forces can, if he chooses, assume with relative ease the highest political office and install his supporters in top echelon policy-making positions. He may even introduce and maintain political institutions. His capacity to implement policy, however, is not visibly enhanced. In the absence of a national focus of orientation or a tradition of confidence in the political system, popular response to persuasion by government—any government —is necessarily negligible. It takes generations to transcend parochial loyalties, to overcome widespread poverty, and to develop a leadership structure which can attract mass support. Simultaneously, rudimentary communications and inefficient and at times unreliable personnel hold the effectiveness of governmental coercion to a narrow range. It takes a long time to build the necessary roads and massive investment to procure sufficient radio sets. It takes a long time and massive investment (to mention only two requirements) to build an efficient and honest administration. Moreover, even within the narrow range of his effectiveness, a military commander must make concessions and compromises. He may be a man of unimpeachable integrity and fervent patriotism. Yet, having seized power by revolutionary means, institutional arrangements or constitutional guarantees can offer only limited security. In the final analysis, his preeminence must rest upon the loyalty of the armed forces and their prolonged ability to deter or destroy organized opposition. He is tied to his military constituency and must respond to the most pronounced aspirations of its members. This is not all. Unless such a military commander is prepared to rule the country exclusively or even primarily through the military command structure, he is compelled to enlist the cooperation of the government apparatus, including the bureaucracy and, as in the case of Pakistan, the judicial hierarchy. This support too must be paid for— in cash or personal favors perhaps, but invariably with a substantial share in decision-making.

Another distinctive feature of guided democracy is

its strategy of increasing political control by the conversion of personal hegemony based largely upon the capacity to coerce into representative institutions relying primarily upon the capacity to persuade. Here again Pakistan's experience seems revealing. It suggests that, at least in the initial stages, the voluntary reduction in coercive control is not accompanied by a compensatory yield in the capacity to persuade. Local elected councils which are adjuncts of the bureaucracy may generate no more public commitment to local government than a pattern of appointed boards chaired by an administrator. Similarly, a legislature controlled by the executive may not visibly enhance the popular feeling of participation in national decision-making beyond the level generated by an authoritarian system. Such local councils and central legislatures may well be essential stages toward fully representative bodies, but only *after* they have been substantially emancipated from executive (bureaucratic) control is the process likely to be rewarded by an increase in popular commitment. Guided democracy as a vehicle of political development apparently faces from its earliest stages until the final breakthrough a progressive *decline in the already precarious control of the political system.*

This decline in control is accentuated by one further feature of Pakistan's experience, namely the singular determination to exclude from decision-making all those who before the Revolution had demonstrated their skill in mobilizing mass support. The hierarchies of small-scale groups have little standing with the regime. The religious leaders and the bar associations are virtually ignored. The student leaders are admonished. Politicians are castigated. It is, of course, possible that a grand coalition of these subnational hierarchies could not be organized behind the program of political development. The traditional leaders may well be determined to subvert such progress. Their focus of orientation is at best the small-scale unit and at worst their own personal ambition. The performance of other postindependence leaders rarely inspires confidence. Nevertheless, unless a genuine effort is made to involve these men, who after all do have a popular following, such a conclusion remains intuitive, and opposition may be by default. Worse still, the exclusion of these leaders not only neglects a possible source of increment in control, it invites massive resistance—even political sabotage.

These observations focus upon the crucial vulnerability of guided democracy. The danger is very real indeed that such decline in control could not be absorbed by the government and that it would dissolve in chaos. Alternatively, intimidated by what appear to be severe reverses even a military commander who sincerely strives to convert his own hegemony into the control of representative institutions will slacken the pace of his program and will seek refuge in coercion. He may find himself gradually but almost irresistibly drawn into the whirlpool of regression that can terminate only in a corrupt and authoritarian rule with little interest and prospect for political development. To guide a program along the narrow and unmarked road which avoids both these pitfalls requires the scarcest commodity in newly independent states (or in the world for that matter): a truly extraordinary measure of statesmanship.

Appendices

A. Memorandum written by
General Mohammad Ayub Khan
Defense Minister of Pakistan, October 4, 1954:

*A Short Appreciation of Present and Future Problems
of Pakistan*

THE AIM

1. The ultimate aim of Pakistan must be to become a sound, a solid and a cohesive nation to be able to play its destined role in world history. This can be achieved only if as a start a constitution is evolved that will suit the genius of the people and be based on the circumstances confronting them, so that they are set on the path of unity, team work and creative progress.

2. Before such a constitution can be devised, it is obvious that certain preliminary steps will have to be taken that will provide the setting for the unhindered evolution of such a constitution. Taking of such preliminary steps therefore becomes the *immediate* aim of Pakistan.

FACTORS

GENERAL

3. (a) The people of Pakistan consist of a variety of races each with its own historical background and culture. East Bengalis, who constitute the bulk of the population probably belong to the very original Indian races. It would be no exaggeration to say that up to the creation of Pakistan, they have not known any real freedom or sovereignty. They have been in turn ruled either by the caste Hindus, Moghals, Pathans or the British. In addition, they have been and still

are under considerable cultural and linguistic influence. As such they have all the inhibitions of downtrodden races and have not yet found it possible psychologically to adjust to the requirements of their newborn freedom. Their peculiar complexes, exclusiveness, suspicion and a sort of defensive aggressiveness probably emerge from this historical background. Prudence, therefore, demands that these factors should be recognized and catered for and they be helped so as to feel equal partners and prove an asset. This can be done only if they are given a considerable measure of partnership.

(b) The population in West Pakistan, on the other hand, is probably the greatest mixture of races found anywhere in the world. Lying on the gateways to the Indian sub-continent, it was inevitable that each successive race should have left its traces here. Consequently, this forced mixture of races has fusion of ideas, outlook and culture, despite linguistic variety obtained. Strategically and economically too, this area is destined to stand or fall as a whole. Lying as it does in the basin of the Indus river and its tributaries, its future economic development must be considered as a whole to achieve maximum results. All this indicates therefore that West Pakistan, in order to develop properly and prove a bulwark of defence from the North or South, must be welded into one unit and all artificial provincial boundaries removed, regardless of any prejudices to the contrary, which are mostly the creation of politicians rather than real. When doing this, however, regard must be had for the prejudices and fears of people, and their future balanced development. This unit should, therefore, be so subdivided that each sub-unit embraces a racial group or groups with a common economy, communications and potentiality for development, and administration decentralized in them to the maximum possible.

(c) The creation of one unit in West Pakistan, however, is possible only if the biggest constituent is prepared to show large-heartedness and make a sacrifice for the common good. Punjab is the biggest and most important province in West

Pakistan with more than half its population. If she insists on proportionate representation, the others will, at once, shy off. Besides, no coalition can work with one dominant partner. Therefore, for its preservation and the glory of Pakistan, Punjab should be asked to accept forty per cent representation in the legislature of this unit, others having representation in proportion to their population. But before such a unit can be brought into being, the existing provincial and States' legislatures and cabinets will have to be done away with so as not to interfere and impede reorganization.

Deductions from the above:

(1) Call East Bengal one unit and give it as much partnership as possible.

(2) Reorganize West Pakistan into one unit and give it similar partnership as above.

(3) Abolish present provincial Ministries and legislatures to speed up reorganization.

(4) Subdivide each unit into convenient sub-units, each embracing a racial group or groups with common economy, communications and prospective development. Administration to be decentralized in these sub-units as much as possible.

(5) In order to remove any fear of domination, Punjab to be asked to accept forty per cent representation in West Pakistan unit legislature.

(6) Both East and West units to have their own legislatures.

4. Given the above, the fear of one unit dividing or dominating others would disappear; harmonious and unfettered development in each unit will be possible, fear of provincialism will be reduced to the minimum; saving in man-power in eliminating so many top-heavy provincial administrations would be effected; expense of administration would be reduced to the minimum and the danger of politicians interfering with the local administrators curtailed. In other words, very valuable gains would have been made by such a reorganization.

The Administrative Structure of Each Provincial Unit

5. Having created two provincial units in Pakistan, the next question is to determine the structure of administration in each unit. Before answering such a question, it would be appropriate to reiterate the fact that our eventual aim must be to develop democracy in Pakistan, but of a type that suits the genius of the people. Our people are mostly uneducated and our politicians not so scrupulous. The people are capable of doing great things, but they can also be easily misled. Unfettered democracy can, therefore, prove dangerous, especially now-a-days when Communism from within and without is so quick to make use of its weaknesses. We, therefore, have to have a controlled form of democracy, with checks and counter-checks. This indicates that legislature finds the Cabinet, whose actions are controllable by a Governor, who in turn is controlled by the Head of the State (President); in certain circumstances, the Governor having the power to remove Ministers or the Ministry. He should also be in a position to protect the rights of the Services and have them carry out their obligations.

6. Connected with the elections of legislatures is the question of franchise. It is too late now to resile from universal suffrage, however great its shortcomings may be. The answer would be to provide checks here too, so as to prevent its becoming irresponsible. We must not forget that democracy is a means to an end and not an end by itself and that there is no set pattern of democracy that can be applied to every country without modifications. It would be advisable, therefore, to enable people to elect a college of people in each sub-unit, who in turn elect members for the Provincial and Central legislatures. Such an electoral system would be more easily manageable and would make for a good deal of responsibility.

7. As to the size and type of provincial and central legislatures, opinions may differ, but the need for strict economy in men and money would indicate that one legislature for each province, of about 150 members each, would do.

Similarly, the central legislature, of which mention will be made later, should not be of a strength more than that.

8. Whilst talking about administration there is the problem of our legal system, which is most expensive, ineffective, dilatory, tyrannical and totally unsuited to our genius. This will need complete overhaul and to be made humane, quick and cheap. The answer would seem to lie in having a *Jirga* cum judicial system and revision of evidence and procedural laws with only one right of appeal. The highest judicial court for dealing with cases other than constitutional will have to be created in each sub-unit. The federal or the provincial High Courts should deal only with cases of a constitutional nature.

Deductions from the above:

(1) In each province there should be one legislature of about 150 members each, headed by a Cabinet. There should be a Governor in each Province appointed by the President with powers of control over the Cabinet and the Services.

(2) The electoral system should consist of election of electoral colleges in each sub-unit by universal suffrage: these colleges to elect members for the provincial legislature, the central legislature and also to elect the President, of which mention will be made later.

(3) The legal system should be simplified and decentralized to sub-units: introduction of *Jirga* cum judicial system to be examined.

(4) Government Servants' Conduct Rules should be revised so as to make summary dealings in case of rewards and punishment possible.

The Structure of the Centre

9. Having created two units of the country, their federation on an equal basis without fear of domination of one over the other becomes a practical proposition. This federation should consist of one legislative house of about 150 strong, equally divided amongst the two units, headed by a Cabinet. This Cabinet should have executive powers as

voted by the legislature, subject to some effective control by the President who should be elected. The President should be made the final custodian of power on the country's behalf and should be able to put things right in both the provinces and the Centre should they go wrong. Laws should be operative only if certified by the President except in cases where they are passed by three-fourths majority. No change in the constitution should be made unless agreed to by the President. In case of serious disagreement between the President and the legislatures, provision should be made for fresh elections of either one or both. Acceptance of the Mohammad Ali Formula for election of the President and passing of laws would perhaps be necessary.

10. For reasons given before, the provinces should have as much partnership as possible and that means that in addition to the subjects already in their hands, Communications, except inter-provincial, Industries, Commerce, Health, etc., should be handed over to the Provinces, leaving Defence, Foreign Affairs and Currency in the hands of the Centre.

11. The quick development of our resources and the raising of the standard of living of our people is one of the main problems which Pakistan has to solve. This can be done effectively only if we overhaul our educational system to prepare our manpower for the task and to have well-controlled and well-financed organizations to undertake major development projects. That indicates organization of Development Boards rather on the P.I.D.C. fashion for education, cottage industries, land and power and hosts of other things in each Province. This arrangement will help relieve local administrations of a lot of headaches and will ensure quick development.

12. But nothing much will be gained unless we carry out land reforms in a scientific fashion. Possession of vast areas of land by a few is no longer defensible nor is acquisition of land without compensation. The Egyptian example is a very good one; they allowed the owner a certain limit of holding, buying the rest for distribution amongst peasants, who will pay the cost in seventy yearly instalments.

13. It was mentioned earlier that the President should be

made the repository of power. He can discharge this duty only if the Services are made directly responsible to him. To do that, a system of Joint Staff headed by a Supreme Commander will have to be introduced. The Supreme Commander should be appointed by the President. In addition to other duties, he should be made the Defence Member and an *ex officio* member of the Cabinet. This will not only knit the Services together, but would put a stop to any attempt by politicians to interfere in the internal affairs of the Services to promote their personal interests.

14. The experience of the last seven years has shown how dangerous the use of ambiguous cliches can be. Everybody said we should have an Islamic Democracy without ever defining what it was and how it differed from the normally understood democracy. Perhaps it is not possible to define it. Would it, therefore, not be correct to say that any variety of democracy when worked in the spirit of the Quran can be called an Islamic Democracy. We shall perhaps do better and avoid many pitfalls if we accept this concept.

OUTLINE PLAN

15. As a preliminary, abolish provincial Ministries and legislatures in West Pakistan and create one Province of it under a Governor with the requisite staff.

16. Create sub-units in East Bengal and West Pakistan equivalent to a Commissioner's Division, each Division containing racial group or groups with common language, common economy and communications and common development potential. Decentralize administration so that the Head of the Division becomes the king-pin of administration.

17. Overhaul the legal system so as to make it cheaper and quicker, placing the highest appellate court in a Division, except for cases involving points of constitutional law, for which a Federal Court or a High Court in each Province should suffice. A *Jirga* cum judicial system should be evolved and procedural law simplified.

18. Create Development Boards in each Province covering

Education, Water and Power, Land Reforms and Development, Cottage Industries, etc.

19. Create a Joint Staff for the three Services headed by a Supreme Commander who in addition to other duties should be the Defence Member and be the *ex officio* member of the Central Cabinet coming finally under the President.

20. The Central Government to consist of one Legislature consisting of about 150 members equally divided between the two Provinces, a Cabinet and the President. The President to have overriding powers to assume control should things go wrong in the Provinces or the Centre. To avoid undue domination of the one Province over the other, apply the Mohammad Ali Formula to the election of President and passage of Bills.

21. The Provincial Government in East Bengal to consist of a legislature of about 150 members headed by a Cabinet with a Governor appointed by the President: the Governor to have some measure of control over the Cabinet and the Services. Same arrangement should apply in Province of West Pakistan, except that the representation of the present Punjab to be forty per cent and the rest of the seats divided amongst others in accordance with their population.

22. Provinces to have maximum partnership possible, the Centre dealing only with Defence, Foreign Affairs, Currency and such communications as are inter-provincial.

23. The Government Servants Conduct Rules should be revised so as to make summary awards or punishments possible.

24. The suffrage should be adult franchise, who should be called upon to elect an electoral college in each Division, who will then elect the President and members of the Central and provincial legislatures.

25. Finally hope and pray that this Constitution is worked in the spirit of the Quran. If so, our solidarity, strength and future is assured.

B. The Constitution of the Republic of Pakistan

(*Extracts*)

PREAMBLE

PART I. THE REPUBLIC AND ITS TERRITORIES

1. (1) The State of Pakistan shall be a Republic under the name of the Republic of Pakistan.

PART II. PRINCIPLES OF LAW-MAKING AND OF POLICY

CHAPTER 1. PRINCIPLES OF LAW-MAKING

6. (1) The responsibility of deciding whether a proposed law does or does not disregard or violate, or is or is not otherwise in accordance with, the Principles of Law-Making is that of the legislature concerned, but the National Assembly, a Provincial Assembly, the President or the Governor of a Province may refer to the Advisory Council of Islamic Ideology for advice any question that arises as to whether a proposed law disregards or violates, or is otherwise not in accordance with, those Principles.

   (2) The validity of a law shall not be called in question on the ground that the law disregards, violates or is otherwise not in accordance with the Principles of Law-Making.

Principles of Law-Making

1. Islam
2. Equality of citizens
3. Freedom of expression
   1. No law should impose any restriction on the freedom of a citizen to give expression to his thoughts.
   2. This Principle may be departed from where it is necessary to do so—
      (a) in the interest of the security of Pakistan;

307

(b) for the purpose of ensuring friendly relations with foreign States;

(c) for the purpose of ensuring the proper administration of justice;

(d) in the interest of public order;

(e) for the purpose of preventing the commission of offences;

(f) in the interest of decency and morality;

(g) for the purpose of granting privilege, in proper cases, to particular proceedings; or

(h) for the purpose of protecting persons in relation to their reputation.

4. Freedom of association
5. Freedom of movement and right to acquire property
6. Freedom to follow vocation
7. Freedom of religion
8. Safeguards in relation to arrest and detention
9. Protection against retrospective punishment
10. Regulation of compulsory acquisition of property
11. Protection against forced labor
12. Public educational institutions
13. Access to public places
14. Protection of languages, scripts and cultures
15. Protection against slavery
16. Practice of untouchability forbidden

CHAPTER 2. PRINCIPLES OF POLICY

7—8. Principles of policy and responsibility

Principles of Policy

1. Islamic way of life
2. National solidarity
3. Fair treatment to minorities
4. Promotion of interests of backward peoples
5. Advancement of under-privileged castes, etc.
6. Opportunities to participate in national life
7. Education
8. Humane conditions of work
9. Well-being of the people

10. Opportunity to gain adequate livelihood
11. Social security
12. Provision of basic necessities
13. Administrative offices to be provided for public convenience
14. Entry into service of Pakistan not to be denied on grounds of race, etc.
15. Reduction in disparity in remuneration
16. Parity between the Provinces
17. Service in the Defence Services
18. Elimination of riba (usury)
19. Prostitution, gambling and drug-taking to be discouraged
20. Consumption of alcohol to be discouraged
21. Strengthening bonds with the Muslim world, and promoting international peace.

PART III. THE CENTRE

Chapter 1. The President

9. There shall be a President of Pakistan, who shall be elected in accordance with this Constitution and the law.

10. A person shall not be elected as President unless—

(a) he is a Muslim;

(b) he has attained the age of thirty-five years; and

(c) he is qualified to be a member of the National Assembly.

13. (1) Not less than one-third of the total number of the members of the National Assembly may give written notice signed by each of them to the Speaker of the Assembly that they intend to move a resolution in the Assembly for the removal of the President from office on a charge that he has wilfully violated this Constitution or has been guilty of gross misconduct.

(2) The notice shall set out particulars of the charge.

(3) The Speaker shall forthwith cause a copy of the notice to be transmitted to the President.

(4) The resolution shall not be moved in the National Assembly earlier than fourteen days, or later than thirty days, after notice of the resolution was given to the Speaker and, if it is necessary to summon the Assembly in order to enable the resolution to be moved within that period or to be considered by the Assembly, the Speaker shall summon the Assembly.

(5) The President shall have the right to appear and be represented before the National Assembly during the consideration of the resolution by the Assembly.

(6) If, after consideration by the National Assembly of the resolution, it is passed by the Assembly by the votes of not less than three-quarters of the total number of members of the Assembly, the President shall forthwith cease to hold office and shall be disqualified from holding public office for a period of ten years from the passing of the resolution.

(7) If less than one-half of the total number of members of the National Assembly vote in support of the resolution, the members who gave notice of the resolution to the Speaker of the Assembly shall cease to be members of the Assembly forthwith after the result of the voting on the resolution is declared.

Chapter 2. The Central Legislature

19. There shall be a Central Legislature of Pakistan, which shall consist of the President and one House, to be known as the National Assembly of Pakistan.

20. (1) There shall be one hundred and fifty-six members of the National Assembly, one half of whom shall be elected in accordance with this Constitution and the law from the Province of East Pakistan and the other half of whom shall be so elected from the Province of West Pakistan.

(2) Three of the seats of members for each Province

shall be reserved exclusively for women, but this clause shall not be construed as making a woman ineligible for election to any other seat in the National Assembly.

21. (1) Unless it is sooner dissolved, a National Assembly shall continue for a term of five years from—
    (a) the declaration of the result of its election of its members; or
    (b) the expiration of the term of the previous National Assembly,
    whichever last occurs.
    (2) On the expiration of the term of a National Assembly, it shall stand dissolved.

22. (1) The President may from time to time summon the National Assembly and, except when it has been summoned by the Speaker, may prorogue it.
    (2) The Speaker of the National Assembly may, at the request of not less than one third of the total number of members of the Assembly, summon the Assembly and, when the Speaker has summoned it, he may prorogue it.

23. (1) Subject to this Article, the President may at any time dissolve the National Assembly.
    (2) The President shall not dissolve the National Assembly at any time when the unexpired portion of the term of the Assembly is less than one hundred and twenty days.
    (4) When the President dissolves the National Assembly, he shall cease to hold office—
    (a) upon the President elected as his successor entering upon his office; or
    (b) upon the expiration of one hundred and twenty days after the date of the dissolution,
    whichever first occurs.
    (5) Paragraph (a) of clause (4) of this Article shall not be construed as preventing a President who dissolves the National Assembly from being re-elected as President.

24. (1) If, at any time, a conflict with respect to any

311

matter arises between the President and the National Assembly and the President considers that it is desirable that the matter should be referred to a referendum, the President may cause the matter to be referred to a referendum in the form of a question that is capable of being answered either by "Yes" or "No."

(2) A referendum under this Article shall be conducted amongst the members of the Electoral College.

25. (1) The President may address the National Assembly and send messages to the Assembly.

(2) A member of the President's Council of Ministers and the Attorney-General shall have the right to speak in, and otherwise take part in, the proceedings of the National Assembly, or of any of its committees, but shall not be entitled to vote.

26. No Bill, or amendment of a Bill, providing for or relating to preventive detention shall be introduced or moved in the National Assembly without the previous consent of the President.

27. (1) When a Bill has been passed by the National Assembly, it shall be presented to the President for assent.

(2) The President shall, within thirty days after a Bill is presented to him—

(a) assent to the Bill;

(b) declare that he withholds assent from the Bill; or

(c) return the Bill to the National Assembly with a message requesting that the Bill, or a particular provision of the Bill, be reconsidered and that any amendments specified in the message be considered,

but if the President fails to do any of those things within the period of thirty days, he shall be deemed to have assented to the Bill at the expiration of that period.

(3) If the President declares that he withholds assent

from a Bill, the National Assembly shall be competent to reconsider the Bill and, if the Bill is again passed by the Assembly (with or without amendment) by the votes of not less than two-thirds of the total number of members of the Assembly, the Bill shall again be presented to the President for assent.

(4) If the President returns a Bill to the National Assembly, the Assembly shall reconsider the Bill and if—

(a) the Bill is again passed by the Assembly, without amendment or with the amendments specified by the President in his message or with amendments which the President has subsequently informed the Speaker of the Assembly are acceptable to him, by the votes of a majority of the total number of members of the Assembly; or

(b) the Bill is again passed by the Assembly, with amendments of a kind not referred to in paragraph (a) of this clause, by the votes of not less than two-thirds of the total number of members of the Assembly,

the Bill shall again be presented to the President for assent.

(5) When the Bill is again presented to the President for assent in pursuance of clause (3) or clause (4) of this Article, the President shall, within ten days after the Bill is presented to him—

(a) assent to the Bill; or

(b) cause to be referred to a referendum under Article 24 the question whether the Bill should or should not be assented to,

but if, within the period of ten days, the President fails to do either of those things and the Assembly is not dissolved, the President shall be deemed to have assented to the Bill at the expiration of that period.

(6) If, at a referendum conducted in relation to a

Bill by virtue of paragraph (b) of clause (5) of this Article, the votes of a majority of the total number of members of the Electoral College are cast in favour of the Bill being assented to, the President shall be deemed to have assented to the Bill on the day on which the result of the referendum is declared.

29. (1) If, at a time when the National Assembly stands dissolved or is not in session, the President is satisfied that circumstances exist which render immediate legislation necessary, he may, subject to this Article, make and promulgate such Ordinances as the circumstances appear to him to require, and any such Ordinance shall, subject to this Article, have the same force of law as an Act of the Central Legislature.

(2) An Ordinance made and promulgated under this Article shall, as soon as is practicable, be laid before the National Assembly.

(3) If, before the expiration of the prescribed period, the National Assembly, by resolution, approves of the Ordinance, the Ordinance shall be deemed to have become an Act of the Central Legislature, but if, before the expiration of that period, the National Assembly, by resolution, disapproves of the Ordinance, it shall cease to have effect, and shall be deemed to have been repealed, upon the passing of the resolution.

(4) If the National Assembly has not approved or has not disapproved of the Ordinance, and it has not been repealed by the President, before the expiration of the prescribed period, it shall cease to have effect, and shall be deemed to have been repealed, upon the expiration of that period.

(5) The power of the President to make laws by the making and promulgation of Ordinances under this Article extends only to the making of laws within the legislative competence of the Central Legislature.

30. (1) If the President is satisfied that a grave emergency exists—
    (a) in which Pakistan, or any part of Pakistan, is (or is in imminent danger of being) threatened by war or external aggression; or
    (b) in which the security or economic life of Pakistan is threatened by internal disturbances beyond the power of a Provincial Government to control,
    the President may issue a Proclamation of Emergency.

    (2) A Proclamation of Emergency shall, as soon as is practicable, be laid before the National Assembly.

    (3) The President shall, when he is satisfied that the grounds on which he issued a Proclamation of Emergency have ceased to exist, revoke the Proclamation.

    (4) If, at a time when a Proclamation of Emergency is in force (whether or not the National Assembly stands dissolved or is in session at that time), the President is satisfied that immediate legislation is necessary to assist in meeting the emergency that gave rise to the issue of the Proclamation, he may, subject to this Article, make and promulgate such Ordinances as appear to him to be necessary to meet the emergency, and any such Ordinance shall, subject to this Article, have the same force of law as an Act of the Central Legislature.

    (5) An Ordinance made and promulgated under this Article shall, as soon as is practicable, be laid before the National Assembly.

    (6) The National Assembly shall have no power to disapprove of the Ordinance but if, before the Ordinance ceases to have effect, the National Assembly, by resolution, approves of the Ordinance, the Ordinance shall be deemed to have become an Act of the Central Legislature.

(8) The power of the President to make laws by the making and promulgation of Ordinances under this Article extends only to the making of laws within the legislative competence of the Central Legislature.

CHAPTER 3. THE CENTRAL GOVERNMENT

31. The executive authority of the Republic is vested in the President and shall be exercised by him, either directly or through officers subordinate to him, in accordance with this Constitution and the law.

33. To assist him in the performance of his functions, the President may, from amongst persons qualified to be elected members of the National Assembly, appoint persons to be members of a Council of Ministers, to be known as the President's Council of Ministers.

35. The President may, from amongst the members of the National Assembly, appoint persons (not exceeding in number the number of divisions of the Central Government established by the President) to be Parliamentary Secretaries, and persons so appointed shall perform such functions in relation to those divisions as the President may direct.

CHAPTER 4. FINANCIAL PROCEDURE OF THE CENTRE

37. All revenues received and all loans raised by the Central Government, and all moneys received by the Central Government in repayment of any loan, shall form part of one consolidated fund, known as the Central Consolidated Fund.

40. (1) The President shall, in respect of every financial year, cause to be laid before the National Assembly, a statement (to be called the Annual Budget Statement) of the estimated receipts into, and the estimated expenditure from, the Central Consolidated Fund for that year.

(2) The Annual Budget Statement shall distinguish expenditure on revenue account from other expenditure, and shall show separately—

316

(a) the sums required to meet expenditure charged upon the Central Consolidated Fund; and

(b) the sums required to meet other expenditure, distinguishing recurring expenditure from expenditure that is not recurring expenditure, and showing the extent, if any, to which that other expenditure is new expenditure.

(4) In this Article—

"new expenditure," in relation to the Annual Budget Statement for a financial year, means—

(a) where expenditure for a project for that year has previously been approved by the National Assembly in pursuance of Article 42 —so much of any expenditure for that project for that year as exceeds the expenditure approved for that year by more than ten per centum of the approved expenditure;

(b) any other expenditure which is not recurring expenditure;

(c) any expenditure which is recurring expenditure and which is for a purpose in respect of which no provision was made by way of recurring expenditure in the Schedule of Authorized Expenditure for the previous financial year; and

(d) so much of any expenditure which is recurring expenditure and which is for a purpose in respect of which provision was made by way of recurring expenditure in the Schedule of Authorized Expenditure for the previous financial year as exceeds that expenditure by more than ten per centum of that expenditure;

"recurring expenditure" means expenditure of a kind that ordinarily recurs from year to year, but does not include expenditure for which provision may be made under Article 42.

317

(5) For the purpose of the definition of "new expenditure" set out in clause (4) of this Article, any Schedule of Authorized Expenditure relating to a Supplementary Budget Statement for a financial year shall be regarded as being incorporated with the Schedule of Authorized Expenditure that relates to the Annual Budget Statement for that year.

41. (1) So much of an Annual Budget Statement as relates to expenditure charged upon the Central Consolidated Fund may be discussed in, but shall not be submitted to the vote of, the National Assembly.

(2) So much of an Annual Budget Statement as relates to other expenditure, not being expenditure specified in the Statement in pursuance of clause (1) of Article 42 in respect of any subsequent financial year, shall be submitted to the National Assembly in the form of demands for grants.

(3) A demand for a grant in respect of a sum that is not shown in an Annual Budget Statement as new expenditure may be discussed in the National Assembly, but subject to clause (4) of this Article, the demand shall not be submitted to the vote of the Assembly and the Assembly shall be deemed to have assented to the demand—

(a) at the expiration of fourteen days after the Statement was laid before the Assembly; or

(b) at the commencement of the financial year to which the Statement relates,

whichever last occurs.

(4) The National Assembly may, with the consent of the President, reduce a demand for a grant referred to in clause (3) of this Article and, in that event, the Assembly shall be deemed to have assented to the demand as so reduced.

(5) The National Assembly may assent to or refuse a demand for a grant in respect of a sum that is shown in the Annual Budget Statement as new

318

expenditure or may assent to the demand in respect of such lesser sum as the Assembly may specify.

(6) A demand for a grant shall not be made except on the recommendation of the President.

42. (2) The National Assembly may, by resolution, approve or disapprove of the expenditure specified for any such subsequent year or may approve of such lesser expenditure for that year as is specified in the resolution.

(3) If, at the expiration of a period of fourteen days after the National Assembly has assented (either with or without reduction) to the demand for a grant in respect of the expenditure specified in the Budget Statement in relation to the project for the year in which the Statement relates, the Assembly has not passed a resolution in pursuance of clause (2) of this Article in relation to the estimated expenditure for a subsequent year, the Assembly shall, at the expiration of that period, be deemed to have approved of the estimated expenditure for that subsequent year.

(4) Notwithstanding the approval of the National Assembly under this Article of any expenditure for a project for a subsequent financial year, the estimated expenditure for that project for that subsequent year shall (whether or not it is the same as the approved expenditure for that year) be included in the Annual Budget Statement for that subsequent year.

44. (1) If, in respect of any financial year, it is found that the amount authorized to be expended from the Central Consolidated Fund for a particular purpose is insufficient, or a need has arisen for expenditure from that Fund for a purpose with respect to which there is no authority for expenditure, the President shall cause to be laid before the National Assembly a Supplementary Budget

Statement setting out the proposed additional expenditure.

(2) If, in respect of any financial year, it is found that money has been expended from the Central Consolidated Fund for a particular purpose and that expenditure is in excess of the amount authorized to be expended for that purpose for that year, the President shall cause to be laid before the National Assembly an Excess Budget Statement setting out the excess expenditure.

46. When, for any reason, the Schedule of Authorized Expenditure for a financial year is not authenticated before the commencement of that year, the President may, pending the authentication of the Schedule, authorize withdrawals from the Central Consolidated Fund of amounts necessary to meet expenditure that is provided for in the Annual Budget Statement for that year and—

(a) is charged upon the Central Consolidated Fund; or

(b) is not specified in the Statement as new expenditure.

47. (1) Except on the recommendation of the President, no Bill or amendment shall be introduced or moved in the National Assembly if—

(a) it would, if enacted and brought into operation, involve expenditures from the revenues or other moneys of the Central Government; or

(b) it makes provision for any of the matters, or any matter incidental to any of the matters, specified below:

(i) The imposition, abolition, remission, alteration or regulation of any tax;

(ii) The borrowing of money, or the giving of any guarantee, by the Central Government, or the amendment of the law relating to the financial obligations of the Central Government;

(iii) The imposition of a charge upon the

Central Consolidated Fund, or the abolition or alteration of any such charge;

(iv) The custody of the Central Consolidated Fund, the payment of moneys into, or the issue of moneys from that Fund;

(v) The custody, receipt or issue of any other moneys of the Central Government;

(vi) The audit of the accounts of the Central Government or of a Provincial Government.

(2) Clause (1) of this Article does not apply to a Bill or amendment by reason only that it provides—

(a) for the imposition or alteration of any fine or other pecuniary penalty, or for the demand or payment of a licence fee or a fee or charge for any service rendered; or

(b) for the imposition, abolition, remission, alteration or regulation of any tax by any local authority for local purposes.

CHAPTER 5. THE SUPREME COURT OF PAKISTAN

49. (1) There shall be a Supreme Court of Pakistan.

(2) The Supreme Court shall consist of a Chief Justice and so many other Judges as may be determined by law, or until so determined, as may be fixed by the President.

50. (1) The Chief Justice of the Supreme Court shall be appointed by the President, and the other Judges shall be appointed by the President after consultation with the Chief Justice.

56. (1) The permanent seat of the Supreme Court shall, subject to clause (3) of this Article, be at Islamabad, but it shall sit in Dacca at least twice a year for such period as the Chief Justice may consider necessary.

(2) Until provision is made for establishing the Su-

preme Court at Islamabad, the seat of the Court shall be at such place as the President may appoint.

57. (1) The Supreme Court shall, to the exclusion of every other Court, have original jurisdiction in any dispute between one of the Governments and one or both of the Governments.

(2) In the exercise of the jurisdiction conferred on it by this Article, the Supreme Court shall pronounce declaratory judgments only.

(3) In this Article, "the Governments" means the Central Government and the Provincial Governments.

61. (1) The Supreme Court shall have power to issue such directions, orders or decrees as may be necessary for doing complete justice in any cause or matter pending before it, including an order for the purpose of securing the attendance of any person or the discovery or production of any document.

(2) Any such direction, order or decree shall be enforceable throughout Pakistan and shall, where it is to be executed in a Province, be executed as if it had been issued by the High Court of that Province.

62. The Supreme Court shall have power, subject to the provisions of any Act of the Central Legislature and of any Rules made by the Supreme Court, to review any judgment pronounced or any order made by it.

PART IV. THE PROVINCES

CHAPTER 1. THE GOVERNORS

66. (1) There shall be a Governor of each Province, who shall be appointed by the President.

(2) The Governor of a Province shall, in the performance of his functions, be subject to the directions of the President.

Chapter 2. The Provincial Legislatures

70. There shall be a Provincial Legislature of each Province, which shall consist of the Governor of the Province and one House, to be known as the Assembly of the Province.

71. (1) There shall be one hundred and fifty-five members of the Assembly of each Province, who shall be elected in accordance with this Constitution and the law.

 (2) Five of the seats of members of the Assembly of each Province shall be reserved exclusively for women, but this clause shall not be construed as making a woman ineligible for election to any other seat in the Assembly.

Chapter 3. The Provincial Governments

80. The executive authority of a Province is vested in the Governor of the Province and shall be exercised by him, either directly or through officers subordinate to him, in accordance with this Constitution, the law and the directions of the President.

81. The Governor of a Province may—

 (a) specify the manner in which orders and other instruments made and executed in pursuance of any authority or power vested in the Governor shall be expressed and authenticated; and

 (b) regulate the allocation and transaction of the business of the Government of the Province and establish departments of the Government.

Chapter 4. Financial Procedure of the Provinces

Chapter 5. The High Courts

91. (1) There shall be a High Court of each Province.

 (2) A High Court shall consist of a Chief Justice and so many other Judges as may be determined by law or, until so determined, as may be fixed by the President.

92. (1) A Judge of the High Court shall be appointed by the President after consultation—

    (a) with the Chief Justice of the Supreme Court;

    (b) with the Governor of the Province concerned; and

    (c) except where the appointment is that of Chief Justice—with the Chief Justice of the High Court.

PART V. PROVISIONS APPLICABLE TO THE CENTRE AND THE PROVINCES

CHAPTER 1. THE CENTRAL AND PROVINCIAL LEGISLATURES

108. (1) After a general election of the members of an Assembly, the Assembly shall, before proceeding to the despatch of any other business—

    (a) choose a member to be the Speaker of the Assembly; and

    (b) choose two other members to be Deputy Speakers of the Assembly, specifying which is the senior of the two.

  (2) So often as the office of the Speaker, or of a Deputy Speaker, of an Assembly becomes vacant, the Assembly shall again choose a member to fill the office.

  (3) When the office of the senior of the Deputy Speakers becomes vacant, the other Deputy Speaker shall become the senior of the Deputy Speakers.

109. There shall be at least two sessions of an Assembly in every period of three hundred and sixty-five days, and not more than one hundred and eighty days shall intervene between the last sitting of an Assembly in one session and its first sitting in the next session.

111. (1) The validity of any proceedings in an Assembly shall not be questioned in any Court.

  (2) An officer or member of an Assembly in whom powers are vested for the regulation of procedure, the conduct of business or the maintenance

of order in the Assembly shall not, in relation to the exercise by him of any of those powers, be subject to the jurisdiction of any Court.

(3) A member of, or a person entitled to speak in, an Assembly shall not be liable to any proceedings in any Court in respect of anything said by him, or any vote given by him, in the Assembly or in any committee of the Assembly.

(4) A person shall not be liable to any proceedings in any Court in respect of the publication by or under the authority of an Assembly of any report, paper, vote or proceedings.

CHAPTER 2. THE CENTRAL AND PROVINCIAL GOVERNMENTS

118. (1) A Governor, a Minister or Parliamentary Secretary appointed by a President, and the Attorney-General, shall hold office during the pleasure of the President, and may be removed from office at any time by the President without any reason being assigned for his removal.

119. (1) A Minister or Parliamentary Secretary appointed by the Governor of a Province, and the Advocate-General for a Province, shall hold office during the pleasure of the Governor of the Province, and, subject to clause (2) of this Article, may be removed from office at any time by the Governor without any reason being assigned for his removal.

(2) A Governor shall not remove a Minister from office without the concurrence of the President.

CHAPTER 3. THE CENTRAL AND PROVINCIAL JUDICATURES

123. (1) In this Article, "Court" means the Supreme Court or a High Court.

(2) A Court shall have power to punish any person who—

(a) abuses, interferes with or obstructs the process of the Court in any way or disobeys any order of the Court;

325

(b) scandalizes the Court or otherwise does anything which tends to bring the Court or a Judge of the Court into hatred, ridicule or contempt;

(c) does anything to prejudice the determination of a matter pending before the Court; or

(d) does any other thing which, by law, constitutes contempt of the Court.

(3) The exercise of the power conferred on a Court by this Article may be regulated by law and subject to law, by rules made by the Court.

128. (1) There shall be a Supreme Judicial Council of Pakistan, in this Article referred to as "the Council."

(2) The Council shall consist of—

(a) the Chief Justice of the Supreme Court;

(b) the two next most senior Judges of the Supreme Court; and

(c) the Chief Justice of each High Court.

(3) If, at any time, the Council is inquiring into the capacity or conduct of a Judge who is a member of the Council, or a member of the Council is absent or is unable to act as a member of the Council due to illness or some other cause, the Judge of the Supreme Court, who is next in seniority below the Judges referred to in paragraph (b) of clause (2) of this Article shall act as a member of the Council in his place.

(4) The Council shall issue a Code of conduct to be observed by Judges of the Supreme Court and of the High Courts.

(5) If, on the information received from the Council or from any other source, the President is of the opinion that a Judge of the Supreme Court or of a High Court—

(a) may be incapable of properly performing the duties of his office by reason of physical or mental incapacity; or

(b) may have been guilty of gross misconduct,

the President shall direct the Council to inquire into the matter.

(6) If, after inquiring into the matter, the Council reports to the President that it is of the opinion—

    (a) that the Judge is incapable of performing the duties of his office or has been guilty of gross misconduct; and

    (b) that he should be removed from office, the President may remove the Judge from office.

(7) A Judge of the Supreme Court or of a High Court shall not be removed from office except as provided by this Article.

PART VI. RELATIONS BETWEEN THE CENTRE AND THE PROVINCES

131. (1) The Central Legislature shall have exclusive power to make laws (including laws having extra-territorial operation) for the whole or any part of Pakistan with respect to any matter enumerated in the Third Schedule.

    (2) Where the national interest of Pakistan in relation to—

        (a) the security of Pakistan, including the economic and financial stability of Pakistan;

        (b) planning or co-ordination; or

        (c) the achievement of uniformity in respect of any matter in different parts of Pakistan,

so requires, the Central Legislature shall have power to make laws (including laws having extra-territorial operation) for the whole or any part of Pakistan with respect to any matter not enumerated in the Third Schedule.

132. A Provincial Legislature shall have power to make laws for the Province, or any part of the Province, with respect to any matter other than a matter enumerated in the Third Schedule.

133. (1) The responsibility of deciding whether a legisla-

ture has power under this Constitution to make a law is that of the legislature itself.

(2) The validity of a law shall not be called in question on the ground that the legislature by which it was made had no power to make the law.

134. When a Provincial Law is inconsistent with a Central Law, the latter shall prevail, and the former shall, to the extent of the inconsistency, be invalid.

135. The executive authority of the Republic extends—

(a) to all matters with respect to which the Central Legislature has exclusive power to make laws under clause (1) of Article 131;

(b) where a law made by the Central Legislature in pursuance of clause (2), clause (3) or clause (4) of Article 131 provides that the law shall be administered by the Central Government—to the execution of that law; and

(c) in relation to a part of Pakistan not forming part of a Province—to all matters.

136. (1) Subject to clause (2) of this Article, the executive authority of a Province extends to all matters with respect to which the Legislature of the Province has power to make laws.

(2) The executive authority of a Province does not extend to the execution of a law made by the Central Legislature to which paragraph (b) of Article 135 applies.

138. The Central Legislature may by law make grants in aid of the revenues of a Provincial Government that may be in need of assistance.

143. Delegation of powers to Provinces.

144. National Finance Commission.

145. (1) As soon as is practicable after the commencing day, the President shall constitute a Council, to be known as the National Economic Council.

(3) The Council shall, from time to time, and whenever so directed by the President, review the overall economic position of Pakistan, formulate

plans with respect to financial, commercial and economic policies and the economic development of Pakistan and inform the Central and the Provincial Governments of those plans.

(4) A primary object of the Council in formulating the plans referred to in clause (3) of this Article shall be to ensure that disparites between the Provinces, and between different areas within a Province, in relation to income *per capita* are removed and that the resources of Pakistan (including resources in foreign exchange) are used and allocated in such manner as to achieve that object in the shortest possible time, and it shall be the duty of each Government to make the utmost endeavour to achieve that object.

PART VII. ELECTIONS

CHAPTER 1. CHIEF ELECTION COMMISSIONER AND ELECTION COMMISSIONS

147. (1) There shall be a Chief Election Commissioner ... who shall be appointed by the President.

CHAPTER 2. THE ELECTORAL COLLEGE AND THE CONSTITUENCIES

155. (1) Each Province shall, in accordance with law, be divided into not less than Forty thousand territorial units, which shall be known as electoral units.

(2) The number of electoral units in each Province shall be the same.

158. (1) The persons enrolled on the electoral roll for an electoral unit shall, in accordance with law, from time to time elect from amongst themselves a person who is not less than twenty-five years of age, who shall be known as the Elector for that unit.

(2) The Electors for all electoral units in both Provinces shall together constitute the Electoral Col-

lege of Pakistan and shall be known as the members of the Electoral College.

160. (1) The Commissioner shall, in accordance with law, from time to time arrange the electoral units of each Province into groups (which shall be known as Provincial Constituencies), so that there are one hundred and fifty such Constituencies in each Province and so that each such Constituency is one undivided area.

(2) The Electors for the electoral units included in a Provincial Constituency shall be the constituents for one seat (not being a seat reserved exclusively for women) in the Assembly of the Province in which the Constituency is included.

161. (1) The Commissioner shall also, in accordance with law, from time to time arrange the electoral units of each Province into other groups (which shall be known as Central Constituencies), so that there are seventy-five such Constituencies in each Province and so that each such Constituency is one undivided area.

(2) The Electors for the electoral units included in a Central Constituency shall be the constituents for one seat (not being a seat reserved exclusively for women) in the National Assembly.

CHAPTER 3. CONDUCT OF ELECTIONS AND REFERENDUMS

165. (1) An election for the office of President shall be decided by the votes of the members of the Electoral College.

166. (1) Except as provided by this Article, a person who is, and has for a continuous period of more than eight years, been holding office as President is not eligible to be re-elected as President.

(2) If a person referred to in clause (1) of this Article is a candidate for election to the office of President, the Commissioner shall inform the Speaker of the National Assembly of the candidature, and the Speaker shall forthwith convene a

joint sitting of the members of the National Assembly and of the Provincial Assemblies (or, if the National Assembly stands dissolved, of the Provincial Assemblies only) to consider the candidature.

(3) If the majority of the members present at the joint sitting, by secret ballot, approve of the candidature, the President shall be eligible for re-election.

167. (1) If the number of candidates for election to the office of President exceeds three, the Commissioner shall inform the Speaker of the National Assembly of the fact, and the Speaker shall forthwith convene a joint sitting of the members of the National Assembly and of the Provincial Assemblies (or, if the National Assembly stands dissolved, of the Provincial Assemblies only) to select three of the candidates for election.

(4) Where the person holding office as President is a candidate for election, his candidature shall be disregarded for the purposes of this Article.

168. (1) The election of a person to a seat (not being a seat reserved exclusively for women) in the National Assembly or a Provincial Assembly shall be decided by the votes of the constituents for that seat.

(2) A general election of members of the National Assembly or a Provincial Assembly shall be held within the period of one hundred and twenty days immediately preceding the day on which the term of the Assembly is due to expire (unless the Assembly has been sooner dissolved), and the results of the election shall be declared not later than fourteen days before that day.

(3) When an Assembly is dissolved, a general election of members of the Assembly shall be held within a period of ninety days after the dissolution.

169. (1) After a general election of members of a Provin-

331

cial Assembly, the persons elected as members shall, before the first meeting of the Assembly, elect five members to the seats in the Assembly reserved exclusively for women, so that there is one woman member for each zone referred to in clause (1) of Article 162.

(2) Subject to clause (3) of this Article, after a general election of the members of the National Assembly, each Provincial Assembly shall, before the first meeting of the National Assembly, elect three members to the seats in the National Assembly reserved exclusively for women, so that there is one woman member for each zone referred to in clause (2) of Article 162.

(3) Where a general election of the members of the National Assembly is held at or about the same time as a general election of the members of a Provincial Assembly, the persons elected as members of the Provincial Assembly may, before the first meeting of that Assembly, conduct the election referred to in clause (2) of this Article.

172. All elections and referendums under this Part shall be decided by secret ballot.

173. Except as permitted by Act of the Central Legislature, any person who, in connection with an election required to be held under this Constitution, holds out himself or any other person as being a member of, or as having the support of, a political party or any similar organisation shall be punishable in such manner as may be prescribed by Act of the Central Legislature, but provision shall be made by law for ensuring—

(a) that each candidate at an election has the opportunity, and so far as it is practicable, equal opportunity with other candidates, of addressing the persons who are entitled to vote at the election; and

(b) that the persons entitled to vote at the election have the opportunity of questioning each candidate, face to face.

332

C. Inaugural Address of
President Mohammad Ayub Khan
March 23, 1965

My dear countrymen,

Assalam-o-Alaikum

On assumption of office as President, my first thoughts are of complete submission to Allah, the Beneficent, the Merciful, Whom we all serve and to Whom we all turn for guidance and protection. May He bless this occasion. And may He also bless my people and my country with whose charge He has entrusted me. It is a very heavy responsibility, which cannot be discharged without Divine guidance.

And it cannot be discharged without full cooperation and active assistance from those who have the welfare of this country at heart. I shall seek that cooperation from the newly elected Central and Provincial Assemblies, from those associated with me in the Government—be they Ministers or Governors—and from all the public services.

But more than these, I seek it from the people at large. It is their country and their future at stake. As their elected leader, they would naturally expect me to show them the way. That I will not fail to do, with the help of Allah.

The elected representatives of the people have now been associated with the Government, not only at the Central and Provincial levels, but also at all lower levels of the Administration, down to the village and the mohallah. My Government would, therefore, be more in touch with the elected representatives of the people than ever before in the history of this subcontinent.

I shall seek cooperation even outside the elected forums, for the nation as a whole has to move. Socio-economic development cannot take place without a national effort. There is a stiff climb ahead of us. It calls for hard work and sacrifices. Individual interests must yield to the national ones.

We are also beset with dangers. The external ones do not worry me so much as the internal ones. We must not play the enemy's game by creating, through word or action, disunity or disaffection among our ranks. We must look for moral or spiritual weaknesses each in his own mind and purify ourselves—if we are to be at peace with ourselves.

I appealed earlier for active assistance in the task of Government. I shall also look for advice and wise counsel. It will be available to me in the Assemblies, the Councils and the public services. But I shall look for it even outside. I have had arrangements made for forums of intellectuals, experts and knowledgeable persons who can be consulted in their respective fields. In any case, I shall welcome a personal letter from any source, if it has an original and workable idea.

I look for ideas in the Press too. It can do a lot to promote national cohesion, constructive thinking and healthy public opinion. I am sure that it will strive to fulfill this role in our national progress.

The nation, in electing me, has approved the programme set out in my election Manifesto. It will call for a new outlook on our social and economic attitudes. I have already initiated action within the Government for the adjustment of our programmes and policies. And I will be seeking the nation's assistance whenever required.

My foreign policy has already received the enthusiastic approval of the people. We need peace to concentrate on the development of the country. But we will defend our freedom, whatever the threat.

We are watching with admiration the heroic struggle of the oppressed people of Jammu and Kashmir to exercise their internationally promised right of self-determination. We shall stand by them through thick and thin.

To us, already blessed with freedom, there is need to appreciate it, to work hard to consolidate it by making our nation united and our country economically sound, so that we can hold our own with others in peace and war. The political and economic stability of the past few years has already, by the grace of Allah, set us on the road to progress. Let us shed petty jealousies, parochial feelings and negative attitudes if they exist anywhere. Let us work together for the greater glory of our beloved country.

335

Index

337

Other books published for
The Center of International Studies
Woodrow Wilson School of Public and International
Affairs

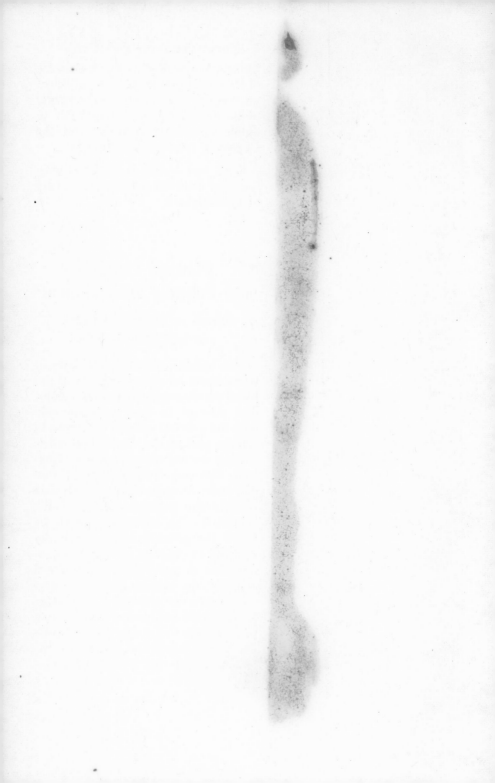